Holt Basic Reading

Freedom's Ground

Bernard J. Weiss
Senior Author
Reading and Linguistics

Loreli Olson Steuer
Reading and Linguistics

Susan B. Cruikshank
Reading and Language Arts

Lyman C. Hunt
General Editor—Satellite Books

Level 14

HOLT, RINEHART AND WINSTON, PUBLISHERS
New York • Toronto • Mexico City • London • Sydney • Tokyo

ISBN 0-03-002387-4
7890 032 9876543

Acknowledgments

Grateful acknowledgment is made to the following authors and publishers:

Atheneum Publishers, Inc., for "Magic and Some Black and Blue," from *Black and Blue Magic.* Copyright © 1966 by Zilpha Keatley Snyder. For "Concrete Mixers," from *8 A.M. Shadows.* Copyright © 1965 by Patricia Hubbell. For "A Commercial for Spring," from *It Doesn't Always Have to Rhyme.* Copyright © 1964 by Eve Merriam. Used by permission.

The Bobbs-Merrill Company, Inc., for "Robert H. Goddard, Father of the Space Age," adapted from *Robert Goddard: Pioneer Rocket Boy* by Clyde B. Moore. Copyright © 1966 by The Bobbs-Merrill Company, Inc. Used by permission.

Brandt & Brandt, for "Clipper Ships and Captains" and "Johnny Appleseed," from *A Book of Americans* by Rosemary and Stephen Vincent Benét. Copyright 1933 by Rosemary and Stephen Vincent Benét, renewed © 1961 by Rosemary and Stephen Vincent Benét; published by Holt, Rinehart and Winston, Publishers. Used by permission.

The Caxton Printers, Ltd., Caldwell, Idaho, for "The Adventures of Paul Bunyan," from *Paul Bunyan Swings His Axe* by Dell J. McCormick. Copyright 1950 by Mrs. Dell J. McCormack. Used by permission.

Wm. Collins + World Publishing Company and Curtis Brown, Ltd., for "By the Light of the Moon," adapted from *Moon in Fact and Fancy* by Alfred Slote. Copyright © 1967 by Alfred Slote. Used by permission.

Control Data Education Company HQAO3Z for an article on computers written by members of the Control Data Staff. Used by permission.

Candida Donadio & Associates, Inc., for "Davie's Wonderful Summer," from *The Runaway Summer of Davie Shaw* by Mario Puzo. Copyright © 1966 by Mario Puzo. Used by permission.

Coward-McCann & Geoghegan, Inc., for "Captain Stormalong Meets a Kraken," adapted from "Captain Stormalong, The Revolution and Clipper Ships," from *Tall Tale America* by Walter Blair. Copyright 1944 by Walter Blair: Used by permission.

Coward-McCann & Geoghegan, Inc., and Hamish Hamilton Ltd., for "The Mud Ponies," adapted from *The Mud Ponies* by Lace Kendall. Copyright © 1963 by Lace Kendall. Used by permission.

Curtis Brown, Ltd., for "Take Off with Books" by Ogden Nash. Copyright © 1967 by Ogden Nash. Used by permission.

Estate of Mrs. Frank Dobie, for "Gretchen and The White Stallion," adapted from *The Mustangs* by Frank Dobie. Used by permission.

Doubleday & Company, Inc., for "Night Journey," from the *Collected Poems of Theodore Roethke.* Copyright 1940 by Theodore Roethke. For "General Moses," from *Freedom Train* by Dorothy Sterling. Copyright 1945 by Dorothy Sterling. Used by permission.

Doubleday & Company, Inc. and World's Work, Inc., for "What Is Gold?" from *Hailstones and Halibut* by Mary O'Neill. Copyright © 1961 by Mary Le Duc O'Neill. For "Feelings About Words" from *Words, Words, Words* by Mary O'Neill. Copyright © 1966 by Mary O'Neill. Used by permission.

E. P. Dutton & Co. Inc., for "Earth, Moon and Sun," also for "Blue," from *Poems of Earth and Space* by Claudia Lewis. Copyright © 1967 by Claudia Lewis.

E. P. Dutton & Co., Inc., and Curtis Brown, Ltd., for "The City of Tomorrow," adapted from the book *Old Cities and New Towns* by Alvin Schwartz. Copyright © 1968 by Alvin Schwartz. Used by permission.

Grosset & Dunlap, Inc., for "Handy Do-it-Yourself Word-Making Kit," adapted from *The Language Book* by Franklin Folsom. Copyright © 1963 by Franklin Folsom. Used by permission.

Harcourt Brace Jovanovich, Inc., for "The Bird of Seven Colors," from *The Three Wishes:* A Collection of Puerto Rican Folktales. Copyright © 1969 by Ricardo E. Alegria. Used by permission.

Holt, Rinehart and Winston, Publishers, for "Steam Shovel" from *Upper Pastures* by Charles

Malam. Copyright 1930, renewed © 1958 by Charles Malam. Used by permission.

Holt, Rinehart and Winston, Publishers, and Eleanor Langdon Associates, for "Alvin and the Secret Code," adapted and condensed from *Alvin's Secret Code* by Clifford B. Hicks. Copyright © 1963 by Clifford B. Hicks. Used by permission.

Holt, Rinehart and Winston, Publishers, Laurence Pollinger, Ltd., and Jonathan Cape, Ltd., for "A Time to Talk," from *Complete Poems of Robert Frost.* Copyright 1916 by Holt, Rinehart and Winston, Publishers. Copyright 1944 by Robert Frost. Used by permission.

Houghton Mifflin Company, for "The Fast Sooner Hound" by Arna Bontemps and Jack Conroy. Copyright 1942 by Houghton Mifflin Company. Used by permission.

Houghton Mifflin Company, Longmans Young Books, and McIntosh and Otis, Inc., for "The Black Pearl," from *The Black Pearl* by Scott O'Dell. Copyright © 1967 by Scott O'Dell. Used by permission.

May Justus, for "The Outlander Teacher" by May Justus from the *Smoky Mountain Sampler.* Used by permission.

Little, Brown and Company, for "Goose, Moose & Spruce" and "Scat! Scitten!" from *Take Sky* by David McCord. Copyright © 1961, 1963 by David McCord. Used by permission.

The Macmillan Publishing Co., Inc., for "Cherry Ann and The Dragon Horse," from *American Adventures* by Elizabeth Coatsworth. Copyright © 1955, 1968 by Macmillan Publishing Co., Inc. For "Poem of Praise" by Elizabeth Coatsworth. Copyright 1934 by Macmillan Publishing Co., Inc., copyright renewed © 1962 by Elizabeth Coatsworth. Used by permission.

The Macmillan Publishing Co., Inc., and Geoffrey Bles Ltd., for "Lucy and the Wardrobe," from *The Lion, the Witch and the Wardrobe* by C. S. Lewis. Copyright 1950 by The Macmillan Publishing Co., Inc. Used by permission.

Eve Merriam c/o International Creative Management, for "Elizabeth Blackwell." Copyright © 1968 by Eve Merriam. Used by permission.

Julian Messner, a division of Simon & Schuster, Inc., for "The Stargazer," adapted from *America's First Woman Astronomer: Maria Mitchell* by Rachel Baker and Joanna Baker Merlen. Copyright © 1960 by Rachel Baker and Joanna Baker Merlen. Used by permission.

Harold Ober Associates, Inc., for "Trip: San Francisco," from the *Langston Hughes Reader.* Copyright © 1958 by Langston Hughes. Used by permission.

Ethelyn M. Parkinson for "One for the Computer," from *The Terrible Troubles of Rupert Piper* by Ethelyn M. Parkinson. Copyright © 1956 by Abingdon Press, renewed © 1977 by Ethelyn M. Parkinson. Used by permission.

May Swenson, for "The Cloud Mobile." Copyright © 1958 by May Swenson. Used by permission.

Helen W. Thurber and Rosemary Thurber Sauers, for excerpt from *Many Moons* by James Thurber. Copyright 1943 by James Thurber, renewed © 1971 by Helen W. Thurber and Rosemary Thurber Sauers. Published by Harcourt Brace Jovanovich. Used by permission.

University of California Press for "Pushing Up the Sky," by Ella E. Clark, from *Indian Legends of the Pacific Northwest* Copyright 1953. Used by permission.

The Viking Press (Viking Penguin Inc.) for "Camp Miller School," from *Blue Willow* by Doris Gates. Copyright 1940, © renewed 1968 by Doris Gates. For "Stranger," from *Song in the Meadow* by Elizabeth Madox Roberts. Copyright 1940 by Elizabeth Madox Roberts, © renewed 1968 by Ivor S. Roberts. For "Ginger's Colt," adapted from *Little Vic* by Doris Gates. Copyright © 1961 by Doris Gates Hall. For "Pie and Punch and You-Know-Whats," adapted from *Centerburg Tales* by Robert McCloskey. Copyright 1951 by Robert McCloskey. Used by permission.

Henry Z. Walck, division of David McKay Co., Inc., for "The Reluctant Dragon," from *Plays and How to Put Them On* by Moyne Rice Smith. Copyright © 1961 by Moyne Rice Smith. For "My Uncle Joe," from *The Life I Live* by Lois Lenski. Copyright © 1965 by Lois Lenski. Used by permission of the author, published by Henry Z. Walck, Inc.

Harry R. Warfel and Octagon Books, Inc., for "Noah Webster: The Word Watcher," from *Noah Webster: Schoolmaster to America* (1936, 1966). Copyright 1936, renewed © 1966. Used by permission.

Art Credits:

N. Jo Smith, pages 12 – 13
Bernie D'Andrea, pages 16 – 31, 98 – 110, 240 – 250, 422 – 435
Ralph Pereida, page 34
Denver Gillen, pages 44 – 63
Muriel Wood, pages 78 – 97, 142 – 160
Len Ebstein, pages 98 – 111
James Barkley, page 112
Joseph Cellini, pages 117 – 127
David Chestnut, pages 128 – 133
Lionel Kalish, pages 162 – 163
Michael Garlin, pages 164 – 169
Mabey Trousdell, pages 167, 178 – 179, 184 – 189, 200 – 203, 207
Jan Pyk, pages 170 – 171
Franklin Luke, pages 172 – 177
Viewpoint Graphics, Inc., pages 180, 205
Ann Toulmin-Rothe, pages 181, 204, 208
Judith Fast, page 206
Karen Berkhart, pages 216 – 226
Melvin Bolden, pages 227 – 236
Dan Kirk, pages 252 – 253
Robert Owens, pages 260 – 261, 280 – 281, 334 – 335
Ted Lewin, pages 262 – 265, 364 – 373, 378 – 383, 468 – 482
Jerry Pinkney, pages 267 – 277
Joseph Smith, pages 288 – 303
Ethel Gold, pages 336 – 359, 488 – 504
Mae Gerhard, pages 384 – 385
Tim and Greg Hildebrandt, pages 386 – 401, 484 – 485

Cover design by Taurins Design Associates
Cover illustration by Jeanette Adams

Photo Credits:

p. 32 top, Culver Pictures; bottom, Visiting Nurse Service of New York. p. 33 top and bottom left, Visiting Nurse Service of New York; bottom right, Brown Brothers. p. 42 top, Ken Wittenberg; bottom HRW Photo by Russell Dian. p. 43 top, Paul Fusco/Magnum; bottom, Ken Wittenberg. p. 64 Shostal Associates. pp. 67 – 69, 71, 73 Joshua Tree. p. 75 Arthur Griffin/Photo Researchers. p. 134 The Bettmann Archive. p. 135 Tyrone Dukes/N.Y. Times. p. 194 left, Warner Brothers, Seven Arts; right, Wide World Photos. p. 195 top, Library of Congress; bottom, National Archives. pp. 196 – 197 HRW Photos by Russell Dian. p. 227 U.S. Defense Mapping Agency. p. 233 Maria Mitchell Museum, Nantucket. pp. 234 – 235 Vassar College Library. p. 237 top, The Permanent Collection of the University of Delaware; bottom, Harvard University News Office. p. 254 Russ Kinne/Photo Researchers. p. 256 Control Data Corporation. p. 257 top and bottom left, Museum of Science, Boston; top right, MIT News Office. p. 258 top, Daniel Brody/Stock Boston; bottom, Erich Hartman/Magnum. p. 259 left, Rene Burri/Magnum; top right, HRW Photo by Brian Hammill; bottom right NASA. p. 278 – 279 NASA. p. 329 Thomas Jefferson Memorial Foundation. p. 330 top left, Chase Manhattan Bank Money Museum; top right, Courtesy of University of Virginia; bottom, Virginia State Travel Service. p. 333 Courtesy of University of Virginia. p. 360 HRW Photos by Russell Dian. p. 362 top left, Constantine Manos/Magnum; top right, Bohdan Hrynewych/Stock Boston; bottom, HRW Photo by Russell Dian. pp. 374 – 377 Marcia Keegan. p. 403 top, Steve Wilson/dpi; bottom, Shostal Associates. p. 408 Golden State Mutual Life Insurance Co./Afro-American Art Collection. p. 417 Collection of the Architect of the Capitol/Library of Congress. p. 443 top and bottom, Courtesy of the Puerto Rican Traveling Theater, N.Y. p. 448 top left and center, M.A. Yuschenkoff/Black Star; top right, Michael E. Bry; pp. 448 – 449 bottom, Fred Lyon/Rapho Guillumette, PR. p. 449 top left, San Francisco Convention & Visitor's Bureau; top right, Hans

Hannan/Rapho Guillumette, PR. p. 464 top, Norman Prince; bottom, Owen Franken/Stock Boston. p. 465 top, Owen Franken/Stock Boston; bottom, Norman Prince. p. 466 top and bottom, George F. Thompson/Photo Researchers. p. 467 top left, Tom McHugh/Photo Researchers; top right, Hans Namuth/Photo Researchers; bottom left, Porterfield Chickering/Photo Researchers; bottom right, G.F. Thompson/Photo Researchers. p. 468 UPI. p. 471 Walker Evans/Courtesy, The Museum of Modern Art, N.Y. p. 473 Dorothea Lange/Library of Congress. p. 475 U.S. Forest Service. p. 476 Arthur Rostein/Library of Congress. p. 479 Walker Evans/Library of Congress. p. 481 Ben Shahn/Library of Congress. p. 486 left, Claus Meyer/Black Star; right, Howard Sochurek. p. 487 top left, Charles Moore/Black Star; top right, bottom left and right, Martin Weaver; bottom middle, New York Convention and Visitor's Bureau, by Allen Green. p. 506 top left, The Art Institute of Chicago; top right, Missouri Historical Society; bottom left, Ralph Crane/Black Star; bottom right, Ezra Stoeller Association. p. 507 top left and right, Joseph W. Molitor; bottom left, Wide World Photos; bottom right, James Sugar/Woodfin Camp & Associates. p. 508 The Traveler's Insurance Co., Hartford, Conn. pp. 510 – 511 © 1967 by The New York Times Co., reprinted by permission. p. 512 Conklin & Rossant. p. 513 left, John Hancock Mutual Life Insurance Company, photo by Peter Benton; right, Cornell Aeronautical Laboratory, Inc.

Table of Contents

UNIT ONE
TAKE OFF WITH BOOKS

UNIT TWO

THE WORLD OF WORDS

UNIT THREE

RIDING HIGH

UNIT FOUR

FOR YOU AND ME

UNIT FIVE

THE ENTRANCE PLACE OF WONDERS

UNIT SIX
TO SEE THE LAND

Welcome to **Freedom's Ground**! Here you will find stories, poems, paintings, and other special features that will carry you from New York to California, from reality to fantasy, from yesterday to tomorrow.

Ride your imagination!

You will meet Gretchen, a German girl who grew up in Texas nearly 200 years ago, Alvin, who finds a mysterious secret code, and Harry, a boy who suddenly sprouts wings. You will also read about legendary characters like Paul Bunyan, and the hound dog who was so fast he could outrun a railroad train. And you will discover the Reluctant Dragon—who doesn't have a fierce bone in his body.

Freedom's Ground is waiting for you.

Get ready for adventure!

1 TAKE OFF WITH BOOKS

Take Off with Books

Take off with books,
Not with the rocket's roar,
Take off in silence
And in fancy soar
At rocket speed
To every land and time,
And see, spread out beneath,
Past, present, future as you higher climb.

Explore those worlds the rocket cannot reach,
Troy, Camelot and Crusoe's lonely beach.
No path forbid, no darkling secret hid;
Books reached the moon before real rockets did.

Ogden Nash

Pie and Punch and You-Know-Whats

ROBERT McCLOSKEY

A Little Bit Bitten

Homer Price and his pal Freddy were just finishing some doughnuts when a stranger opened the door of Uncle Ulysses's lunchroom.

"Good evening," he said softly. He was carrying a flat parcel. "I have brought a recording to put in your jukebox," he said, nervously fumbling with the strings and paper of his parcel. "It will be number one on the *bit*—" The stranger broke off suddenly. Then, after a moment, he repeated, "It will be number one on the Hit Parade!" He finished undoing his package and took out a recording, which he carelessly tossed almost to the ceiling. Then he stood motionless, watching it drop. The record landed with a *crash!* on the lunchroom floor. Homer and Freddy gasped, but the stranger laughed.

"Unbreakable!" he said, chuckling. He picked up the record and bent it almost double. "Absolutely, disgustingly unbreakable! I've *tried* to break it—goodness knows I've *tried,*" he said. He unlocked the glass front of the jukebox. "I'll put it right here," he said, sliding the record into the stack. Then he quickly snapped the glass case shut and locked it. "There!" he said with great relief. "That's that!"

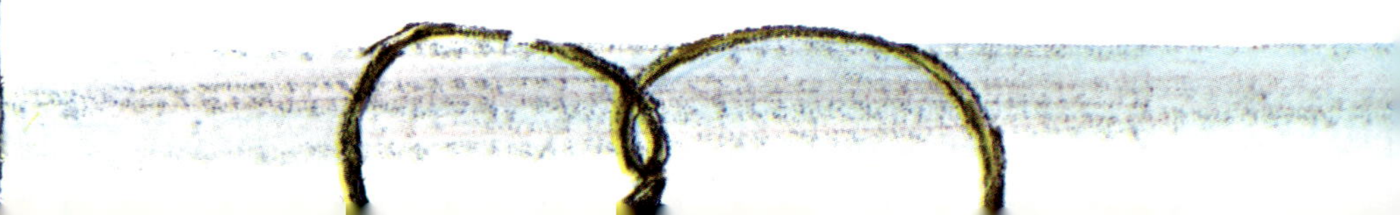

The two boys felt relieved, too. They had been startled by the sudden appearance of this odd stranger. Homer, remembering what his job was, put down the book he had been holding and went behind the counter. He often took over the counter while Uncle Ulysses visited his friends in the barbershop.

"Would you care for a snack to eat, sir? A sandwich and a cup of coffee?" he asked. "Some nice fresh doughn—"

"Uht! Uht! Uht! Uht!" the stranger interrupted, wagging his finger violently, before Homer could finish saying "doughnuts."

"I *never, never* eat them," he said. Then, leaning way over, he whispered, "They're positively full of *holes,* you know! They're simply full of *whole holes!* I must go now. I really must be going," he said, turning toward the door. He appeared eager to be gone before something dreadful could happen.

"Hey, mister," Freddy called, "you forgot to put a name for the new record here next to the selector buttons!"

"Oh," said the stranger, pausing with his hand on the door, "it hasn't any name. It's—ah—just one of those things. And by the way," he added, *"don't play it!"*

Then, without the least trace of humor, the stranger laughed, "Hah, hah, hah! But you will," he whispered.

The door closed and the stranger was gone.

"What can happen from playing a record?" Freddy demanded. "I don't see why we shouldn't play—"

"I'm not afraid to play it!" Homer interrupted. He jammed his hand into his pocket and pulled out a dime. Then he marched straight up to the jukebox, jammed his dime into the slot, and poked one of the buttons, *the* button, the one without a name.

There was a loud *cl-l-lick!* and mysteriously and silently the disgustingly unbreakable record slid out of the stack and began to spin. Both Homer and Freddy watched out of the corners of their

eyes, wondering what kind of a weird noise or music or even a scream might come blaring out of the jukebox. They stood, hands ready to clap over their ears, prepared to dash out of the door.

As the music began flowing out of the jukebox, they sighed with relief and began to smile. It was only a gay little tune with a bouncing rhythm!

"That's sure a surprise!" said Homer, nodding his head in time with the music.

"There's nothing wrong with that music!" said Freddy, beginning to tap his foot. "Boy, that's a catchy tune!"

After a few more measures of the catchy rhythm, a man's voice began to sing:

"Sing hi-diddle-diddle,
For a silly little vittle.
Sing get-gat-gittle,
Got a hole in the middle.
Sing dough-de-dough-dough,
There's dough, you know.
There's not no nuts
In you-know-whats.
In a whole doughnut
There's a nice whole hole.
When you take a big bite,
Hold the whole hole tight.
  If a little bit bitten,
  Or a great bit bitten,
  Any whole hole with a hole bitten in it
  Is a holey whole hole
  and it JUST---PLAIN---ISN'T!"

When the record stopped playing, Freddy cried, "That's about the best tune I've ever heard, Homer, and the words are sort of good, too. I'm gonna play that record *again!*"

Freddy put a dime in the jukebox, and once more he and Homer nodded and tapped time to the tricky music and listened to the tricky words. Before the song was halfway through, they were singing gaily along with the voice coming from the jukebox.

"There just plain isn't anything wrong with that record," said Homer when the record stopped.

"Na-aw!" said Freddy. He giggled and hummed a few measures of the catchy tune.

"I could sit around," said Homer, "for a holey whole day and not do a thing but listen to it play."

"Say, Homer," said Freddy, starting to laugh, "do you-know-whats? You're talking a little vittle bit funny!"

"Hawh!" Homer grinned at Freddy. "You're talking *notes*, just like *music*, and a little bit bitten funny, too."

"That's not nut-nothing," Freddy started to sing, "to get-gat-gittle excited about."

"No, not a bit bitten," Homer agreed.

"Not a little bit bitten," Freddy sang.

"Or a great bit bitten," Homer joined in.

"And any whole hole with a hole bitten in it is a holey whole hole, and it JUST PLAIN

ISN'T!" They ended up singing as loud as they could sing and stamping time with their feet.

"That was just plain swell!" Freddy sang happily when they had finished.

"But, Freddy," Homer sang sadly, "we're a little bit bitten!"

"Or a great bit b—" Freddy stopped singing suddenly, and the smile faded from his face. *"Holey whole holy smoke!"* he sang forte-forte.

"Yes, holey whole holy smoke," Homer encored in a sad piano-piano.

A Holey Whole Hole

The barber put down the cards he had been dealing to Uncle Ulysses, Posty Pratt, and the mayor and answered the telephone. "Oh, Homer, it's you," he said. "Yes, he's here. I'll call him to the phone." He jerked his thumb at Ulysses. "Homer is on the line. Says you better get-gat-gittle back to the lunchroom. Funny thing," the barber continued, "sounds just as though he were *singing!*"

"Hello, Homer," said Uncle Ulysses. "What? What? What's that you're singing?" He listened for a while and then asked, "But the jukebox hasn't stopped *working,* has it? Oh, good," said Uncle Ulysses, "then there's nothing to worry a bit bitten about. Say, Homer, that's a good number you're singing," Uncle Ulysses said. "Sing it just once more, please, from the beginning."

Uncle Ulysses, with the receiver pressed tight to his ear, stood swaying and tapping time with one foot, then with two feet, and then he started singing:

> "In a whole doughnut
> There's a nice whole hole."

When he had sung the song through, Uncle Ulysses sang, "Thank you, Homer, that was just plain swell!" He turned to the barber, the mayor, and Posty Pratt, singing, "Drop your cards and get all set, this song is swell for a male quartet!"

And it certainly was. After three practice tries they sang it in perfect four-part harmony. Each time they sang it the holey whole hole way through, they sang it a little bit bitten better. By the time they discovered they could not stop singing, they had already set a nonstop record for barbershop quarteting. Finally four desperate

men burst out of the barbershop and went singing off in all directions.

Uncle Ulysses came high-diddle-diddling through the door of the lunchroom where he started singing in the same key as Homer and Freddy and about two dozen customers. As the people had arrived in the lunchroom, they, too, had joined in, and one by one they, too, had discovered that they could *not stop* singing.

Homer was singing and trying, along with everybody else, to forget the clever words and the charming little melody. "What if we *never* stop!" Homer began to worry. "Somebody has to think of a cure," he thought. He remembered that something like this had happened to him once before. It was last September, when he had read a verse in a library book and couldn't stop repeating it. He remembered that there was a cure in the story. Now if he could only recall the name of that book or the name of that story!

Homer looked at the clock and saw that it was five minutes of nine. In five minutes the library would close. And the librarian was going on vacation with the sixth-grade teacher. They wouldn't be back for two weeks!

"We just got to find that book right away!" Homer thought. "We just got to get-gat-gittle that book from the library, no matter what!" He jumped up on the counter and soloed, "Everybody follow me-e-e, over to the librar-re-e-e!"

And they all danced out of the door after Homer, singing:

"... hi-diddle-diddle,
For a silly little vittle.
Sing get-gat-gittle,
Got a hole in the middle."

It was closing time, and the librarian glanced quickly around the library to see that everything was in its place. "Now," she thought happily, "I can go on my vacation. *This* is the moment I have been waiting for!"

And *that* was the moment that Homer danced diddledy-viddledy in and *crash!* tripped over the standing sign that said, "Quiet, please."

He was followed by about half the town, including the mayor, the judge, and a couple of city legislators, all singing and dancing in a dignified manner. Posty Pratt was there, singing his way in at the head of his family of wife, daughters,

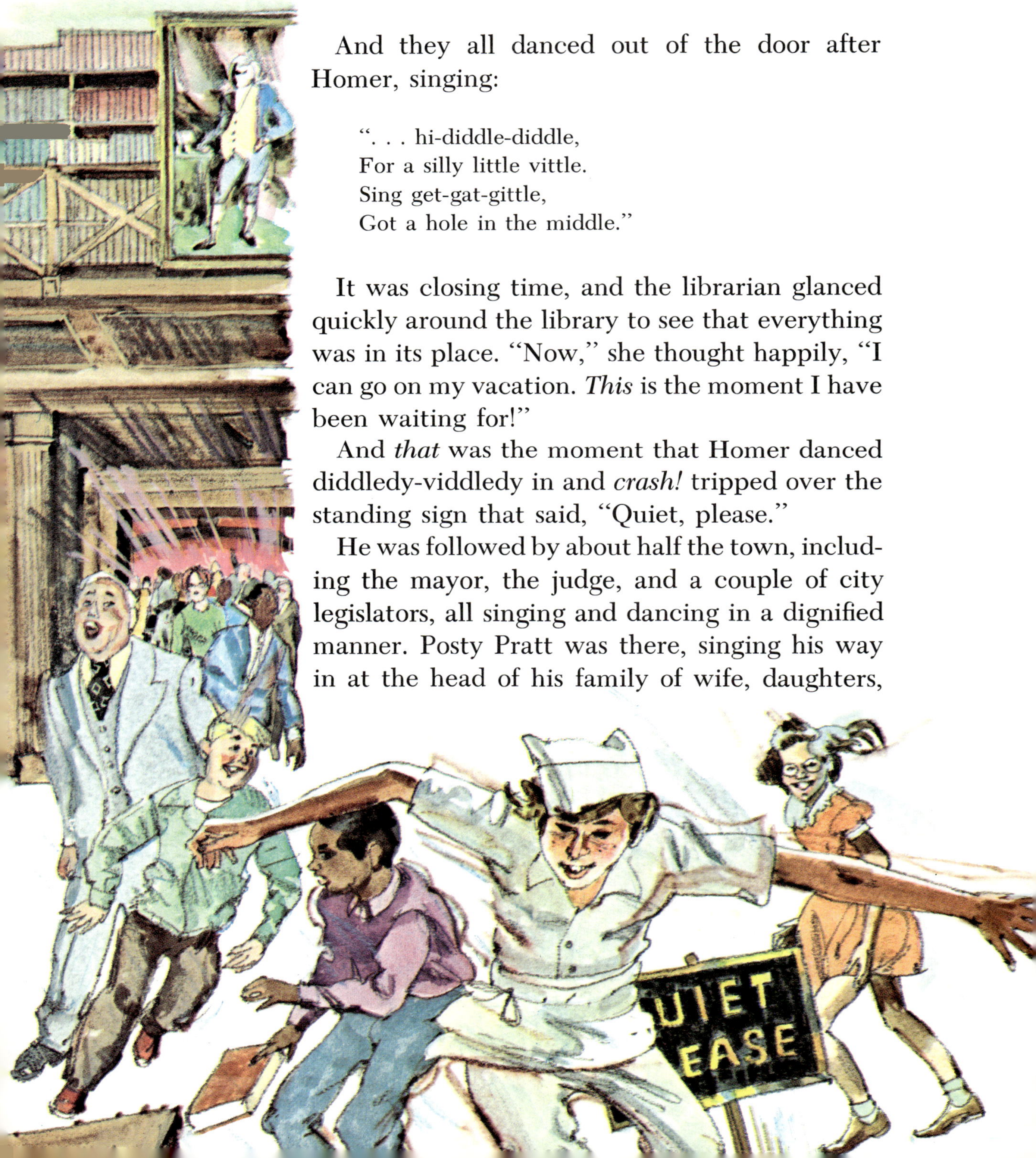

sons-in-law, eight grandchildren, and an elderly second cousin of Mrs. Pratt's, who was having herself a high old time keeping time with her cane.

Homer wiggled to his feet and danced straight for the librarian. "We're a little bit bitten!" he sang.

And the entire group chorused, "A little bit bitten, or a great bit bitten . . ." They sang the whole song for her, better than they had ever sung it.

The librarian, though worrying about catching her train, began to have an irresistible urge to sing, too. "What can I do to help?" she whimpered, trying her utmost not to sing the question.

"There's a book here on the shelves that'll tell us how to cure ourselves," Homer soloed.

"What's the title?" yelled the librarian, losing complete control of her library manner. "Do you know the author's name? What's the book's catalog number?" she screamed.

"Dough-de-dough-dough, I do not know," sang Homer. "Those things I cannot remember, but I read it last September."

"Then there's nothing I can do, get-gat-gittle, I can't help you," the librarian chanted, beginning to be a wee bit bitten herself.

"We have to find a black-backed book, or maybe it's a brown-backed book," sang Homer. "And I think it was a little bit battered!"

A Little Bit Battered

Then everybody, the poor librarian included, joined in singing, "Find a black-backed book that's a little bit battered, or a brown-backed book that's a little bit battered." And at the same time everybody, the poor librarian included, started dancing past the shelves, snatching out for Homer every single brown-backed and black-backed book they came to.

"In a whole doughnut there's a nice whole hole," everybody was singing and then singing some more. The more they sang, the more they danced past the shelves. The more they danced past the shelves, the more books they collected. Before very long Homer was perched in the middle of a tremendous pile of brown-backed and black-backed books that were a little bit battered, more or less. But Homer still hadn't found the book that he had read last September.

Freddy started dancing along the balcony, and books started sailing over the railing to Homer, who caught them expertly without skipping a single beat in the rhythm. Suddenly the books that Freddy was lobbing from the balcony started sailing right on past Homer, because Homer was giving his undivided attention to a story in a slightly battered brown-backed book.

Almost before you could sing "high-diddle-diddle," everybody had gathered in a swaying group around the mountain of books.

"Looky-look-look, it's a brown-backed book," someone sang.

"Get-gat-gittle, he's got a story in the middle," Uncle Ulysses sang hopefully.

Suddenly Homer stopped swaying and bobbing. He smiled and kept reading, and then he started to sway and bob again. But while everybody else was swaying, Homer was bob-bobbing, and when the others bobbed, Homer swayed. Homer was caught by a *new* rhythm all his own. Then from the top of the pile of books, he began to shout at the top of his voice:

"Conductor, when you receive a fare,
Punch in the presence of the passenjare!
A blue-trip slip for an eight-cent fare,
A buff-trip slip for a six-cent fare,
A pink-trip slip for a three-cent fare,
Punch in the presence of the passenjare!

Chorus

Punch, brothers, punch with care!
Punch in the presence of the passenjare!"

Before Homer started shouting the second chorus of "Punch, brothers, punch with care!" the singers began to falter in their rhythm for the first time that evening. Then one by one they began to shout along with Homer, "A pink-trip slip for a three-cent fare," until everybody, yes, everybody, began to stamp his tired feet for joy and shout, "Punch, brothers, punch with care! Punch in the presence of the passenjare!"

That is, everybody except Homer. He sat smiling and out of breath on his perch atop the pile of books. Everybody else was yelling, *"Punch, brothers, punch!"* and stamping so hard that the walls shook. But not Homer. Homer was cured. After he had rested for a moment and caught his breath, he slid down the pile of books.

"A blue-trip slip for an eight-cent fare!" Everybody was shouting and stamping so loud and so hard that Homer was completely ignored. He dodged through the group without being stamped on. Homer needed somebody to help complete the cure—anybody who had not yet heard the "Punch, brothers, punch" jingle. He rushed out of the door to bring back the very first person he should meet. He had a good idea who that person would be. And there she was, coming right up the library steps. It was the sixth-grade teacher!

"What has happened to Lucy?" she cried, meaning the librarian. "It's almost train time!"

"You've got to help," Homer said. "Come inside."

As they came in through the door, Homer shouted as he had never shouted before. "Tell it to her!" he bellowed, pointing to the sixth-grade teacher.

And they told her:

> "Punch, brothers, punch with care!
> Punch in the presence of the passenjare!"

They very generously told her two times, all the way through, without holding back a single *Punch* or *Pink-trip slip.*

Like all sixth-grade teachers, she was very quick to catch on.

> "A pink-trip slip for a three-cent fare,
> Punch in the presence of the passenjare!"

Then, as suddenly as they had started shouting and stamping out the jingle, everybody stopped, just as Homer knew they would—everybody, that is, except the sixth-grade teacher. She'd caught it just too perfectly, and she went right on shouting and stamping. Everybody else sat down, gasping for breath, right where they were, to rest their tired and aching feet.

Freddy edged his way over to where Homer stood. "Now, what," he asked, nodding at the howling, stamping sixth-grade teacher, "are we going to do with *her?*"

"She'll be all right," Homer said, "as soon as she tells it to somebody else. Just like I was cured when I told it to you, and you were cured when you told it to her."

"You mean that after you tell that jingle to somebody, you forget it and are cured?" Freddy asked.

"Yep, that's the way it goes," said Homer, "just like in the book."

Freddy thought for a moment and then asked, "And the person she tells it to has to tell it to somebody else?"

"Yep, Freddy, somebody's *always* going to be saying it," Homer admitted.

"Gets to be monotonous, doesn't it, Homer?" Freddy commented. He shook his head sadly toward the sixth-grade teacher, who was just beginning another chorus. "It will be terrible to

have to listen to somebody around town keep on saying and saying that jingle forever and ever!"

"That will be better than having everybody in Centerburg keep on singing forever and ever," Homer argued. "And besides," he continued, "she's going on a vacation, isn't she? We'll just have to make sure that she gets on that train without telling somebody, and all our troubles will be over! C'mon, Freddy, we've got to get busy."

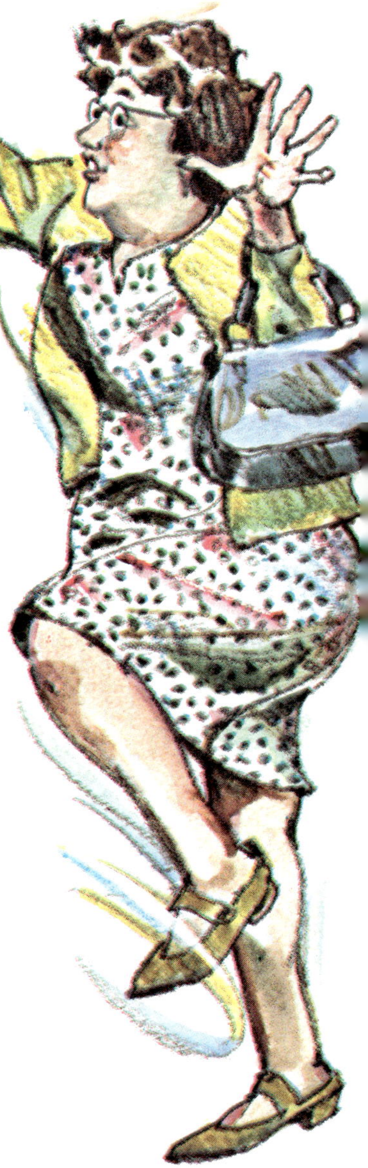

Reflections

1. What did the stranger say that made it almost certain that the boys would play the record?
2. Your teacher probably will not let you read the song that was on the record out loud. Why would doing that be dangerous?
3. What is the first hint you get in the story that the song is catchy?
4. In the story, the record does not have a name. What would you call it?
5. Have you ever been unable to get a tune out of your head? What made you stop singing it over and over?
6. Pretend you are the last person in the world who has not heard the song. Write a paragraph telling how you would cure yourself after hearing it.

Settlement Houses

JANE ADDAMS (1860–1935)

In 1889, Jane Addams, the daughter of a wealthy lawyer, moved into the middle of a poor immigrant section of Chicago. There she opened a neighborhood center, or *settlement house.* In this center, called Hull House, babies were cared for while their mothers worked. Children were fed and medicine was given to the sick. People of all ages and nationalities came together there for classes and games and parties.

Jane Addams believed that even more should be done for the poor and the helpless. She made speeches and wrote books calling for laws to improve housing, working conditions, and health care for the poor.

After a lifetime devoted to helping others, she won the Nobel Peace Prize in 1931.

LILLIAN WALD (1867–1940)
Lillian Wald also left a pleasant life to provide one of the things new Americans needed most—medical care. After training as a nurse, she and several other nurses moved into a house on Henry Street in New York City. From there they went into people's homes to help them. The nurses often went from roof to roof to save climbing the many flights of stairs in the old tenements. This service—which grew into one of the first visiting nurse programs—and the Henry Street Settlement House are still going strong today.

Grandma's Diary

RITA GOLDEN GELMAN

Our house was getting pretty crowded and Dad finally decided to fix up the attic.

"We can put two rooms up there," he said.

I was really excited. At last I could have a room of my own.

"But you'll have to help clean it out, Judy," Mother said. "We'll have to go through everything that's been stored up there all these years."

"Sure," I said. I would have agreed to anything.

I started the very next day. As I looked at all the boxes there were to unpack, I was glad it was raining.

I opened a box. It was filled with pictures. Mostly they were of people in old-fashioned clothes, all standing in a line. Then I saw a small black book, tied with a red ribbon. The ribbon fell apart when I untied it. And on the front page was Grandma's name:

This is the diary of:

1918

Deborah Judith Miller

Ten years, two months, and seven days

100 Rivington Street

New York City

I opened the diary to the first page. . . .

TUESDAY, JANUARY 1

Last week we had to write a list of New Year's resolutions for school. I wrote ten, but the one I really want to keep is to cook a potato in the vacant lot. The older kids are always doing it. They build a fire, and throw potatoes in until they cook. My best friend Ida and I are definitely going to do it—soon!

There is nothing so good in the world as a hot potato cooked in a fire on a cold day. Besides the taste (which is better than any other taste in the world), the hot potato keeps your fingers warm.

WEDNESDAY, JANUARY 2

Ida and I brought our potatoes to school today. We met by the flagpole at three o'clock. Then we ran all the way to the lot, dodging in and out of pushcarts. In case you don't know it, Diary, Orchard Street is loaded with pushcarts. They sell everything there—tomatoes and potatoes and beans and every kind of vegetable, and coats and belts and dresses. And the pickles and herring smell wonderful. It drives me crazy whenever I walk by.

But today, Ida and I weren't noticing. We raced through the jumble of people and carts and into the back corner of the lot where we had been saving a big pile of sticks and paper. Then we waited for Ida's sister Margie. But she never came, and we're not allowed to build a fire ourselves.

THURSDAY, JANUARY 3

Margie came today! She lit the fire and we put our potatoes in. Ida and I were in charge of keeping the fire going.

After a very long time (potatoes take forever to cook), we were almost ready to eat the potatoes when these two little kids ran across the lot. They came right up to where we were standing and tried to hide behind us. The older looked about eight, and the little one looked about six.

Two seconds later Mr. Zacks arrived. He has a pushcart on Orchard Street and he sells fruits and vegetables and things like that. Well, he grabbed those kids by their coats and started shaking them and screaming about how they belonged in jail.

Then he reached into their coat pockets and pulled out two apples.

~~FRIDAY, JANUARY 4~~

Mr. Zacks held up the apples. "Look," he hollered. "They have bites! Who's going to pay me for these apples?"

I looked at Ida. Ida looked at me. Then we both looked at the scared kids.

"We can't **pay** you, Mr. Zacks, but we'll deliver vegetables for you. Won't that pay for the apples?"

"You shouldn't protect criminals," he said. "But all right." And he left.

Both of the children burst into tears. "Mommy's gone," said the older one. We found out later that their names are Joan and Bobby Levy.

"They took Mommy away," said Bobby.

Then we got the whole story. It was very sad. Their father was killed in the war, and yesterday morning their mother got sick. An ambulance came and picked her up. Bobby and Joan were left alone. Ida and I gave them our potatoes and took them to my house.

On the way home, we tried to cheer them up. We counted horses and played hide and seek in and out of the pushcarts. Bobby and Joan were giggling by the time we got to the house.

Mama gave them some soup and made a dinner package for them to take home. Ida and I walked them back to their apartment. Joan had a key tied to a shoelace around her neck and she opened the door. We stayed with them until dinner time.

Just as we were ready to go, somebody banged on the door. Bobby ran to the door screaming, "It's Mommy!" But it wasn't. It was their upstairs neighbor who had just heard about Mrs. Levy. She said they could stay with her. Ida and I promised to visit tomorrow.

Friday, January 4

A boring day. Bobby and Joan weren't home when we went to visit. And we didn't have any more potatoes. And I'm glad I used up all the space in the diary yesterday.

MONDAY, JANUARY 7

Ida and I went to see Bobby and Joan after school. Mrs. Levy was home from the hospital but she had to stay in bed. She just kept thanking us and thanking us for helping Joan and Bobby.

The apartment was freezing and there was no food in the house. Ida and I didn't have any money to buy coal for the stove, but we decided that we were going to get some food. We walked up and down Orchard Street and asked every pushcart man for a contribution. When we were finished collecting, we had a huge bagful of vegetables—cabbage, potatoes, onions, stringbeans, and carrots. Then we went to the butcher, who gave us some soup bones. Ida and I made a giant pot of soup. It was great, and Mrs. Levy was so happy.

I wanted to keep two potatoes (there were plenty) so we could cook them in the lot, but Ida said that was dishonest. Well, someday we'll get to roast those potatoes.

SUNDAY, JANUARY 13

We picked up Bobby and Joan and took them to the candy store with us. Ida and I usually go to the candy store on Sundays and wait for phone calls. None of the people in the buildings near the candy store have telephones, so their relatives call them at the candy store and we run and get them. We usually get a penny for the trip.

This morning we had five calls. Then we bought a big bag of penny candy and had a feast.

MONDAY, JANUARY 14

Ida and I were very busy in school today. Mrs. Levy needs coal to heat her apartment and we promised to bring her some. So we made a speech in each class. Tomorrow every kid who can is going to bring in a piece of coal. Ida and I are going to bring in bags and collect it.

TUESDAY, JANUARY 15

Ida and I went around to all the classes today. We got three big bags of coal. Mrs. Levy cried when we brought it. She can walk around now.

WEDNESDAY, JANUARY 16

After school today Ida and I delivered vegetables for Mr. Zacks. We pulled the huge bags on the wagon we made last summer out of an orange crate and a pair of broken roller skates. We hit a lot of bumps and practically dumped the whole load about a thousand times.

We worked for a lot longer than two apples were worth, but when we finished, Mr. Zacks gave us two potatoes.

THURSDAY, JANUARY 17

At last! Our fire was beautiful. (Margie helped us again. But mostly Ida and I were in charge. We just need Margie 'cause her mother says she has to supervise.)

Anyway, this time we got to eat the potatoes ourselves. They were hard and crusty and hot on the outside and mushy and delicious on the inside. Nothing ever tasted so good!!!

I closed the diary. I could finish it later and this seemed like a good place to stop. It was strange to think of my grandmother as a girl in school. Tomorrow Mom and I are going into the city. I'm going to ask her to take me to Rivington Street. Maybe we can find the house where Deborah Miller once lived.

Reflections

1. How old was Deborah Miller when she started her diary? In what year was she born? How did you figure it out?
2. In what sorts of ways do you think life has changed since Grandma wrote her diary?
3. Why was Mr. Zacks so upset when the children took two apples from his pushcart? Do you think he made much money selling fruit from the pushcart? What reasons might he have for being angry besides the money he lost?
4. How did the girls pay for the stolen apples? How did the two girls get coal for the family? What things could you do for someone who needed help?
5. Would you like to keep a diary? Why or why not? If you do keep a diary, what kinds of things do you write in it? Do you think you would like your grandchild to read it someday? Why or why not?
6. Although Deborah Miller did not describe herself in her diary, we learn about her from the things she did. Write a description of Deborah, using examples from her diary to support your opinions.

In the Community

In every town and city there are people who need help. And there are many people who work to help them.

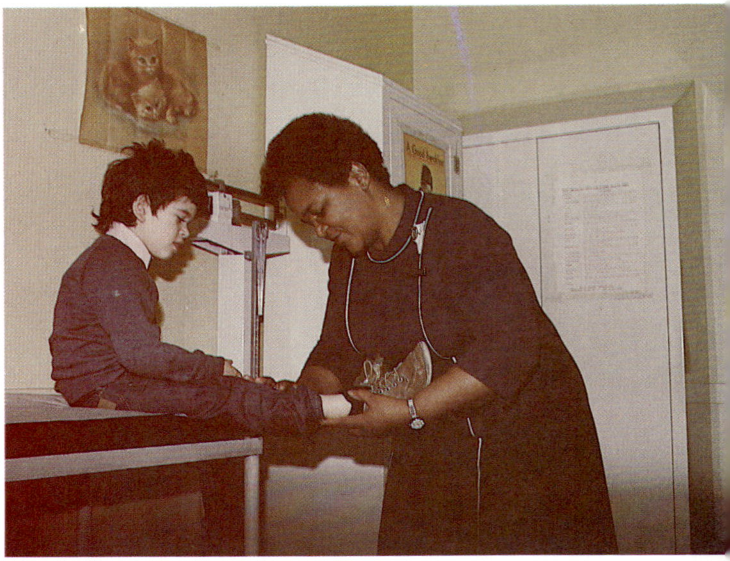

Doctors and nurses *(top)* often help people in community clinics. They examine children and give their parents advice about caring for them.

Many old people cannot climb stairs to go out to shop for food. Some may even find it too hard to cook their own meals. For such people, some cities provide a service called "Meals on Wheels." Here *(bottom)*, dinner is being delivered to an elderly woman.

(top) People who like to work with young children can find opportunities in day-care centers. There, teachers and their helpers take care of the children while their mothers work.

After-school centers often provide activities for older children. Here *(bottom),* children in a recreation center paint a mural to decorate its walls.

The Black Pearl

SCOTT O'DELL

A boy named Ramón Salazar tells this story, which takes place in Baja California. Ramón grew up knowing that one day he would become a partner with his father, who was a pearl merchant.

Ramón also knew the stories told about the Manta Diablo. This monster of the sea had a shape like a kite. He was supposed to be as large as the largest ship in the harbor, with seven rows of teeth in his mouth.

But Ramón wasn't thinking of the Manta Diablo as he watched his father's fleet leave on a pearling trip. He was wondering when his father would allow him to learn to dive. And he was dreaming about the great pearl he would discover—the Pearl of Heaven all divers longed to find.

A Chance Comes

I was standing at the desk, with a pen over my ear and the leather-bound ledger open in front of me. I was watching a canoe that moved around the tip of the lizard tongue. It was a red canoe and came swiftly, so I knew it belonged to the Indian Soto Luzon.

I was glad to see old Luzon. He had sold pearls to my father for many years. He came about every three months and never brought more than one, but it always was a pearl of good quality. Soon after I began to work with my father, Luzon had brought in a beautiful pearl of more than two carats.

As I watched Luzon beach the canoe and come up the path, I hoped he was bringing another like it, for the yield from our last trip had been poor. Five boatloads of shells had yielded no round or pear-shaped pearls and only a handful of buttons and baroques, all of them dull.

I opened the door at his timid knock and invited him to come in and sit down.

"I have traveled all night," Luzon said. "If it pleases you, I would like to stand."

Luzon never sat. He had an Indian's thin legs but a powerful chest and thick arms that could wield a paddle for hours and not grow tired.

"I passed your boats this morning," he said. "They were near Maldonado."

"They are going to Isla Cerralvo."

The old man gave me a shrewd look. "The pearling is not good around here?"

"Good," I said. It was not wise to say that it was poor when he had come to sell a pearl. "Very good."

"Then why, señor, do your father's boats go to Cerralvo?"

"Because my father wants to search there for the black ones."

The old man fumbled in his shirt and pulled out a knotted rag and untied it. "Here is a black one," he said.

I could see at a glance that it was round and of a good quality, like the pearl I had bought from him three months before. I placed it on the scales and balanced it against the small copper weights.

"Two and a half carats," I said.

My father never haggled with Luzon and always gave him a fair price and had told me to do the same. For that reason old Luzon always brought his pearls to Salazar and Son, although four other dealers were in our town.

"Two hundred pesos," I said.

This sum was about fifty pesos more than my father would have offered, but a plan was taking shape in my mind, and I needed the old man's help. I counted out the money, and he put it in his shirt, probably thinking to himself that I was not so smart as my father.

"You always bring in good pearls. Black ones," I said. "There must be many in your lagoon. If you permit me, I will come and dive there. All the pearls that I find I will pay you for."

The old man looked puzzled. "But you are not a diver," he said.

"You can teach me, señor."

"I have heard your father say many times, since the time you were a child, that he did not

raise you to drown in the sea or to give an arm or a leg to a burro shell."

"My father," I said, "has gone to Cerralvo, and he will not return for a week or more."

"And your mother and your sister, what will they say?"

"They will say nothing because today they go to Loreto." I paused. "You will teach me to dive, and I will look for the big one. And when I find it, I will pay you what it is worth."

"The big one I have searched for for many years," Luzon said. "How is it found in a week?"

"You can find the big one in a single dive."

The old man pulled at his stubbly chin. He was thinking, I knew, about his wife and his two unmarried daughters and his three young sons and all those mouths he had to feed every day.

"When do you wish to go?" he said.

"I wish to go now."

Luzon hitched up his trousers. "After I buy a sack of frijoles and a sack of flour, then we go."

The old man left, and I put the pearls away and locked the safe. I took the bundle from under the desk—my pants, a shirt, and the knife. I closed the door and locked it. As I walked down to the beach, I thought about the great pearl I had dreamed of.

It was a dream so wild that only a very young man and a stupid one could dream it. And yet, as happens sometimes, the dream came true.

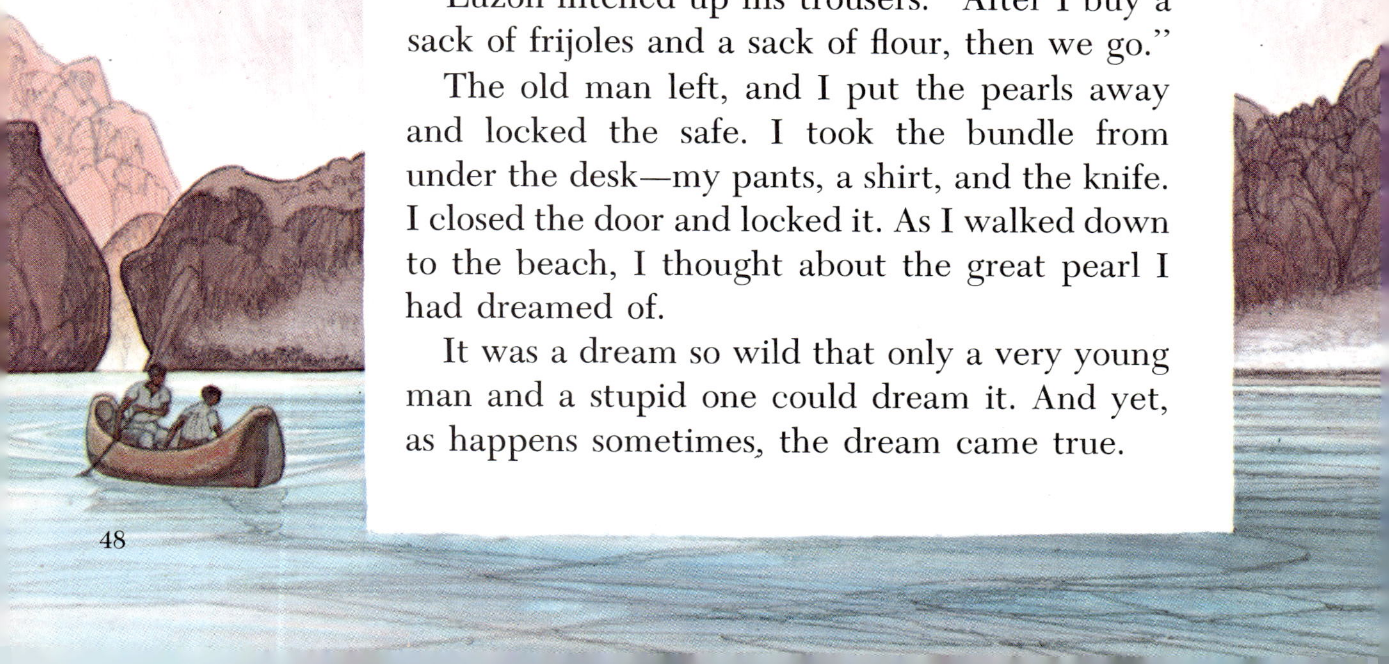

El Diablo

The lagoon where the old man lived was about seven leagues from La Paz, and we should have reached it by midnight. But the currents and the wind were against us, so it was near dawn before we sighted the two headlands that marked the lagoon's hidden entrance.

You could pass this entrance many times and think that it was only an opening in the rocks that led nowhere. But as soon as you passed the rocks, you came to a narrow channel that wound like a snake between the two headlands for a half mile or farther.

The sun was just rising when the channel opened out, and suddenly we were in a quiet oval-shaped lagoon. On both sides of the lagoon, steep hills came down to the water, and at the far end lay a shallow beach of black sand. Beyond were two scraggly trees and beneath them a cluster of huts where breakfast fires were burning.

It was a peaceful scene that lay before me, much like many other lagoons that dot our coast. But there was something about the place that made me feel uneasy. At first I thought it must be the barren hills that closed in upon the lagoon and the coppery haze that lay over it and the beach of black sand and the quiet. I was soon to

hear that it was something else, something far different from what I thought.

Carefully raising and lowering the paddle as if he did not want to disturb the water, the old man paddled slowly across the lagoon. And though he had talked most of the time before we reached the lagoon, he now fell silent. A gray shark circled the canoe and disappeared. He pointed to it but said nothing.

Nor did he speak again until we beached the canoe and were walking up the path to the huts. Then he said, "It is well to hold the tongue and not to talk needlessly when you are on the lagoon. Remember this when we go out to dive, for there is one who listens and is quickly angered."

Indians think that the moon and the sun and some animals and birds, especially the coyote and the owl, have special powers. So I was not surprised that he wished to warn me.

"Who is it that listens and grows angry?" I asked him.

Twice he glanced over his shoulder before he answered. "The Manta Diablo," he said.

"El Diablo?" I asked, holding back a smile. "He lives here in your lagoon?"

"In a cave," he answered, "a big one which you can see just as you leave the channel."

"The channel is very narrow," I said, "barely wide enough for a canoe. How does a giant like

El Diablo swim through it? But perhaps he does not need to. Perhaps he remains here in your lagoon."

"No," the old man said. "He travels widely and is gone for many weeks at a time."

"Then he must swim through the channel somehow."

"Oh, no, that would be impossible, even for him. There is another opening, a secret one, near the place where you enter the channel. When he swims out to sea, it is this one he uses."

We were nearing the huts clustered beneath the two scraggly trees. A band of children came running out to meet us, and the old man said nothing more about El Diablo until we had eaten breakfast, slept the morning away, eaten again, and gone back to the lagoon.

As we floated the canoe and set off for the pearling reefs, Luzon said, "When the mist goes, that means El Diablo has gone, too."

It was true that the red mist was gone, and the water now shone green and clear. I still smiled to myself at the old man's belief in El Diablo, yet I felt a little of the excitement that I had felt long ago when my mother threatened me with the monster.

"Now that he is gone," I said, "we can talk."

"A little and with much care," Luzon replied, "for he has many friends in the lagoon."

"Friends?"

"Yes, the shark you saw this morning and many small fish. They are all friends, and they listen, and when he comes back, they tell him everything, everything."

"When he leaves the lagoon, where does he go?"

"That I do not know. Some say that he takes the shape of an octopus and seeks out those pearlers who have done him a wrong or spoken ill of him. It is also said that he takes the shape of a human and goes into the town and seeks his enemies there in the streets and sometimes even in the church."

"I should think that you would fear for your life and leave the lagoon."

"No, I do not fear El Diablo. Nor did my father before me. Nor his father before him. For many years they had a pact with the Manta Diablo, and now I keep this pact. I show him proper respect and tip my hat when I come into the lagoon and when I leave it. For this he allows me to dive for the black pearls which belong to him and which we now go to search for."

Silently the old man guided the canoe toward the south shore of the lagoon, and I asked no more questions, for I felt that he had said all he wished to say about the Manta Diablo. In two fathoms of water, over a reef of black rocks, he dropped anchor and told me to do the same.

"Now I teach you to dive," he said. "First we start with the breathing."

The old man lifted his shoulders and began to take in great gulps of air, gulp after gulp, until his chest seemed twice its size. Then he let out the air with a long whoosh.

"This is called taking the wind," he said. "And because it is very important, you must try it."

I obeyed his command but filled my lungs in one breath.

"More," the old man said.

I took in another gulp of air.

"More," the old man said.

I tried again and then began to cough.

"For the first time it is good," the old man said. "But you must practice this much so you stretch the lungs. Now we go down together."

We both filled our lungs with air and slipped over the side of the canoe feet first, each of us holding a sink stone. The water was as warm as milk, but clear, so that I could see the wrinkled sand and the black rocks and fish swimming about.

When we reached the bottom, the old man put a foot in the loop of the rope that held his sink stone, and I did likewise with my stone. He placed his hand on my shoulder and took two steps to a crevice in a rock that was covered with trailing weeds. Then he took the knife from his belt and thrust it into the crevice. Instantly the crevice closed, not slowly but with a snap. The old man wrenched the knife free and took his foot out of the loop and motioned for me to do the same, and we floated up to the canoe.

The old man held out the knife. "Note the scratches which the burro shell leaves," he said. "With a hand or a foot it is different. Once the burro has you, he does not let go, and thus you

drown. Take care, therefore, where you step and where you place the hand."

We dived until night came. The old man showed me how to walk carefully on the bottom, so as not to muddy the water, and how to use the knife to pry loose the oysters that grew in clumps and how to get the shells open and how to search them for pearls.

We gathered many baskets that afternoon but found nothing except a few baroques of little worth. And it was the same the next day and the next. Then on the fourth day, because the old man had cut his hand on a shell, I went out on the lagoon alone.

It was on this day that I found the great Pearl of Heaven.

In the Cave

A red haze hung over the water as I floated the canoe on the morning of the fourth day and began to paddle toward the cave where the old man said the Manta Diablo lived.

The sun was up, but the haze hung so thick that I had trouble locating the channel. After I found it, I searched for almost an hour before I sighted the cave. It was hidden behind a rocky pinnacle and faced the rising sun. The opening was about thirty feet wide and the height of a tall man and curved downward like the upper lip of a mouth. Because of the red mist, I could not see into the cave, so I drifted back and forth and waited until the sun rose higher and the mist burned away.

I had talked to the old man the night before about the cave. We had eaten supper. The women and children had gone to bed, and the two of us were sitting around the fire.

"You have fished everywhere in the lagoon," I said, "but not in the cave."

"No," he said. "Nor did my father, nor did his father."

"Big pearls may grow there."

The old man did not answer. He got up and put wood on the fire and sat down again.

"The great one itself, the Pearl of Heaven, may lie there," I said.

Still he did not answer, but suddenly he looked across the fire. It was a fleeting look that he gave me, and yet its meaning was as clear as if he had spoken to me and said, "I cannot go to the cave to search for pearls. I cannot go because I fear the Manta Diablo. If you go there, then it is alone. El Diablo cannot blame me."

And that morning when I went down to the beach, he did not go with me. "The wound on my hand hurts very much," he said, "so I will stay behind." And the look he gave me was the same I had seen the night before.

At last, about midmorning, the sun burned

away the mist, and I could see for a short distance into the cave. I paddled through the mouth and soon found myself in a vast vaultlike room. The walls of the room were black and smooth and shone from the light that came in through the opening.

Near the mouth of the cave, the water was very clear. I picked up my basket and sink stone, took a deep breath, and slipped over the side of the canoe, remembering all that the old man had taught me.

I reached the bottom after about a fathom and a half. I looped my foot in the rope tied to the sink stone and waited until the bubbles that had risen behind me disappeared and I could find the bed of shells I had noticed from above. The bed was five steps away toward the mouth of the cave. I walked carefully in the sand as I had learned to do.

The shells were the largest I had ever seen. They were half the length of my arm and thick through as my body and covered with weed that looked like a woman's hair. I chose the nearest one, which seemed to be easier to get at than

the others. I took my knife and worked quietly, but a school of small fish kept swimming in front of my eyes, so I failed to pry the shell loose before my lungs began to hurt and I had to go up.

On my second dive I had no sooner reached the bottom than a shadow fell across the bed where I was working. It was the shadow of a gray shark, one of the friendly ones, but by the time he had drifted away, my breath was gone.

I dived six times more and worked quickly each time I went down, hacking away with my sharp knife at the base of the big shell where it was anchored to the rock. But it had been growing there for many years, since long before I was born, I suppose, and it would not come free from its home.

By this time it was late in the afternoon, and the light was poor. Also my hands were bleeding, and my eyes were half blind with salt from the sea. But I sat in the canoe, thinking of the many hours I had spent for nothing.

I filled my lungs and took the sink stone and went down again. With the first stroke of my knife, the shell came free. It toppled over on one side, and I quickly untied the rope from the sink stone and looped it twice around the shell and swam back to the surface. I pulled the big shell up, but it was too heavy for me to lift into the canoe, so I tied it to the stern and paddled out of the cave.

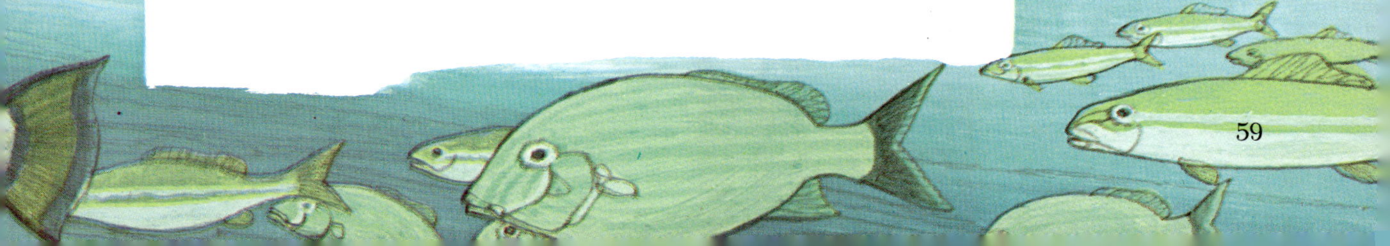

Across the lagoon I could see the old man standing among the trees. From time to time during the day, I had caught glimpses of him standing there with his eyes fixed on the cave. I knew that I could drown and he would not try to save me and that he was telling El Diablo all along that he had not wanted me to go to the cave and that he was therefore not to blame. But I also felt that if I found a pearl, he would be willing to take his share because he had nothing to do with finding it.

He came out from the trees as I paddled across the lagoon and strolled down to the beach as if he did not care whether I had found a pearl or not. I suppose this was to show El Diablo and his friends the fish and the long, gray shark that Soto Luzon was without blame.

"A big one," he said when I dragged the shell ashore. "In my life I have never seen such a monster. It is the grandfather of all oysters that live in the sea."

"There are many in the cave bigger than this one," I said.

"If there are so many," he answered, "then the Manta Diablo cannot be mad that you have taken only one of them."

"Perhaps a little mad," I said and laughed, "but not much."

The mouth of the oyster was closed, and it was hard to put my blade between the tight edges of the shell.

"Lend me your knife," I said. "Mine is blunted from use."

The old man placed his hand on the hilt of his knife and pulled it from the sheath and then slipped it back again.

"I think it is better if you use your own knife," he said, and his voice began to tremble as he spoke.

I wrestled a long time with the oyster. At last the hard lips began to give a little. Then I could feel the knife sink through the heavy muscles that held them together, and suddenly the lips fell apart.

I put my finger under the frilled edge of the flesh as I had seen my father do. A pearl slid along my finger, and I picked it out. It was about the size of a pea. When I felt again, another the same size rolled out and then a third. I put them on the other half of the shell so they would not be scratched.

The old man came and leaned over me as I knelt there in the sand and held his breath.

Slowly I slid my hand under the heavy tongue of the oyster. I felt a hard lump, so monstrous in size that it could not be a pearl. I took hold of it and pulled it from the flesh and got to my feet and held it to the sun, thinking that I must be holding a rock that the oyster had swallowed somehow.

It was round and smooth and the color of smoke. It filled my cupped hand. Then the sun's light struck deep into the thing and moved in silver swirls, and I knew that it was not a rock that I held but a pearl, the great Pearl of Heaven.

"Of Heaven," the old man whispered when he saw it.

I stood there and could not move or talk. The old man kept whispering over and over, "The Great Pearl of Heaven."

Darkness fell. I tore off the tail of my shirt and wrapped the pearl in it.

"Half of this is yours," I told him.

I handed the pearl to him, but he drew back in fear.

"You wish me to keep it until we reach La Paz?" I said.

"Yes, it is better that you keep it."

"When shall we go?"

"Soon," he said hoarsely. "El Diablo is away, but he will come back. And his friends will tell him then about the pearl."

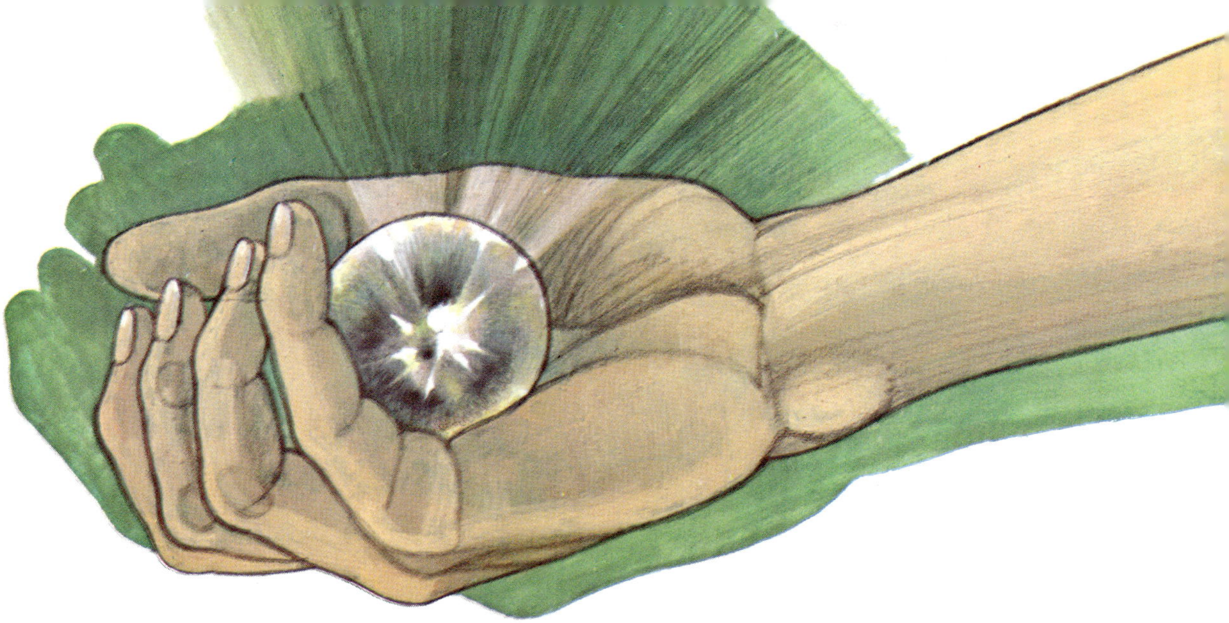

Reflections

1. Why do you think Mr. Salazar did not want Ramón to learn to dive? Do you think Luzon was right to take Ramón diving without Mr. Salazar's permission? Why or why not?
2. How do you think Ramón felt when he was in the cave? What do you think was his major concern?
3. Luzon would not go to the cave with Ramón because he was afraid of angering El Diablo. Why then do you think he was willing to share in Ramón's find? Do you think Luzon exhibited good reasoning? Explain.
4. What do you suppose Mr. Salazar said when he learned that Ramón had gone diving and had found the Pearl of Heaven?
5. Ramón's dream was to find the Pearl of Heaven. Write about something you have wanted very much. Be sure to tell how you went about getting it or how you plan to get it.

Ginger's Colt

DORIS GATES

A Small Victory

He was born in the bluegrass country on a spring morning. When his mother pushed her gentle nose against him, he got to his feet. He didn't want to stand up. He was not at all sure about his legs. They didn't feel strong under him. For a minute he stood without moving and looked with surprised brown eyes at this strange new world.

There was not much to see—just the four sides of his box stall and a thick covering of straw on the floor. He moved one of his tiny hoofs in the straw.

He felt his mother's nose upon his back. It made him brave. He took a step. Then from inside him a new feeling sent a signal into his beautiful little head. It was his stomach telling him that it would like some milk. The colt was hungry. Suddenly he moved closer to his mother's side. His own small nose bumped against her ribs and felt along her side. Then he took one more step. This brought him within reach of his breakfast.

It was about an hour later that a boy came into the barn. He went straight to the box stall where Ginger stood with her new colt beside her.

"Well, old lady," said the boy, his face lighting with joy. "Well!" He opened the door into the stall and slowly went inside. Ginger moved so that she stood between the boy and the colt.

"Come now, old lady," the boy said. "You know me better than that!"

He stood for a minute, watching the horse. Then, on the other side of her, the boy could hear something stirring. He knew it was Ginger's baby, and he waited. Soon a little nose peeped out at him from under Ginger's neck. Two small ears were pointed toward him. Two wide eyes stared at this strange two-legged animal. Between the eyes was a white star.

"By all that is wonderful," breathed the boy, "another Victory! Only smaller. Come here, Little Vic."

Victory was the colt's father. He was a son of Man o' War, who, some people think, was the greatest racehorse of all time. Victory was a great racehorse in his own right. And now here was a colt of his with the same wide space between his eyes and with a white star upon it.

The little colt seemed interested in the boy. He edged out from behind his mother. Ginger did not seem to care, so the colt came a step nearer. The boy took a step farther into the stall and put out his hand. But Ginger sniffed the hand and blew loudly. It was a warning to the colt, who recognized it as such. He quickly backed up under his mother's neck again.

The boy smiled and lowered his hand. He went out of the stall and closed the door. Then he rested his arms on the top of it and looked at Ginger and her son. You could tell from the way he looked at them that he thought they were the two most beautiful things in the world.

"Take your time, old lady," he said to Ginger. He kept his voice low and quiet. "He has a large number of things to learn about this big old world. You're wise to make him take it easy. I'm glad, though, that I'm the first person he ever set eyes on. I'm going to be glad about that for as long as I live."

The boy's name was Jonathan Rivers, but nobody ever called him that. When his mother was alive and feeling cross, she would say "Jonathan" in a special way. But she was gone now, and the name was lost to him for good. It didn't matter, though. From the time he could walk almost, he had been known as Pony. Pony Rivers was now his name. It suited him, for Pony cared nothing about anything except horses. He could not remember when he had not loved horses. He thought he must have come into the world loving them.

Pony Rivers had come to Spring Valley Farm about six months ago. He had arrived one stormy night when the rain beat against the windows of the big house and the wind blew puffs of smoke now and then down the big chimney. He had come on a freight train from New York because he had no money with which to buy a seat on the passenger train. All the clothes he had were on his back, and they were wet through.

He had spent that first night curled up in a corner of the barn. One of the farmhands had found him there asleep the next morning. He had taken Pony to the man who ran the farm, and the man had not been glad to see the boy.

"What do you mean by hiding in our barn?" Mr. Barby had asked him.

"I was not hiding," said Pony. "I just wanted to get out of the rain until morning. Then I planned to ask you for a job."

Mr. Barby looked at him, and he didn't like what he saw. The boy standing before him was a little fellow. He didn't look more than twelve years old at first sight.

"What's your name?" he asked.

"Pony Rivers," said the boy.

"That is not a name," said the man.

"It's my name," answered the boy.

"Why do you have a name like that?"

"It's because I like horses so much. Horses are all I care about. That's why I came down here to the horse country, to the bluegrass. I want to live all my days with horses."

"But you said you were from New York. How could you get to know anything about horses up there?"

"My father rode racehorses until he was killed in a race. Then my mother took in roomers. Most of them worked around the racetrack. They used to let me go there with them every chance I got. They taught me things about horses and riding. A month back I lost my mother. I lived with an aunt after that, but I didn't like it. She wanted me to get a job selling papers. I tried that, and I didn't like any part of it. So I ran away. I had heard about this country. I knew the great horses came from here. So I decided to head this way. I came straight to this place."

"Why?"

"Because I knew that Victory was at this farm."

Mr. Barby looked long and thoughtfully at the boy who waited before him. He looked as if he might be the son of a racetrack rider. He was small. He had a quiet way about him that would go well around horses. Perhaps everything was just as he had said.

"Okay," said Mr. Barby at last. "We'll give you a try. But I won't pay you much. You've got to show me you know something about horses first."

"I don't care about the pay," said Pony.

A Great Little Victory

Six months had now gone by. In that time Pony Rivers had more than earned his pay. Though he was young, he had a way with horses.

Spring Valley Farm was one of the biggest farms in the bluegrass country. It was known far and wide for its fine string of racehorses. Each spring a new crop of foals was born at Spring Valley Farm. Many of them were the sons and daughters of the farm's greatest treasure, Victory. In the days before he left the track, Victory had been the best-known horse in the country next to his father, Man o' War. It was believed that any foal of his would be a great racehorse, too. And so his foals were always watched with interest as they grew old enough to train.

Pony Rivers had known for years about Spring Valley Farm. He had seen Victory race. Pony's father had always hoped that someday he would have a chance to ride Victory, but the chance had never come. He had talked to his small son about riding and had told Pony many good things to know. All Pony wanted was to live and work with horses. And, he decided, as long as he wanted to live on a horse farm, to choose the one where Victory lived.

Now here he was, the first person to be looking at a new son of Victory's. It was the first of his colts to be born at the farm since Pony Rivers had arrived. Pony thought there could never be a more promising colt born anywhere than the lovely little animal he was watching.

After a while he left the barn and went up to the big house. Mr. Barby was there.

"Ginger has her colt," said Pony, very proud to be the first one to spread the good news.

"Are they both all right?" asked Mr. Barby.

"I'll say they are," said Pony. His eyes were shining so that Mr. Barby had to smile. "He looks just like Victory, only smaller."

Mr. Barby's smile grew wider. "Sounds like a lucky break for the farm," he said. "And the first colt of the season, too."

"He's a real little Victory, all right," said Pony. He was watching Mr. Barby's face closely as he said it. But the man seemed not to have heard.

Pony Rivers knew that naming the horses on such a farm as Spring Valley was a very important job. It was always done by the owner or the owner's wife. Then the names had to be given to the people who make the rules about racing in America. He knew that a racehorse's name is almost as important as a person's. But he had called the new colt Little Vic, and he knew that, for him, Little Vic would always be his name.

"Don't you think Little Vic would be a good name for him, Mr. Barby?"

Pony would never know what made him say it. He felt foolish the minute the words were out. He wished with all his heart that he could call them back. Suppose he had made Mr. Barby mad enough to fire him!

But all Mr. Barby did was to look at Pony in a surprised sort of way, and all he said was, "Let's take a look at the colt."

Pony let out a thankful breath and never said another word all the way to the barn.

Mr. Barby was not very well pleased with Ginger's baby, however. "He looks small," he said, tipping his head to one side and looking at the colt out of the tail of his eye. "He looks small. But then you can't always tell. Some of them born big don't shape up well later. Time will tell."

"But don't you think he looks just like Victory?" Pony asked.

Mr. Barby tipped his head to the other side. The colt stared back at him as if waiting for his answer. "Yes," said the man slowly. "He has the same dark coat and the star. But it seems to me there was something different about Victory when he was born. I can't seem to remember just what it was. Something about the way he held his head perhaps, the flash of his eye."

He turned to look at the boy standing beside him. It was clear that Pony had stopped listening a good many words back. Now he was just feasting his eyes on the lovely colt. He didn't know it, but a smile was playing around his mouth. He looked like a person who is seeing something wonderful, something that no other person can quite see.

"You look as if you've fallen hard for this colt," said Mr. Barby.

Pony jumped. He had forgotten the man at his side. "Yes," he said quietly. "He's the most beautiful thing in this world."

Mr. Barby laughed and slapped Pony on the back. "All right then. If you feel that way about him, I'll turn him over to you. From this day until he starts training, he's going to be your own special care. Do a good job with him."

It had been a long time since Pony's eyes had known tears. And then they had not been happy ones. But now tears were once more filling his eyes, though the boy tried hard to fight them back. Through them the walls of the box stall became all wavy, and Ginger and her colt looked wavy, too. When at last he thought it was safe to speak, his words sounded foolish to him.

"Do you mean it?" he said and wiped his eyes with the back of his hand.

"Sure, I mean it," said Mr. Barby. He waited a minute for Pony to get hold of himself. "Doc will be along to check them over." He took a quick look at Pony. "Ginger kind of put one over on Doc, didn't she? He wasn't expecting the colt for another week."

Pony Rivers said nothing, but he was thinking as Mr. Barby walked out of the barn, "It wasn't Ginger who put one over. It was Little Vic. He isn't ever going to do anything the way people think he will. But he's going to be great just the same!"

Reflections

1. What did Mr. Barby think of Pony when he first met him? Why did Mr. Barby change his mind?
2. Ginger warned her colt to stay away from Pony. How did this make Pony feel?
3. Why did Pony cry at the end of the story?
4. What do you suppose Pony meant at the end when he said to himself, "He isn't ever going to do anything the way people think he will"?
5. What do you think will happen to Pony and Little Vic? Write another part to this story telling what the future might bring to the boy and the colt.

Lucy and the Wardrobe

C. S. LEWIS

Lucy Looks into a Wardrobe

Once there were four children whose names were Peter, Susan, Edmund, and Lucy. This story is about something that happened to them when they were sent away from London because of the air raids during the war. They were sent to live in the house of an old professor in the heart of the country, ten miles from the nearest post office. He had no wife, and he lived in a very large house with a housekeeper called Mrs. Macready and three servants. (Their names were Ivy, Margaret, and Betty, but they do not come into the story much.)

He himself was a very old man with shaggy white hair, which grew over most of his face as well as on his head, and the children liked him almost at once. But on the first evening when he came out to meet them at the front door, he was so odd looking that Lucy (who was the youngest) was a little afraid of him, and Edmund (who was the next youngest) wanted to laugh and had to keep on pretending that he was blowing his nose to hide it.

As soon as they had said good night to the professor and had gone upstairs on the first night, the boys came into the girls' room, and they all talked it over.

"We've fallen on our feet and no mistake," said Peter. "This is going to be perfectly splendid. That old chap will let us do anything we like."

"I think he's an old dear," said Susan.

"Oh, come off it!" said Edmund, who was tired and pretending not to be tired, which always made him bad-tempered. "Don't go on talking like that."

"Like what?" said Susan. "And anyway, it's time you were in bed."

"Trying to talk like Mother," said Edmund. "And who are you to say when I'm to go to bed? Go to bed yourself."

"Hadn't we all better go to bed?" said Lucy. "There's sure to be a row if we're heard talking here."

"No there won't," said Peter. "I tell you this is the sort of house where no one's going to mind what we do. Anyway, they won't hear us. It's about ten minutes' walk from here down to that dining room, and any amount of stairs and passages in between."

"What's that noise?" said Lucy suddenly. It was a far larger house than she had ever been in before, and the thought of all those long passages and rows of doors leading into empty rooms was beginning to make her feel a little creepy.

"It's only a bird, silly," said Edmund.

"It's an owl," said Peter. "This is going to be a wonderful place for birds. I shall go to bed now.

I say, let's go and explore tomorrow. You might find anything in a place like this. Did you see those mountains as we came along? And the woods? There might be eagles. There might be stags. There'll be hawks."

"Badgers!" said Lucy.

"Snakes!" said Edmund.

"Foxes!" said Susan.

But when the next morning came, there was a steady rain falling, so thick that when you looked out of the window, you could see neither the mountains nor the woods nor even the stream in the garden.

"Of course it *would* be raining!" said Edmund. They had just finished breakfast with the professor and were upstairs in the room he had set apart for them—a long, low room with two windows looking out in one direction and two in another.

"Do stop grumbling, Ed," said Susan. "Ten to one it'll clear up in an hour or so. And in the meantime we're pretty well off. There's a wireless and lots of books."

"Not for me," said Peter, "I'm going to explore in the house."

Everyone agreed to this, and that was how the adventures began. It was the sort of house that you never seem to come to the end of, and it was full of unexpected places. The first few doors they tried led only into spare bedrooms, as everyone had expected that they would. But soon they came to a very long room full of pictures, and there they found a suit of armor. After that was a room all hung with green, with a harp in one corner.

Then came three steps down and five steps up and then a kind of little upstairs hall and a door that led out onto a balcony and then a whole series of rooms that led into each other and were lined with books—most of them very old books and some bigger than a Bible in a church. And shortly after that they looked into a room that was quite empty except for one big wardrobe—the sort that has a looking glass in the door. There was nothing else in the room at all except a dead bluebottle on the windowsill.

"Nothing to do there!" said Peter, and they all trooped out again—all except Lucy. She stayed behind because she thought it would be worthwhile trying the door of the wardrobe, even though she felt almost sure that it would be locked. To her surprise it opened quite easily, and two mothballs dropped out.

What Lucy Found There

Looking inside, she saw several coats hanging up—mostly long fur coats. There was nothing Lucy liked so much as the smell and feel of fur. She immediately stepped into the wardrobe and got in among the coats and rubbed her face against them, leaving the door open, of course, because she knew that it is very foolish to shut oneself into any wardrobe. Soon she went further in and found that there was a second row of coats hanging up behind the first one. It was almost quite dark in there, and she kept her arms stretched out in front of her so as not to bump her face into the back of the wardrobe. She took a step further in, then two or three steps, always expecting to feel woodwork against the tips of her fingers. But she could not feel it.

"This must be a simply enormous wardrobe!" thought Lucy, going still further in and pushing the soft folds of the coats aside to make room for herself. Then she noticed that there was something crunching under her feet. "I wonder, is that more mothballs?" she thought, stooping down to feel it with her hands. But instead of feeling the hard, smooth wood of the floor of the wardrobe, she felt something soft and powdery and extremely cold. "This is very queer," she said and went on a step or two further.

Next moment she found that what was rubbing against her face and hands was no longer soft fur

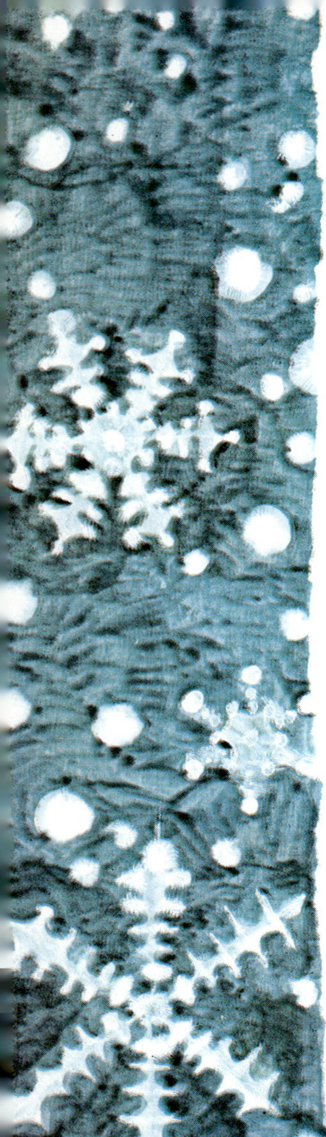

but something hard and rough and even prickly. "Why, it is just like branches of trees!" exclaimed Lucy. And then she saw that there was a light ahead of her, not a few inches away where the back of the wardrobe ought to have been, but a long way off. Something cold and soft was falling on her. A moment later she found that she was standing in the middle of a wood at nighttime, with snow under her feet and snowflakes falling through the air.

Lucy felt a little frightened, but she felt very inquisitive and excited as well. She looked back over her shoulder, and there, between the dark tree trunks, she could still see the open doorway of the wardrobe and even catch a glimpse of the empty room from which she had set out. It seemed to be still daylight there. "I can always get back if anything goes wrong," thought Lucy. She began to walk forward *crunch-crunch,* over the snow and through the wood towards the other light.

In about ten minutes she reached it and found that it was a lamppost. As she stood looking at it, wondering why there was a lamppost in the middle of a wood and wondering what to do next, she heard a pitter-patter of feet coming towards her. And soon after that a very strange person stepped out from among the trees into the light of the lamppost.

He was only a little taller than Lucy herself, and he carried over his head an umbrella, white with snow. From the waist upwards he was like a man, but his legs were shaped like a goat's (the hair on them was glossy black), and instead of feet he had goat's hoofs. He also had a tail, but Lucy did not notice this at first because it was neatly caught up over the arm that held the umbrella so as to keep it from trailing in the snow. He had a red woolen muffler round his neck, and his skin was rather reddish, too.

He had a strange but pleasant little face with a short, pointed beard and curly hair, and out of the hair there stuck two horns, one on each side of his forehead. One of his hands, as I have said, held the umbrella. In the other arm he carried several brown paper parcels. What with the parcels and the snow, it looked just as if he had been doing his Christmas shopping. He was a Faun. And when he saw Lucy, he was so surprised that he dropped all his parcels.

"Goodness gracious me!" exclaimed the Faun.

"Good evening," said Lucy. But the Faun was so busy picking up his parcels that at first he did not reply. When he had finished, he made her a little bow.

"Good evening, good evening," said the Faun. "Excuse me—I don't want to be inquisitive—but should I be right in thinking that you are a Daughter of Eve?"

"My name's Lucy," said she, not quite understanding him.

"But you are—forgive me—you are what they call a girl?" asked the Faun.

"Of course I'm a girl," said Lucy.

"You are, in fact, human?"

"Of course I'm human," said Lucy, still a little puzzled.

"To be sure, to be sure," said the Faun. "How stupid of me! But I've never seen a Son of Adam or a Daughter of Eve before. I am delighted. That is to say—" and then he stopped as if he had been going to say something he had not intended but had remembered in time. "Delighted, delighted," he went on. "Allow me to introduce myself. My name is Tumnus."

"I am very pleased to meet you, Mr. Tumnus," said Lucy.

"And may I ask, O Lucy, Daughter of Eve," said Mr. Tumnus, "how you have come into Narnia?"

"Narnia? What's that?" said Lucy.

"This is the land of Narnia," said the Faun, "where we are now. All that lies between the lamppost and the great castle of Cair Paravel on the eastern sea. And you—you have come here from the wild woods of the west?"

"I—I got in through the wardrobe in the spare room," said Lucy.

"Ah!" said Mr. Tumnus in a rather melancholy voice, "if only I had worked harder at geography when I was a little Faun, I should no doubt know all about those strange countries. It is too late now."

"But they aren't countries at all," said Lucy, almost laughing. "It's only just back there—at least—I'm not sure. It is summer there."

"Meanwhile," said Mr. Tumnus, "it is winter in Narnia, and has been for ever so long, and we shall both catch cold if we stand here talking in the snow. Daughter of Eve from the far land of Spare Oom where eternal summer reigns around the bright city of War Drobe, how would it be if you came and had tea with me?"

"Thank you very much, Mr. Tumnus," said Lucy. "But I was wondering whether I ought to be getting back."

"It's only just round the corner," said the Faun, "and there'll be a roaring fire and toast and sardines—and cake."

"Well, it's very kind of you," said Lucy. "But I shan't be able to stay long."

"If you will take my arm, Daughter of Eve," said Mr. Tumnus, "I shall be able to hold the umbrella over both of us. That's the way. Now—off we go."

Of Nymphs, Dryads, and Fauns

And so Lucy found herself walking through the wood arm in arm with this strange creature as if they had known one another all their lives.

They had not gone far before they came to a place where the ground became rough and there were rocks all about and little hills up and little hills down. At the bottom of one small valley, Mr. Tumnus turned suddenly aside as if he were going to walk straight into an unusually large rock, but at the last moment Lucy found he was leading her into the entrance of a cave. As soon as they were inside, she found herself blinking in the light of a wood fire. Then Mr. Tumnus stooped and took a flaming piece of wood out of the fire with a neat little pair of tongs and lit a lamp. "Now we shan't be long," he said and immediately put a kettle on.

Lucy thought she had never been in a nicer place. It was a little, dry, clean cave of reddish stone with a carpet on the floor and two little chairs ("one for me and one for a friend," said Mr. Tumnus) and a table and a dresser and a mantelpiece over the fire and above that a picture of an old Faun with a gray beard. In one corner there was a door which Lucy thought must lead to Mr. Tumnus's bedroom, and on one wall was a shelf full of books. Lucy looked at these while he was setting out the tea things. They had titles like *The Life and Letters of Silenus* or

Nymphs and Their Ways or *Men, Monks, and Gamekeepers: a Study in Popular Legend* or *Is Man a Myth?*

"Now, Daughter of Eve!" said the Faun.

And really it was a wonderful tea. There was a nice brown egg, lightly boiled, for each of them and then sardines on toast, then buttered toast and then toast with honey, then a sugar-topped cake. And when Lucy was tired of eating, the Faun began to talk.

He had wonderful tales to tell of life in the forest. He told about the midnight dances and how the Nymphs who lived in the wells and the Dryads who lived in the trees came out to dance with the Fauns; about long hunting parties after the milk-white Stag who could give you wishes if you caught him; about feasting and treasure-seeking with the wild Red Dwarfs in deep mines and caverns far beneath the forest floor; and then about summer when the woods were green and old Silenus on his fat donkey would come to visit them, and sometimes Bacchus himself, and then the streams would run with punch instead of water, and the whole forest would give itself up to jollification for weeks on end.

"Not that it isn't always winter now," he added gloomily. Then to cheer himself up, he took out from its case on the dresser a strange little flute that looked as if it were made of straw and began playing. And the tune he played made Lucy want to cry and laugh and dance and go to sleep all at the same time.

It must have been hours later when she shook herself and said, "Oh, Mr. Tumnus, I'm so sorry to stop you, and I do love that tune, but really, I must go home. I only meant to stay for a few minutes."

"It's no good *now*, you know," said the Faun, laying down his flute and shaking his head at her very sorrowfully.

"No good?" said Lucy, jumping up and feeling rather frightened. "What do you mean? I've got to go home at once. The others will be wondering what has happened to me." But a moment later she asked, "Mr. Tumnus! Whatever is the matter?" for the Faun's brown eyes had filled with tears, and then the tears began trickling down his cheeks, and soon they were running off the end of his nose. At last he covered his face with his hands and began to howl.

"Mr. Tumnus! Mr. Tumnus!" said Lucy in great distress. "Don't! Don't! What is the matter?

Aren't you well? Dear Mr. Tumnus, do tell me what is wrong." But the Faun continued sobbing as if his heart would break. And even when Lucy went over and put her arms round him and lent him her handkerchief, he did not stop. He merely took the handkerchief and kept on using it, wringing it out with both hands whenever it got too wet to be any more use, so that presently Lucy was standing in a damp patch.

"Mr. Tumnus!" bawled Lucy in his ear, shaking him. "Do stop. Stop it at once! You ought to be ashamed of yourself, a great big Faun like you. What on earth are you crying about?"

"Oh—oh—oh!" sobbed Mr. Tumnus, "I'm crying because I'm such a bad Faun."

"I don't think you're a bad Faun at all," said Lucy. "I think you are a very good Faun. You are the nicest Faun I've ever met."

"Oh—oh—you wouldn't say that if you knew," replied Mr. Tumnus between his sobs. "No, I'm a bad Faun. I don't suppose there ever was a worse Faun since the beginning of the world."

"But what have you done?" asked Lucy.

"My old father, now," said Mr. Tumnus, "that's his picture over the mantelpiece. He would never have done a thing like this."

"A thing like what?" said Lucy.

"Like what I've done," said the Faun. "Taken service under the White Witch. That's what I am. I'm in the pay of the White Witch."

Under Her Thumb

"The White Witch? Who is she?"

"Why, it is she that has got all Narnia under her thumb. It's she that makes it always winter. Always winter and never Christmas; think of that!"

"How awful!" said Lucy. "But what does she pay *you* for?"

"That's the worst of it," said Mr. Tumnus with a deep groan. "I'm a kidnapper for her, that's what I am. Look at me, Daughter of Eve. Would you believe that I'm the sort of Faun to meet a poor innocent child in the wood, one that had never done me any harm, and pretend to be friendly with it, and invite it home to my cave, all for the sake of lulling it asleep and then handing it over to the White Witch?"

"No," said Lucy. "I'm sure you wouldn't do anything of the sort."

"But I have," said the Faun.

"Well," said Lucy rather slowly (for she wanted to be truthful and yet not to be too hard on him), "well, that was pretty bad. But you're so sorry for it that I'm sure you will never do it again."

"Daughter of Eve, don't you understand?" said the Faun. "It isn't something I *have* done. I'm doing it now, this very moment."

"What do you mean?" cried Lucy, turning very white.

"You are the child," said Mr. Tumnus. "I had orders from the White Witch that if ever I saw a Son of Adam or a Daughter of Eve in the wood, I was to catch them and hand them over to her. And you are the first I ever met. And I've pretended to be your friend and asked you to tea, and all the time I've been meaning to wait till you were asleep and then go and tell *her.*"

"Oh, but you won't, Mr. Tumnus," said Lucy. "You won't, will you? Indeed, indeed, you really mustn't."

"And if I don't," said he, beginning to cry again, "she's sure to find out. And she'll have my tail cut off and my horns sawn off and my beard plucked out, and she'll wave her wand over my beautiful cloven hoofs and turn them into horrid solid hoofs like a wretched horse's. And if she is extra and especially angry, she'll turn me into stone, and I shall be only a statue of a Faun in her horrible house until the four thrones at Cair Paravel are filled—and goodness knows when that will happen, or whether it will ever happen at all."

"I'm very sorry, Mr. Tumnus," said Lucy. "But please let me go home."

"Of course, I will," said the Faun. "Of course, I've got to. I see that now. I hadn't known what humans were like before I met you. Of course, I can't give you up to the Witch, not now that I know you. But we must be off at once. I'll see you back to the lamppost. I suppose you can find the way from there back to Spare Oom and War Drobe?"

"I'm sure I can," said Lucy.

"We must go as quietly as we can," said Mr. Tumnus. "The whole wood is full of *her* spies. Even some of the trees are on her side."

They both got up and left the tea things on the table, and Mr. Tumnus once more put up his umbrella and gave Lucy his arm, and they went out into the snow. The journey back was not at all like the journey to the Faun's cave. They stole along as quickly as they could, without speaking a word, and Mr. Tumnus kept to the darkest places. Lucy was relieved when they reached the lamppost again.

"Do you know your way from here, Daughter of Eve?" said Mr. Tumnus.

Lucy looked very hard between the trees and could just see in the distance a patch of light that looked like daylight. "Yes," she said, "I can see the wardrobe door."

"Then be off home as quick as you can," said the Faun, "and—c-can you ever forgive me for what I meant to do?"

"Why, of course, I can," said Lucy, shaking him heartily by the hand. "And I do hope you won't get into dreadful trouble on my account."

"Farewell, Daughter of Eve," said he. "Perhaps I may keep the handkerchief?"

"Rather!" said Lucy and then ran towards the far-off patch of daylight as quickly as her legs would carry her. And presently, instead of rough branches brushing past her, she felt coats, and instead of crunching snow under her feet, she felt wooden boards. All at once she found herself jumping out of the wardrobe into the same empty room from which the whole adventure had started. She shut the wardrobe door tightly behind her and looked around, panting for breath. It was still raining, and she could hear the voices of the others in the passage.

"I'm here," she shouted. "I'm here. I've come back. I'm all right."

Reflections

1. At first the Faun said he was delighted to meet Lucy. Then he said, "That is to say—" and stopped. To judge from the rest of the story, what did he probably start to say?
2. Would you have gone to the Faun's house as Lucy did? Why or why not?
3. In many stories, creatures who are half human, half animal are quite frightening. What was there about Mr. Tumnus's appearance that would keep you from being especially afraid of him?
4. This selection is only part of a larger story. Do you suppose that Lucy ever goes back to Narnia? Give reasons for your answer.
5. What do you suppose the other children said when they heard Lucy's story? Write a dialogue between Lucy and one of her brothers. Have Lucy tell him about her adventure. How will he answer her? How will she try to convince him that she is telling the truth?

Cherry Ann and the Dragon Horse

ELIZABETH COATSWORTH

Just before World War II began, Cherry Ann Su and her mother left China. They came to San Francisco to join Cherry Ann's father, who had already been in California for years. Mr. Su grows flowers, and every day he brings them to the city in his flower wagon to sell them.

When the story begins, World War II is still going on. Cherry Ann is ten years old. She has been living near San Francisco for over four years, but she is still torn between Chinese traditions and American ways.

Off to Market

Cherry Ann felt happy. When she was with Mother, she was always a little homesick for China. But with Father she seemed almost to belong to this great, bustling America, so strange to her in so many ways. Father had lived in California for years. But Mother and Cherry Ann had left their village in southern China to join him just before the war began. Her heart was divided between two countries and two ways of living, so that she didn't really belong anywhere. Sometimes it was a horrid feeling.

But alone with Father Cherry Ann forgot her troubles. She loved getting up before sunrise on a summer morning to drive along the bay into San Francisco. And she loved to sit on the high seat of the flower wagon with the old horse, Precious White Jade, clop-clop-clopping along. This morning the mist lay over everything, almost hiding the water and headlands and islands.

They drove for a while in pleasant silence. Out of the mist a great ship was seen slowly making its way down the harbor toward the Golden Gate.

"Another troopship," sighed Mr. Su.

A few minutes later a smaller boat followed. "Supply boat," he said. "The war in Europe is over, but still Japan has not surrendered. And people are suffering."

It was just then that Cherry Ann saw the envelope that lay almost out of sight on the floor of the flower wagon, with one corner showing.

She reached down and picked it up. It was unopened and addressed to her father.

"This is something for you, Father," she said, handing it to him. "It must have dropped here out of sight when we got the mail yesterday."

Mr. Su gave the reins to Cherry Ann and read the letter carefully three times to make sure that he understood it perfectly. Then he folded it, put it back into its envelope, and slipped the envelope into his pocket.

When they reached their usual corner, Mr. Su stopped the wagon and said, "I am leaving you in charge of Precious White Jade and the flowers, Cherry Ann. I must go to see the draft board. I have been called up for service."

"You are going to be a soldier, Father?" she asked in a low voice.

Her father looked out over the heads of the crowd.

"This is my country now," he said, after a little while.

"You will go away, Father?"

"Yes, after my training is finished."

"But what will Mother do? She can't speak English."

"You will take my place as far as speaking

English goes. You have been in this country for over four years now, and you have gone to school and learned quickly. You will be ears and mouth for your mother."

"But her heart will follow you, Father."

Mr. Su sighed. "It cannot be helped. We will all be sad, but it is right for me to carry my share of the load." And with a smile he was gone.

For the first time in her life, Cherry Ann was alone in San Francisco.

She wanted to cry, but at ten she thought she was too old for tears. So she smiled instead and looked straight ahead, although things were so blurred that she could see nothing.

About noontime her father returned. He looked at the flowers in the wagon. "You have done well, Cherry Ann."

"Father?" she began.

"Yes?"

"Father, what was decided?"

"I am to be ready to go into training in ten days. For a butterfly ten days is a whole life."

Mr. Su turned to answer a customer, and for a few minutes he was busy. Then he spoke again to Cherry Ann.

"You and I will be butterflies for ten days, Cherry Ann. Mother, too. Now give Precious White Jade his food bag, and we will have our lunch."

Sorrow

That evening Cherry Ann's mother seemed just as usual, but very, very quiet. Her hands were hard at work, but her thoughts seemed far away.

It was a beautiful evening of many stars, and after a while the moon came up. Usually Cherry Ann loved working with her sharp clippers up and down the long rows of flowers, filling the flower baskets and smelling the sweet scent as she worked.

But now the evening seemed filled with sorrow—her mother's sorrow, and her sorrow, and the sorrow of all the other families whose loved ones were in danger. Before this she had not really understood how they felt.

The next day her father did not take her to San Francisco with him. She stayed home to help her mother. Mrs. Su did not talk of Mr. Su's going away, but all day she talked of the village where she had been born.

Several times Cherry Ann found her mother staring at the portraits of Grandfather and Grandmother hanging on one wall of the bedroom. Cherry Ann knew that her mother was asking the ancestors to help them. But when you were in America, you couldn't expect ancestors in China to do very much for you.

The next day Cherry Ann went with her father. It was a bright, sunshiny day, and there were ships coming and going in the harbor. On its hills, with the bay at its feet, San Francisco seemed like a golden city. Her father, following her glance, said, "It is a beautiful place. America has been good to us."

Mr. Su looked forward. He was an American. Mrs. Su looked back to China. And Cherry Ann stood between them, one hand in the hand of each of her parents and her heart never quite at ease.

A Plan

Time passed slowly. On the evening of the eighth day, Cherry Ann brought a pail of water to Precious White Jade in the little shed where he had his stall.

In only two days her father would go away. Cherry Ann wanted to stop him, but she didn't know what to do.

"Precious White Jade," she said, "what do *you* advise?"

The horse blew softly at her. Cherry Ann raised a hand and stroked the muzzle resting on her shoulder.

"What shall we do?" she asked again.

"You must go to the Kong Chow Temple," answered Precious White Jade. "There in a corner you will find a statue of Kwan Ti's horse. He is black and his name is Lung Mah, Dragon Horse. You will find gold paper money heaped on his saddle, and his front knees are tied together by red strings. Each string is a prayer to keep someone from going away. Lung Mah is the proper one to help you."

Cherry Ann thanked Precious White Jade and gave him extra oats and patted his long white neck. Then she went off, deep in thought.

Had Precious White Jade really spoken to her or had she made up words to go with his soft breathing? Was it she, Cherry Ann, or Jade who had remembered Lung Mah, the Dragon Horse, at the temple?

That evening Cherry Ann thought about Lung Mah as she ate her rice and fish, her chopsticks pausing between bowl and mouth until she saw her father glance at her in surprise.

Suddenly she had a wonderful idea.

"Father," she said respectfully, "tomorrow is the last day you will take the flowers to the city. May I go with you?"

Her father thought for a moment.

"I see no reason against it."

Cherry Ann was full of plans, but she didn't tell them. Only, before she went to bed that night, she said to her mother, "May I take some of the gold money for the temple from the chest, Mother?"

Mrs. Su raised her head and looked at Cherry Ann.

"But ordinarily children do not go to the temple."

"But this is not an ordinary time, Mother."

"You are right," said Mrs. Su in a low voice. "This is not an ordinary time."

To the Temple

Early the next morning Cherry Ann climbed into the flower wagon. On any other day it would have been fun to go to the city with Father, and she was careful to appear to be having a good time. Her father seemed just as usual. She wondered if his heart felt as heavy as hers did. This morning the traffic made her feel dizzy, and the motor horns sounded loud and threatening.

In the late morning Cherry Ann went off to the temple. It was not far away, but several times she had to ask for directions before she found it.

The temple was dim and crowded with carved gold altars, and the figures of gods and goddesses stared at her out of the shadows.

Cherry Ann bowed to them all and, with her heart in her shoes, followed her guide to the corner where stood Lung Mah, the Dragon Horse. He was about the size of a merry-go-round horse, carved from wood and painted black. His tail and mane were blown back and his head was high and his nostrils were wide as though he had been running. But he seemed to pause and look at Cherry Ann to hear what she had to say before he ran on.

Cherry Ann put the gold paper money she had brought with her on the saddle with the money already there.

Then she knelt and told Lung Mah all the story. "It is because of my mother that I dare trouble you," she said. "She is gentle and good as a flower, and I am afraid that the black frost of loneliness and sorrow will wither her."

Cherry Ann prayed for a long time, and Lung Mah seemed to listen, always with that wild air of being about to run off as soon as she was done. When she had finished, Cherry Ann took a red string and tied it about his knees where at least a dozen other red strings were already tied.

"Please, Lung Mah! Please!" she begged. "It was our horse, it was Precious White Jade, who told me to come to you."

But Lung Mah's head was held as high as ever. He looked as if he must go. How could a few red strings stop a horse like that? What were prayers, especially the prayers of a child?

Bowing respectfully to the dim, crowding gods and goddesses, Cherry Ann tiptoed out of the temple.

Going Tomorrow

The hours went by slowly that day, and on the way home the clop-clop-clopping of the old white horse's hoofs seemed to be saying, "*Going* tomorrow, *going* tomorrow, *going* tomorrow," until Cherry Ann had to cover her ears, and then her heart beat the same heavy tune.

All Cherry Ann's dreams that night were troubled. Once or twice she cried out in a nightmare, and her father wakened her and comforted her. The next morning, after a friend of Father's took the flowers to market in his wagon, time dragged. Now, in these last hours, nothing seemed worth doing.

The afternoon went by as slowly as the morning. Mr. Su and Mrs. Su and Cherry Ann just sat there looking at one another, smiling when they wanted to be crying.

Then, when the sun was halfway down the sky, the noise began. There was a distant siren and then another. Factory whistles blew; horns began to honk.

"What is it? What has happened?" cried Mrs. Su in alarm.

"It must be an air-raid drill," said Mr. Su.

'But people are shouting," said Cherry Ann. "They are calling to each other from the cars, and their voices sound happy."

At that moment a neighbor burst in, all breathless.

"The war's over!" she cried. "The war's over! Japan has surrendered! We just heard it over the radio. Your father won't have to go away after all, Cherry Ann!"

"What's that?" asked Mrs. Su. "I don't understand."

Only when Mr. Su had explained everything to her in Chinese did she dare to smile.

"It's peace, Mother!" echoed Cherry Ann. "Everything's all right! Father won't go away!"

And as the relief came over Cherry Ann suddenly in a flood, she found that her joy was not only for Mother and Father and herself, but for all the boys and girls at school whose families had been in danger and for all the friendly customers whose relatives were overseas. Her relief was for everyone in the country. They were part of her and she was part of them.

Cherry Ann slipped away to the shed, her hands filled with sugar.

Precious White Jade mumbled and bumbled over the sugar, blowing away half of it with his big breaths. Sticky-handed, Cherry Ann threw her arms about his neck.

"Could we have done it, you and I and Lung Mah?" she whispered.

But it didn't matter why the war had stopped. It was over, and for Cherry Ann more than the war was over. She felt doubly at peace. Her

unhappiness had made her understand how other people felt, but it was her joy mingling with their joy that made her really one of them. Now at last her loyalties were no longer divided. She had stopped looking back to the village in China. She was like Father; she was an American.

Reflections

1. When Mr. Su finds out he must become a soldier in ten days, he says to Cherry Ann, "For a butterfly, ten days is a whole life. You and I will be butterflies for ten days." What does he mean?
2. Cherry Ann is filled with sorrow because her father must go to war. How does this feeling make her understand Americans better?
3. Do you think Precious White Jade told Cherry Ann about the Dragon Horse, or do you think she simply remembered the Chinese custom?
4. Cherry Ann feels that her mother's prayers to her ancestors won't help. But what does Cherry Ann do to keep her father from leaving? How do you think this action will help Cherry Ann understand her mother better?
5. At the end of the story, Cherry Ann feels that she has become an American. Write a paragraph that explains why she finally feels this way.

Poem of Praise

ELIZABETH COATSWORTH

Swift things are beautiful:
swallows and deer,
and lightning that falls
bright-veined and clear,
rivers and meteors,
wind in the wheat,
the strong-withered horse,
the runner's sure feet.

And slow things are beautiful:
the closing of day,
the pause of the wave
that curves downward to spray,
the ember that crumbles,
the opening flower,
and the ox that moves on
in the quiet of power.

Mostly Beginnings

ELIZABETH COATSWORTH

No More Latin

I was brought up in my Grandmother Coatsworth's house, first in the heart of the city of Buffalo, but soon on the outskirts, where three elm-bordered parkways met, leading to the city park, with its lake and great meadow. There we lived, my grandmother, my gentle mother, my tall father, my older sister, Margaret, and I, a rather plump and docile child, then called Bess.

Buffalo even at that time was a true city, but it seemed more like a town. It lies at the very eastern end of Lake Erie, and the west winds blow down the Great Lakes to cool it pleasantly in summer. In winter these same winds bring cold and snow and gray skies. When our father, on his way to business, drove Margaret and me to school in the light sleigh, one runner would be so far up the banked snow near the curb that once we tipped over, and down came Father and Margaret and Bess, all in a heap, and I was at the bottom of it.

Margaret and I went to a private school, very strictly run. It took boys up to the sixth grade, after which they went to a separate school. We studied Latin in the fifth grade, French in the seventh, and if one went on to the end, as I did not, German was taught in the ninth grade and

Greek in the eleventh. We were dismissed at 3:10 in the afternoon, but if we had whispered or if our desks were out of order or if we had borrowed so much as a pencil during the day—no borrowing of any kind was allowed—we had to report ourselves and await our turn to learn and recite poetry before being excused. We seldom ran down the front steps until nearly four o'clock, and in winter four o'clock was already dusk. As summer drew near, we all chanted (under our breaths):

> "Seven more days and we'll be free
> From this school of misery,
> No more Latin, no more French,
> No more sitting on the hard wood bench!"

Although we had little fun at this school, I am grateful to it for its training in concentration. But oh! Each year when it was over, how gratefully we welcomed the carefree summers in our cottage on the Canadian lakeshore about twelve miles from Buffalo. Off with shoes and stockings, not to be put on again until autumn! On with our dark-blue, white-dotted cotton dresses and bloomers! If we were home at mealtimes, the rest of the day was ours to do with as we pleased.

As I look back on those summers, the weather seemed always to have been perfect. We climbed trees or played jacks or cut out paper dolls. For hours we carried about on our shoulders our

white rats, Columbus and Queen Isabella, or threw sticks for Bob, the Boston terrier. Sometimes we explored the back country or went on picnics to the Indian burying ground. In those days it was the older children, not some expert, who taught the younger children how to swim, paddle, and sail. At night, now and then, we had bonfires on the beach, around which we sat singing (though I can't sing) and telling ghost stories. It was an enchanted life.

This all ended when I was fourteen and Father sold his business and we went to Pasadena in southern California. We rented a house in an orange grove, a large, ugly house in a most beautiful garden at the edge of an arroyo, with a river running through it, wide and noisy in the springtime. The mountains and the fields of wild California poppies, the orange orchards in bloom, the long walks in the arroyo with my uncle's two Airedales, Robin and Bangle—all these were a delight.

As for our school here, it scarcely seemed like school at all. We studied outdoors on verandas at the back of the building; and when, during class, the mathematics teacher couldn't solve an algebra problem, she simply erased it from the blackboard and said no more about it. After my hard training at the Buffalo school, I didn't really like such easy schoolwork. But I really did love the beautiful, uncrowded California of those days and have gone back there for a few months at a time all my life.

Our family often traveled. Once we went to Mexico for a long Christmas vacation (Father was always sure we children could make up any schoolwork we might lose). We saw Mexico City at the holiday season. Every afternoon the *pasadas* passed below our balcony, the ladies driving in open carriages in one direction, while the gentlemen walked in the opposite direction along the sidewalks so that everyone might bow to friends and stare at strangers.

Father was a born explorer, and Mother loved travel almost as much as he did. We saw the pyramids near Mexico City and the great one at Puebla; then we went down to far-off, little-visited Oaxaca. At the governor's house in Mitla, we spent some days exploring the ruins there. On another occasion Father and Margaret and I even rode horseback to Monte Alban, which then was only an overgrown mountain where a goatherd guarded his flock. A double row of slabs carved with grinning figures seemed to lead straight into the shaggy hilltop. They were then the *only* hint of the temples and palaces and gold treasures which would later be unearthed to the wonder of the world.

At the moment I was more interested in taking my first real horseback ride. For years I had been afraid of getting into a saddle after an early fall from our old Morgan mare, Dolly. But now I was riding, and when we came to a narrow ditch, my horse jumped it—certainly not at my wish—but there we both were, still in one piece, on the other side.

That Fabulous Year

After two years in Pasadena, we came back to Buffalo, and this time I went to the Buffalo Seminary, in its new building across the parkway from our house. But my grandmother, who had read aloud to us for so many hours when we were little, was ill. During my first year of college at Vassar, both she and my father died, and the house of our childhood was sold. Now my mother, Margaret, and I were sometimes traveling and sometimes living with my mother's mother in California. The year after I graduated from Vassar College, I spent a winter in New York, while I took my master of arts degree at Columbia University.

That year I explored the city from the Van Cortlandt mansion to the north to the crown of the Statue of Liberty to the south. Once I remember riding on the last horsecar in the city, and perhaps in the whole United States. After

Columbia came that fabulous year which my mother, Margaret, and I spent in the Far East. We had no prearranged plans, no guides, no caution, though I sometimes trembled in my shoes, as on the day when my sister and I sat down to rest on what appeared to be a bench in an animal shop in Singapore. Only when a roar sounded beneath us did we realize that we were sitting on the carrying cage of a newly caught jungle tiger. But by that time we were already out in the street.

We saw the princesses dance in Java and were guests in Buddhist monasteries high in the Diamond Mountains of Korea. For ten days while Mother stayed in a hotel at the end of the road, Margaret and I rode horseback along the narrow mountain trails of the head-hunting Igorots in the Philippines. In China, north of Peking, we slept in one of the Ming tombs. Most of that night we lay awake, in fear of the bandits who, the bearers said, might come down from the hills to kidnap us for ransom. We went, too, through the blowing dust of spring past that dragon, the Great Wall of China, climbing along the endless mountains at the frontier. At last we reached the city of Kalgan, where, since there was no hotel, we stayed with an American couple.

The morning after our arrival, our host took Margaret and me out riding on Mongolian ponies to see the nomads come in from the Gobi desert.

At the city gate we passed the body of a man with his head lying a little way off. We were told he had been a bandit, executed that morning. A little further on stood the low inns, with camels kneeling before them. Here the Mongols smoked and drank tea and bargained with Chinese dealers for the sheepskins which their camels had carried from far-off Mongolia.

Some of the camels were used for riding, with saddles between their twin humps. Immediately we wanted to ride them. Our host went into one of the inns to talk to their masters, who thought it a great joke. So, up we climbed on two of the kneeling camels. Too late I realized that the stirrups were like a jockey's. The straps were so short that one sat on one's heels when riding. Only a single cord, knotted in the camel's nostrils, could be used to steer the beast by.

Up got the camels, lurching, and off we started toward the Gobi desert, amid the grins of the gathered Mongols. For a very little while it was not too bad, but suddenly the camels remembered their far-off pastures and broke into a run. Margaret was a good rider and rode from the knee. I have never been a good rider but have made do well enough by riding with a light rein and balancing from the stirrups. With these horrible short stirrups, any balancing was impossible. At every stride of my camel, I rose high in the air and was lurched sideways so that I hung out

of the saddle directly above the earth. Somehow like a Yo-Yo, each time I was hurled back into place and then once again tossed sideways out into the air. Of course, I grabbed for the camel's hump in front of me. Vain hope! After weeks in the desert, that hump was only a hairy jelly, without enough firmness to have supported the paw of a mouse.

By this time Margaret and I were both trying to turn our camels, pulling and pulling on the cords that guided them, while they grunted with discomfort and kept on running. Out of the corner of my eye, I could see our host galloping his pony after us, far, far behind.

But at last, before I crashed, our camels turned. Sulkily they faced away from their beloved Gobi desert. At an unwilling walk they started back for their masters and the inns. My head was spinning. My legs ached from their horrible doubled-up position, but I was still alive. Margaret felt something of this, but far less, being (as I have said) the better rider.

Winters in California, winters in Carthage or Sicily, a rented apartment now and then, and so we drifted for a few years until Margaret married a New Englander and settled down in a town south of Boston. Mother and I bought an eighteenth-century house not far away, looking out over Hingham Harbor toward Boston Light.

Like my sister, I married a Massachusetts South Shore man, Henry Beston. He was a writer and naturalist, who also wrote fairy tales once in a while. I am a tall woman, but Henry was more than three inches taller than I am. In time we had two daughters and later eight small grandchildren who liked their grandfather's stories of chipmunks and birds, foxes and lions as much as their mothers had liked them when they were little.

The Result of Many Things

Meantime I went on writing. It began during a summer in England between my junior and senior years at Vassar. Margaret and I walked most of that summer along the coast of Cornwall and Devon and through the English Lakes, while Mother rode in one of the last of the coaches with their four horses, with the coach horns sounding so sweetly as they drove into a village. I was overcome by the beauty of the countryside and found myself writing poems about it, often hurriedly on the backs of menus while waiting for lunch to be served.

It was not until some years later during a visit to New York that I wrote my first book for children. One of my close friends at Vassar was Louise Seaman, later Mrs. Bechtel, who was the first head of a department for children's books in any publishing house. We used to talk about the authors she was meeting and the books she was publishing. One day I said, "I think I could write a book," and she challenged, "Prove it!" So in a week I had written *The Cat and the Captain.* And ever since then I have gone on writing for children.

As time went on, I wrote novels and essays as well. Writing books is the result of many things. For me, first of all, something must have interested me so much that I want to tell about it. Some authors say that they hate writing and only

do it because they hate *not* writing even more. But I love writing, and when I am at work, I am filled with "tranquillity and delight." These are to me now and have always been the two most beautiful words in the world.

At all times a writer's own personal life goes on. For a couple of years we lived in the old house at Hingham, and then we bought Chimney Farm by a Maine lake. For years we had a garden, which was plowed each spring by a pair of oxen. At first the hay was cut and raked and carried away by horse-driven reapers and rakes and hay wagons. Now it is all done by machine.

During those first years we used to picnic every fine day, while my husband read out loud after we had eaten. In summer we swam every warm day, and the canoe was in frequent use. In the fall, when the mosquitoes were out of the woods, we spent hours cutting trails, often following overgrown logging roads. In the winter we explored the coves and shoreline on snowshoes, watching for moose and otter tracks. My husband wrote a book called *Northern Farm,* and I, too, put down the things we saw and did.

While our daughters, Meg and Kate, were growing up, we spent six months of the year in Hingham in the old house on Hingham Harbor, only coming to the farm in the winter, a week or two at a time. In the early days the place was heated by wood stoves and lighted by oil lamps. But when Meg and Kate went to college, we added electricity and a furnace and came to Maine for good. Later my husband gave his little house on the outer Eastham Beach of Cape Cod to the Massachusetts Audubon Society. It is now a National Literary Monument, for during the year he lived there, he wrote a book called *The Outer-Most House,* which became a classic.

In the spring of 1968 my husband died. Meg and her husband and three little girls and one boy are back in our country again after two years in Greece. They come to see me when they can. Kate lives far away in California. She has a husband, two boys and two girls, four dogs and three horses, as well as a homely fat Shetland pony and the pony's colt. There are cats, too, and if the bantams have escaped the coyotes, there are tiny fluffy chicks and little roosters crowing on the brick wall above the rose trees.

Usually Kate comes East for part of the summer and brings with her some of the children. Last time only my namesake, Liz, came with her. She is the oldest of all the grandchildren.

So with the years, my life has changed, growing quieter and simpler. Sometimes I think I take more pleasure in small things than I used to do. At this moment the light from my bedroom windows falls on a pale pink cyclamen plant. The flowers look like swans with wings uplifted in midflight rising from a green bank.

Then the sunlight slants in to fall on a figure of a seated Buddha. The statue came from a ruined jungle temple. It is about three feet high and covered with gold leaf, except on the forehead, the arms, and the soles of the feet. On these spots the gold leaf has been worn down to the black lacquer beneath by the many hands of jungle people who have prayed to it by touching the places where they were in pain. The statue is Siamese and is about four hundred years old. I am fonder of this than of anything else I have brought back from my travels. I never glance at it without remembering the peaceful, gentle Orient we knew so long ago.

Hidden in and out of my poems and books are many parts of my own life. Sometimes it would

be hard to tell which they are, but they are always there. Like sorcerers they change forms and can grow very large or small enough to be hidden under a clover leaf. But they are always there, and what is true of me is true of all writers.

When we write a book, we give you part of ourselves.

Reflections

1. Why do you think Elizabeth Coatsworth calls her autobiography "Mostly Beginnings"?
2. What does Elizabeth Coatsworth mean when she says, "When we write a book, we give you part of ourselves"?
3. What do you think is as important to a writer as having wide and various experiences? Why do you think Elizabeth Coatsworth remembers playing jacks as vividly as she remembers riding a camel?
4. Based on Elizabeth Coatsworth's description, which country would you most like to visit? In a short essay, explain the reasons for your choice.

Elizabeth Blackwell

EVE MERRIAM

What will you do when you grow up,
nineteenth-century-young-lady?
Will you sew a fine seam and spoon dappled cream
under an apple tree shady?

• • •

"I'm not very nimble with a needle and thread.
"I could teach music—if I had to," she said,
"But I think I'd rather be a doctor instead."

"Is this some kind of joke?"
asked the proper menfolk.
"A woman be a doctor?
Not in our respectable day!
A doctor? An M.D.! Did you hear what she said?
She's clearly and indubitably out of her head!"

"Indeed, indeed, we are thoroughly agreed,"
hissed the ladies of society all laced in and prim,
"it's a scientific fact a doctor has to be a him.
"Yes, sir,
"'twould be against nature
"if a doctor were a her."

Hibble hobble bibble bobble
widdle waddle wag
tsk tsk
twit twit
flip flap flutter
mitter matter mutter
moan groan wail and rail
Indecorous!
Revolting!
A scandal
A SIN
their voices pierced the air like a jabbing hat-pin.
But little miss Elizabeth wouldn't give in.

To medical schools she applied.
In vain.
And applied again
and again
and again
and one rejection offered this plan:
why not disguise herself as a man?
If she pulled back her hair, put on boots and pants,
she might attend medical lectures in France.
Although she wouldn't earn a degree,
they'd let her study anatomy.

Elizabeth refused to hide
her feminine pride.
She drew herself up tall
(all five feet one of her!)
and tried again.
And denied again.
The letters answering no
mounted like winter snow.

Until the day
when her ramrod will
finally had its way.

After the twenty-ninth try,
there came from Geneva, New York
the reply
of a blessed
Yes!

Geneva,
Geneva,
how sweet the sound;
Geneva,
Geneva,
sweet sanctuary found. . . .

. . . . and the ladies of Geneva
passing by her in the street
drew back their hoopskirts
so they wouldn't have to meet.

Psst, psst,
hiss, hiss
this sinister scarlet miss.

Avoid her, the hoyden, the hussy,
lest we all be contaminated!
If your glove so much as touch her, my dear,
best go get it fumigated!

When Elizabeth came to table,
their talking all would halt;
wouldn't so much as ask her
please to pass the salt.

In between classes
without a kind word,
Elizabeth dwelt
like a pale gray bird.

In a bare attic room
cold as a stone,
far from her family,
huddled alone

studying, studying
throughout the night
warming herself
with an inner light:

don't let it darken,
the spark of fire;
keep it aglow,
that heart's desire:

the will to serve,
to help those in pain—
flickered and flared
and flickered again—

until
like a fairy tale
(except it was true!)
Elizabeth received
her honored due.

The perfect happy ending
came to pass:
Elizabeth graduated . . .
. . . at the head of her class.

And the ladies of Geneva
all rushed forward now to greet
that clever, dear Elizabeth,
so talented, so sweet!

Wasn't it glorious
she'd won first prize?

Elizabeth smiled
with cool gray eyes

and she wrapped her shawl
against the praise:

how soon there might come
more chilling days.

Turned to leave
without hesitating.

She was ready now,
and the world was waiting.

Dr. Elizabeth

ELIZABETH BLACKWELL (1821–1910)

Elizabeth Blackwell, born in England, came to America with her family at age eleven. The Blackwells settled in Ohio. When Elizabeth became a young woman she went to Kentucky to teach. There she nursed an elderly friend through a last illness, and decided to become a doctor.

After graduating from medical school, Dr. Blackwell could find no American hospital to work in, so she went to France. She wanted to become a surgeon. Again, finding no hospital that would take a woman doctor, she entered a French hospital as a nursing student. She worked long hours making beds, washing patients, and scrubbing floors, but she watched operations whenever she had a chance.

While caring for a baby who had an eye infection, Elizabeth, too, became ill. After suffering for many months she recovered to find that she had lost the sight of one eye. Her chance of becoming a surgeon was gone. But just when Elizabeth was most discouraged, she received an invitation to study at St. Bartholomew's Hospital in London.

When she returned to the United States, Dr. Elizabeth founded the New York Infirmary for Women and Children. There she was joined by Dr. Maria Zakrzewska, and later by her sister, Dr. Emily Blackwell.

Today, the New York Infirmary treats over 34,000 patients yearly. And its staff of physicians has grown from two when Dr. Blackwell began her work to more than five hundred women and men. In 1975 the hospital celebrated its hundredth anniversary in its present location on New York's Stuyvesant Square.

Wearing 19th century costume, members and supporters of the New York Infirmary celebrate its 100th anniversary. Actress Mildred Dunnock, with doctor's bag, is dressed as Dr. Blackwell.

WAYS TO ACHIEVE STYLE

Just as people differ in the way they live, so do authors differ in the way they write. Each author seeks a writing style that reflects the way he or she sees the world. They relate their writing style to their purpose.

Robert McCloskey in "Pie and Punch and You-Know-Whats" has a lively, interesting, and humorous style. His story is fast moving and funny. It is a tale of today. In "Cherry Ann and the Dragon Horse," Elizabeth Coatsworth tells a story that seems to be about real people and real events, and her style is serious.

Both of these stories are very different in style from "Lucy and the Wardrobe," which introduces fantasy and make-believe into the lives of the characters in the story.

Repetition

Do you remember the lines in "Pie and Punch and You-Know-Whats" that are repeated several times?

> "Punch, brothers, punch with care!
> Punch in the presence of the passenjare!"

These repeated lines are called a refrain. In this refrain how many words begin with the letter *p*? The repetition of words beginning with the same letter in a sentence is called alliteration.

In the poem at the top of page 137, no line is repeated, but one word, *gold,* is repeated a dozen times. Repetition of a word gives emphasis, or importance, to the word. In "What Is Gold?" the repetition also creates a special sound effect which is made stronger by other words that use the sound of *o* heard in *gold.*

What Is Gold?

Gold is a metal
Gold is a ring
Gold is a very
Beautiful thing.
Gold is the sunshine
Light and thin
Warm as a muffin
On your skin.
Gold is the moon
Gold are the stars;
Jupiter, Venus
Saturn and Mars.
Gold is the color of
Clover honey
Gold is a certain
Kind of money.
Gold is alive
In a flickering fish
That lives its life
In a crystal dish.
Gold is the answer
To many a wish
Gold is feeling
Like a king
It's like having the most
Of everything—
Long time ago
I was told
Yellow's mother's name
Is gold. . . .

—Mary O'Neill

Imagery

How many different word pictures, or images, does the poet use in the above poem to give you a feeling of what gold is? How does the dictionary definition of *gold* differ from the definitions you get in the poem?

With images or word pictures, the poet makes you use your different senses to get the feeling of the poem. Sometimes a word picture is given to make you see, or hear, or smell, or taste, or have the sense of touch.

What images do you find above that make you experience some of these things? When you read that "Gold is a metal," do you feel something hard and bright? In "Gold is a ring," do you sense gold as both shape and sound? Does gold as "sunshine light and thin" come through as a touch of warmth? Does gold "warm as a muffin" appeal to both touch and taste? To which of your senses does gold "the color of clover honey" appeal? And what image can you find that appeals to your sense of motion?

Personification

What word do you see in *personification*? When an author describes nonliving or nonhuman things by having them do things that only a person can do, the author is using personification. When poets say that leaves whisper or flowers dance, they are personifying the leaves and flowers.

Another way of using personification is to describe nonliving things by comparing them to animals. In the following poem the poet has written about a steam shovel as if it were a living dinosaur. How many dinosaur actions can you find in the poem?

Steam Shovel

The dinosaurs are not all dead.
I saw one raise its iron head
To watch me walking down the road
Beyond our house today.
Its jaws were dripping with a load
Of earth and grass that it had cropped.
It must have heard me where I stopped,
Snorted white steam my way,
And stretched its long neck out to see,
And chewed, and grinned quite amiably.

—Charles Malam

Similes and Metaphors

A simile tells how a person or a thing is similar to or like someone or something else. Use a simile to complete the following:

1. When I am happy, I sing like ____.
2. When I am angry, I roar like ____.
3. When I am hungry, I eat like ____.
4. He runs as rapidly as ____.
5. She dances as gracefully as ____.

Similes are a part of our everyday speech. They are introduced by the words *like* or *as*. Good authors often need similes, and, when they do, they try to be original and different. See how many different similes you can make to complete the examples on page 138.

Metaphors, like similes, are comparisons, but they do not use the words *like* or *as.* A metaphor simply calls one thing by another name. For example, we might say of a good swimmer, "John is a real fish," or "That boy is a dolphin." Most of us use metaphors very often in everyday speech because they give us a more interesting way of saying things. Authors like to create new and different metaphors. What is the metaphor in "Steam Shovel" on page 138?

Here are some metaphors to describe the streets of a city.

1. The streets of the city are the *endless legs of a giant centipede.*
2. The streets of the city are the *curving claws of eagles' feet.*
3. The streets of the city are *giant's fingers reaching far into the suburbs.*

Complete the following examples by making up a metaphor for each one.

1. The circling airplanes above the airport are ____.
2. The shelves in the supermarket are ____.
3. Happiness is ____.

You have seen how authors use repetition, alliteration, personification, and similes and metaphors to help them get certain effects in their writing. These are only a few of the devices that writers may use to improve the style of their stories or poems. When you understand how these different devices work, you are finding another way to break the reading code.

2 THE WORLD OF WORDS

Feelings About Words

Some words clink
As ice in drink.
Some move with grace
A dance, a lace.
Some sound thin:
Wail, scream and pin.
Some words are squat:
A mug, a pot,
And some are plump,
Fat, round and dump.
Some words are light:
Drift, lift and bright.
A few are small:
A, is and all.
And some are thick,
Glue, paste and brick.
Some words are sad:
"I never had . . . ."
And others gay:
Joy, spin and play.
Some words are sick:
Stab, scratch and nick.
Some words are hot:
Fire, flame and shot.
Some words are sharp,
Sword, point and carp.
And some alert:
Glint, glance and flirt.
Some words are lazy:
Saunter, hazy.
And some words preen:
Pride, pomp and queen.
Some words are quick,
A jerk, a flick.
Some words are slow:
Lag, stop and grow,
While others poke
As ox with yoke.
Some words can fly—
There's wind, there's high;
And some words cry:
"Good-by. . . .
  Good-by. . . ."

Mary O'Neill

hazy

HOT

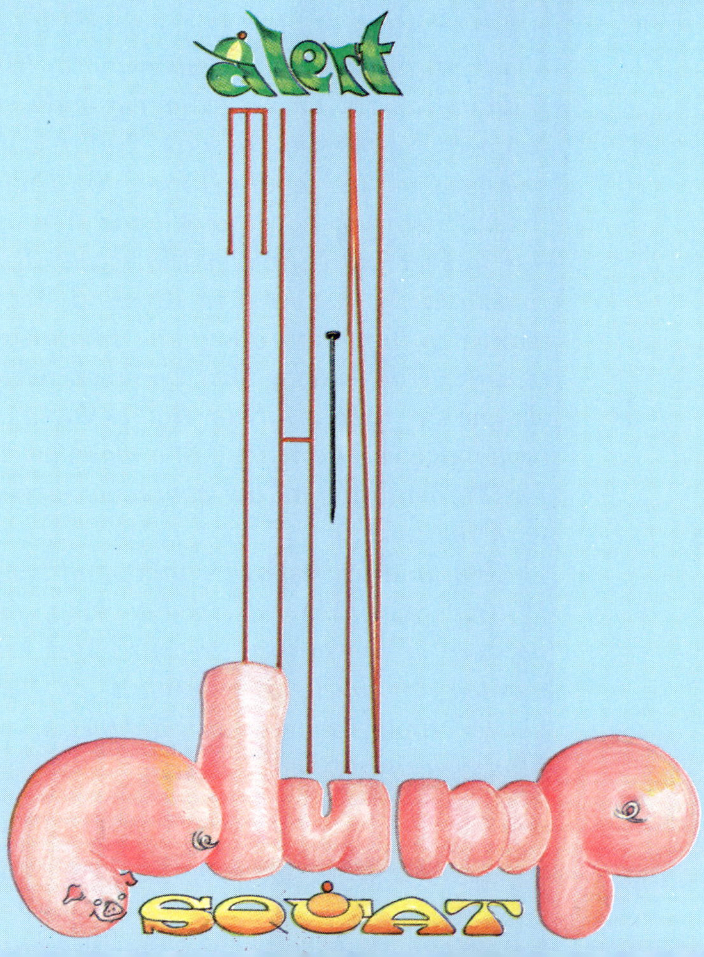
alert
plump
SQUAT

Alvin and the Secret Code

CLIFFORD B. HICKS

Somehow, Alvin Fernald was always finding himself in the middle of an adventure. For instance, there was the time Miss Alicia Fenwick called on Alvin's father, Police Sergeant Fernald. She had come from Mississippi to Riverton, Indiana, to ask for Sergeant Fernald's help in recovering a missing treasure. The treasure had belonged to her family during the Civil War.

Miss Fenwick had thought the treasure was lost forever until she recently received a letter from a Mr. J. A. Smith in Riverton. Mr. Smith wanted information about the treasure. If the treasure still existed, Miss Fenwick felt that it should be used to help the children in her orphanage in Mississippi. She was now looking for Mr. Smith to find out how he was connected with the treasure.

Alvin and his sister, Daphne, and his friend, Wilfred Shoemaker, decided to help solve the mystery of the missing treasure. But first they wanted to finish their project of becoming master cryptographers. Little did they know what a wise decision they made.

Adventure in the Library

The Riverton Public Library was really an old home presented to the town many years ago. A high iron fence ran all the way around the grounds. There was only one gate, at the front.

Three secret agents walked into the library: Alvin Fernald (a twelve-year-old expert on codes and ciphers, alias the Magnificent Brain or Secret Agent K–21½), Daphne (his little sister who always tagged along), and Wilfred Shoemaker (called Shoie or Secret Agent Q–3). Aside from Miss Jackson, the librarian, there was only one other person in the library. He was a big man, seated at a table covered with books and papers.

Alvin, Shoie, and Daphne walked up to Miss Jackson. "We're studying up on codes and how to break them," Alvin whispered to her. "Do you have any good books?"

"Just a minute," said Miss Jackson. She pulled out the small drawer of a card file, flipped

through the cards, and wrote some numbers on a slip of paper. "Here are the catalog numbers of two books on codes. They were donated to the library by Mr. Link. You'll find them over in those stacks." She waved her hand toward the far corner.

"Oh yes," the three children said. "We know Mr. Link. He was a spy, and he knows all about breaking secret codes. He even gave us advice when we decided to become cryptographers."

Over at the stacks, Alvin looked carefully along the shelves. When he came to the spot where the two code books should have been, he saw only an empty space. "Somebody must have them out," he said. "That's strange. I'll bet Miss Jackson knows who's taken out almost any book in this library. And I'll bet those code books aren't checked out very often. Seems like she'd know if they had been checked out. We'd better talk to her."

Back they marched toward the desk. As they passed the big man at the table, Alvin glanced down, then stopped so suddenly that the other two bumped into him, sending him reeling into a reading lamp. There was a loud pop, the tinkle of glass, and a blinding flash of light. The big man sprang to his feet and started brushing the pieces of the broken bulb off his clothing. Alvin looked over at Miss Jackson.

"I'm sorry," she called over to the man, who was staring angrily at Alvin. "Don't try to clean it up," she added. "The library will be swept out as soon as we close. Why don't you move to another table?"

The man snatched up a book and some loose papers and began moving them to another table. When Alvin picked up a book and an old piece of paper from the table to help, the man grabbed them out of his hand. "Why don't you watch what you're doing?" he said.

Alvin poked Shoie and looked at Daphne. He motioned for them to follow him back to the stacks. In the far corner, among the shelves, he whispered, "Did you see what that man was doing?"

"Studying," said Q–3.

"Right," said Alvin. "But, old bean, did you notice *what* he was studying?"

"It looked like arithmetic," said Daphne.

Then Alvin said very slowly, "The two books on that table are the code books we're looking for. And on those sheets of paper are a lot of scribbles that don't make sense. *That man is trying to break a secret code!*"

"Wow!" said Q–3. "Are you sure?"

"Yes," said Alvin. "And I'll tell you something else: That old piece of paper he had in front of him is a message in code. It was written way back during the Civil War, and it tells exactly where Miss Fenwick's treasure is buried!"

"How do you know?" asked Shoie.

"It's the only explanation that makes sense. A mysterious Mr. Smith wrote a letter from right here in town to Miss Fenwick, so there *must* be a Mr. Smith around here somewhere—even though Smith may not be his real name. And the bushwhacker who buried Miss Fenwick's treasure was a spy during the Civil War, so he must have known all about secret codes. He probably wrote down the location of the buried treasure in code to protect his secret after he died."

"Maybe," said Shoie, "but then how did Mr. Smith get the code message?"

"I don't know," said Alvin. "But we can guess one other thing. Our mysterious Mr. Smith can't read that secret message, or he wouldn't be studying code books. I'll bet he's trying to learn how to break codes."

"Let's go home and tell your dad," said Shoie. "I speel kind of fooky. I mean I feel kind of spooky."

"Not yet," said K–$21\frac{1}{2}$. "First we have to get a copy of that secret message."

"How are you going to do that?" asked Shoie.

"I'm not. *You* are."

Shoie grabbed a shelf for support. "Doggone it. You get some of the wildest ideas, Alvin. How am I going to get that message? He's bigger than I am!"

"This is how," said Alvin. "First, take a book off the shelf and go sit down at the same table with him. Then I'll get him away from the table. While he's gone, you copy the secret message— the one that is on a very old and very dirty piece of paper. Copy it *exactly* as it looks, even though it doesn't make sense. Got it?"

"Got it. But I don't like it."

"Okay, go to it." Alvin took a book from a shelf and handed it to Shoie.

The Escape

Trying to appear calm, Shoie strolled over and sat down across from the man. He opened the book and began reading as though he could hardly wait to get to the next word.

"He's holding the book upside down," whispered Daphne.

Alvin popped out from the shelves, carrying some books, and walked over to stand beside Shoie. Meanwhile, Daphne went over and started talking to Miss Jackson to keep her from noticing what was going on.

"Good book?" Alvin asked Shoie just a bit too loudly.

The man looked up. "Shut up!" he growled.

"Sorry," he said. "Oh, *you* have the books I was looking for. The ones on secret codes, I mean. No

hurry, but I'd like to see them when you're through."

"Get out of here, kid," snapped the man.

"Sorry," said Alvin again. "I was just looking for books on secret codes. There's only one other in the library, but it's not on *making* codes. It's on *breaking* them."

The man looked up quickly. For the first time there was interest on his face. "You say there's a book here on how to *break* codes?"

"Yep. But I don't want that one. All I want is . . ."

"Where is it?" the man broke in.

"Back there in the shelves. Saw it just a minute ago. But I don't want . . ."

"Can you find it for me?"

"Sure," said Alvin. "Glad to." He glanced at Shoie on purpose, then walked back toward the shelves. As soon as he got to the shelves, he raced all around one row and ducked up another. Now he had to gain time, so Shoie could copy the message. He could hear the man walking down the rows looking for him. Moments passed. Then, when he heard footsteps approaching, he tipped one of the books forward as though he were reading the title.

"Hi," he said as the man walked up. "I think it's right around here somewhere."

The man looked at him suspiciously. "Are you trying to fool me, kid?"

"No. I saw it right along here." Alvin continued to look through the books.

"What's the name of it?" growled the man.

"Let's see." The Magnificent Brain thought fast. "If I remember right, the title is *A Master Spy's Secrets of Breaking Codes and Ciphers,* written by Alvin Fernald," said Alvin.

Suddenly the man grabbed Alvin's arm. "What's your game, kid? You know there isn't any book on codes here. What are you up to?"

Alvin began to panic. He said the first thing that came into his head, the words tumbling out one after the other. He *had* to gain time, so Shoie could copy the message. "There is too such a book. It was given to the library by Mr. Link. He lives over on Fourth Street. He was a real spy, and he knows all about breaking secret codes. He can break any code there is. And he told me about this book that's here in the library. I can't help it if I made a mistake about where the book is. Maybe it's on the next row of shelves. Let go of my arm, mister, you're hurting . . ."

Just then, the man *did* let go. He whirled around and dashed out through the stacks. He had suddenly realized he'd left his secret message unguarded.

Alvin raced down another row at top speed. He rounded the corner just as the man came out from behind the shelves.

"Run, Shoie!" shouted Alvin, heading toward the door himself.

He saw Shoie leap to his feet, crumple a piece of paper in front of him, and slip it into his pocket. Out of the corner of his eye, he saw Daphne start running, too. Shoie reached the door first. Right at his heels was Daphne, and Alvin brought up the rear. As Alvin darted through the door, he glanced back over his shoulder. The man had stopped just long enough to snatch up the old scrap of paper. Then he, too, was running.

Shoie and Daphne were halfway to the front gate when Alvin heard the big man pounding along behind him. Then he thought of a plan of escape. Searching through his pockets, he pulled out the wrapper from an old jelly sandwich. He began to wave the wrapper wildly, yelling, "I've got a copy of that message!" Then he turned suddenly, and, instead of heading for the front gate, he ran for his life round toward the back of the library. With every step that he took, he could hear the man gaining. When they reached the back of the library, it was apparent in the moonlight that there was no opening in the high iron fence except for the front gate on the other side of the building.

"Got you now!" muttered the man.

Alvin imagined fingers on the back of his neck, but he knew something that the man didn't know. For years he had been crawling between the bars at the corner of the fence to get to the library. Lately, since he had grown so much, it had become a test to him. Could he still squeeze through or not? The last time he'd tried was about six months ago.

He dived through some bushes that grew just inside the fence and heard the branches snap back and hit the man in the face, slowing him. Now Alvin was at the corner of the fence. For the first time he knew exactly how a trapped animal must feel. Poking his head through the iron bars, he wriggled one shoulder through. Then, with a final heave, he pulled himself through the bars. He ran a few steps. Suddenly he stopped and turned around. He knew he was safe now.

The man stood with his hands squeezing the bars of the fence. He knew he couldn't get through, and there was no way to climb the high fence. He looked at Alvin with hatred in his eyes.

"I'm going to find you," the man said slowly and softly. "I'm going to find you and take care of you good. I don't know why you're meddling in my business, but you've meddled just a little too much. You'd better keep looking behind you, because sometime soon I'll be there."

Alvin felt a chill crawl up his spine. He turned and ran for home.

Alvin Fernald, Cryptographer

Shoie and Daphne were waiting on the front steps.

"Oh, Alvin!" said Daphne. "We were so worried!"

"Hurry! Come on inside," said Alvin, looking over his shoulder down the street.

They went straight up to Alvin's room.

"How'd you get away, old bean?" asked Shoie.

He told them, and he felt himself shuddering as he described the man on the other side of the fence. "That man is dangerous," he said.

Daphne was worried. "Alvin, hadn't we better tell Daddy?"

"I've been thinking about that. I don't think we should—yet. After all, we *were* meddling with *his* papers. There's no way anybody can prove he is the mysterious Mr. Smith. Dad couldn't arrest him just for sitting in the library."

"What are we going to do, old bean?" asked Shoie. "I don't want to walk the streets with that guy looking for me."

"I was wrong a minute ago when I said there's no way to prove that he has anything to do with the treasure," said Alvin. "There *is* a way, one way."

"What's that?" asked Shoie.

"Suppose," said Alvin slowly, "suppose we could break the code message that we got from him. And suppose it tells us where to find the treasure. And suppose, by using the message, we find the treasure before he does. That will be mighty strong evidence that he's the mysterious Mr. Smith who wrote Miss Fenwick." The more Alvin talked, the more excited he became. "Shoie, let's take a look at your copy of the message!"

From his pocket Shoie removed the crumpled piece of paper. They smoothed it on the bed. In Shoie's scrawl appeared a jumble of letters:

SREWO TETIN ARGNE EWTEB GIDDN
ASECA PEVLE WTTHG IRNRU TKCOR
DAEHE LTRUT OTHTR ONOGT SEWHT
RONTS EWSEC APNEE TFIFO GREDL
UOBEG RALMO RFFFU LBTSE PEETS
FOESA BTALO OPRET AWRAE LCDNI
FSFFU LBREV IROTS ELIME ERHTT
SEWHT UOSEK IRTSA NAIDN INOTR
EVIRD ELLAC EGALL IVOTO GXXXX

"Gosh," said Daphne, "who could read that?"

Alvin turned and answered Daphne's question. "*I* can read the secret message," he said. Then he added, "As soon as I've broken the code."

Alvin spent a restless night. In a nightmare, he was running down a dark street, looking back over his shoulder at huge letters that were chasing him.

The next day after school, Alvin went alone to his secret code room. He sat down and stared at the message. Each part of the message had five letters, so Alvin knew it was not split into real words. This made a solution more difficult. But Alvin saw that certain letters appeared more often than others. Remembering what he had learned from the spy Mr. Link, Alvin decided to run a letter-frequency check on some of the letters. It took half an hour, but when he was through, he felt he had made some progress.

Letters Used in the Message Lined Up According to the Number of Times They Appear

E–32	L–13
T–25	I–12
R–19	N–11
O–17	F–9
A–14	D–7
S–13	H–6

Frequency Table of the English Language

The four letters that appear most often in English are *E, T, A,* and *O*. They are the first four letters of what is called the Frequency Table of the English Language. The complete order is as follows:

ETAONRISHDLFCMUGYPWBVKXJQZ

Alvin knew that unless the message was very long, it would not match the Frequency Table *exactly*. But this came mighty close. He was certain now that the letters stood for themselves and not some other letters of the alphabet. They seemed to be scrambled in some way. He worked for an hour but still could make no sense out of the message. Then he reviewed again what Mr. Link had told him, seeking a clue that would lead to the solution. Messages, Mr. Link had said once, are much easier to decipher if you know something about the person who has coded them and about the situation in which the message was written. Thoughtfully, Alvin made a list of everything he knew. But the letters of the message still seemed scrambled beyond understanding.

Alvin finally gave up and went outside. But as soon as he was outside, he found himself looking back over his shoulder. He returned to the house feeling ashamed of himself. The problem bothered him so much that he returned to his room, locked the door, and again worked on the code. He *had* to solve it for many reasons. The most important was that he had boasted that he could. Still, the letters seemed to dance in front of his eyes.

Then, suddenly, Alvin realized that if he started with the last letter at the end and read backwards, the five-letter groups began to split up into words that made sense. He had broken the code!

The first three words of the message were "Go to village . . ." Feverishly, Alvin broke the rest of the message apart until he had read all of it. Now he knew that he had the key to help Miss Fenwick locate her family's long-hidden buried treasure.

The Treasure

The story of the Fenwick treasure spread like wildfire through town, and the next morning a procession of cars headed out toward Treasure Bluffs. In the lead was a police car containing the Fernald family, Shoie, and Miss Fenwick.

As he drove, Sergeant Fernald told Alvin what he'd found out about Mr. Smith.

"Seems he is a great-great-nephew of the man who stole the treasure," said Sergeant Fernald. "He discovered the coded message in the attic of an old house belonging to the family."

Alvin was trying to pay attention, but suddenly he interrupted. "Dad, tell the rest of the story later. Here we are at the bluffs, and right now I want to try to find the treasure." His heart began to beat a little faster. What if this whole thing were a flop? What if there *weren't* any treasure? Or what if someone, years ago, had found it?

Sergeant Fernald stopped the car, and a crowd began to gather around.

"All right, Alvin," said his dad quietly, "lead the way."

Alvin walked down the slope. At the bottom, near a pool of still water, he stopped and took the decoded message from his pocket. "This is where the treasure trail starts," he announced.

There was a look of puzzlement and awe on the faces of everyone around him as Alvin began to read the message. Silently the crowd trooped behind Alvin as he started to follow the decoded instructions.

At a spot between two towering rocks, Alvin stopped suddenly and said, "We dig here." His dad was carrying a shovel and began to dig where Alvin pointed.

By the time the hole was three feet deep, there was still no sign of the treasure. Sergeant Fernald stopped to rest, and Shoie grabbed the shovel. A couple of minutes later, Shoie suddenly whispered to Alvin, "Quick, K–21$\frac{1}{2}$, I've hit something!"

Alvin leaped into the hole. There, beside the tip of the shovel, half-covered by dirt, was a rotten board. The boys went down on their hands and knees, scooping out the dirt and small stones with their fingers. Suddenly the board gave way, and the top of an iron chest appeared.

The old lock pulled off easily, and Alvin swung open the lid. His eyes almost popped out at the sight of the treasure. Inside the chest were beautiful silver knives, forks, and spoons. There were pitchers, cups, and platters of solid silver and gold. In one corner of the chest, in an old leather bag, were brooches and rings, necklaces and lockets, bracelets and pins. In another corner of the chest, Alvin saw strange coins by the dozens.

Shoie was the first to speak. "Wow!" was all he could say.

Then someone in the crowd said, "You found the treasure, Alvin. What will you do with it?"

But Sergeant Fernald quickly replied, "Not so fast. The courts will have to decide who owns the treasure. However, I do remember a case where money was found buried in the ground, and it was awarded to the finder."

"If it's mine because I found it," said Alvin, "I'll give it to Miss Fenwick to take back to the orphanage. I think the money would do more good there than anywhere else."

There was such a long silence that Alvin finally looked up to see if anything was wrong. His father was looking proudly down into the hole, not at the treasure, but at him. Next to Dad's face was Miss Fenwick's, tears running down her cheeks.

Then someone back in the crowd started to clap, and soon the bluffs across the river were echoing back the cheers for Alvin Fernald, Secret Agent and Cryptographer.

Reflections

1. Think of your favorite hiding places, shortcuts, and secret routes. Which ones are impossible for grown-ups to use? Which of them have you recently grown too big to use?
2. What is a code? Do you think writing is a code? Explain why or why not.
3. Every library uses a certain type of code. What is it? Explain to the class how it is used.
4. Alvin wanted to break the code primarily because he had boasted he could. What have you claimed you could do before you were able to do it? What effect, if any, did the boasting have on your final ability?
5. Do you think this story could really have happened? Why or why not? Give your opinion and the reasons for it in a short essay.

Scat! Scitten!

DAVID McCORD

Even though
  a cat has a kitten,
  not a rat has a ritten,
  not a bat has a bitten,
  not a gnat has a gnitten,
  not a sprat has a spritten.
  That is that—that is thitten.

Goose, Moose & Spruce

DAVID McCORD

Three gooses: geese.
Three mooses: meese?
Three spruces: spreece?

Little goose: gosling.
Little moose: mosling?
Little spruce: sprosling?

The Outlander Teacher

MAY JUSTUS

The family in this story lives in the hill country of the Southeastern United States during the 1930s. They are farmers, and they have little to do with people from outside their county. Then one day an outlander teacher comes to their highland school, and she's not at all what people expect.

Five miles from Far Beyant, Kettle Creek curls like a grapevine around the foot of Little Twin. On the other side, the mountain known as Big Twin looks down on its little brother. Here and there are homes of the highland folks—gray, weather-beaten log cabins.

The Allisons lived in such a cabin: Glory and Matt, Mammy and Grandy.

On the morning that this story began, the Allisons got up early to get a hop-and-jump ahead of the sun. There was a good reason for this: it was Monday morning, the first Monday in August—the first day of school! On Little Twin, school began early because in the mountain country the children are let out when field work begins in the spring.

Grandy went out to the barn. Glory and Matt hung about the kitchen to give a hand's turn now and then to help Mammy.

When they sat down to breakfast, Glory wasn't hungry. Mammy noticed right away.

"What ails you, honey?" she said. "What makes you so mincey with your victuals? Do you feel a little dauncy?"

"No, Mammy, I don't feel dauncy," Glory said. "But seems like there's no room for anything but the gladsome feeling inside me when I think of this being the first day of school!"

"Humph!" muttered Matt.

"You must have a misery with you, Matt," Mammy said.

"I know what ails him," Glory spoke up. "He's mully-grubby in his mind 'cause he has to start school."

Mammy crossed her knife and fork before replying. "This notion has come to you all

of a sudden. Will you tell me why and when you got so set against school?"

"I don't want to go to school to any gal teacher," Matt said. "This one's not mighty much bigger than your fist. Miss Judy Bird—an outlander teacher with a lot o' biggety ways."

"Humph!" It came from Grandy this time. He seemed to pay no attention to the talk around him, but he hadn't missed a word. Something like a chuckle came from his throat.

"I need a hand in the corn patch today."

He got up and left the table without a sideways look at Matt, but Matt's gaze followed him out the door.

"I reckon I'll try it for one day," he said.

Mammy nodded. "All right, Son. Grandy does need a hand."

Matt drew a long breath. "I—I mean school," he stammered, and Glory giggled.

Mammy smiled, and her blue eyes twinkled. "All right, Son," she said again. "You had better set off now. The sun ball's over the mountain. You mustn't be late the first day."

Glory and Matt got their books and lunch basket and walked through the front gate. They crossed Kettle Creek and followed the trail through Darksome Hollow. Three miles down the hollow, they came to the schoolhouse in a clearing of pine trees. It was built of logs with a chimney at one end. In the crowd gathered around the door were many familiar faces.

"There's Noah Webster!" said Matt.

"Come on, Matt! Come and choose with me for a ball game!" Noah shouted as they drew nearer.

Glory took Matt's books and went inside the schoolhouse to put their things away.

When she came back out to the playground, the choosing for the ball game had stopped, but one more player was needed by each side.

"I'll take Glory!" Noah yelled.

Matt looked as if he had just dropped a piece of bread and butter upside down. "There's nobody else to play on my side," he said.

The teacher stepped out. "If you will take me, I'll play on your side," she told him.

Somebody laughed, and Matt blushed. They weren't used to a teacher taking part in any of their games. But Matt was obliged to say, "All right."

The game began with Matt in the field. After Noah's team had two outs, Glory bunted a ball and got to first base. Bud O'Dell, Noah's best player, sent his ball flying into left field.

"Run after that, somebody!" Matt yelled, starting on his run.

But a miracle had happened. The new schoolteacher had caught the ball, caught it without any trouble.

"Third out! Change sides!" Matt's team yelled. As she came up with the ball in her hand, Matt turned to say to the teacher, "Next time you can hold first base."

But another miracle was to come a little later. There was one out, and the bases were full. Matt went up to bat—and flied out.

"Two out now," his team groaned.

"Count it three," Noah yelled from the pitcher's box. The teacher had the bat, and Noah sent a swift curve around home plate. But it didn't seem to fool the batter. She stood there smiling and waiting for the next one.

"Don't make an out!" somebody begged her.

Crack! Her bat swung out and hit the ball.

"Whoopee!" Matt's players were yelling. "Look! Looky! Look-a-there it goes! Clear the bases, everybody!"

They were clearing them as fast as they could. And here came the teacher.

"Home run!" they all shouted.

She made it amid wild cheers: "Whoopee! Hurrah for Miss Judy!"

A minute later, she went to ring the bell, saying over her shoulder, "We'll finish out the inning at recess."

Glory, standing near Matt in line as they marched in, heard him say to someone, "I like that teacher a sight better than I thought I would. She can play on my side any time."

Reflections

1. Matt says he doesn't want a "gal" teacher. What does Matt think Miss Judy will be like?
2. When Miss Judy catches the ball, Matt thinks a miracle has happened. Was it really a miracle? Explain.
3. What words do the highland people in this story use for each of the following things?
   a. helping hand
   b. food
   c. stuck up or snobbish
   d. sun
4. In the story, Matt changes his mind about Miss Judy. Write about a time when you changed your mind about someone. Include what you first thought about the person, what you now think, and why you changed your mind.

Calico Pie

EDWARD LEAR

Calico Pie,
The little Birds fly
Down to the calico tree,
Their wings were blue,
And they sang "Tilly-loo!"
Till away they flew—
And they never came back to me!
They never came back!
They never came back!
They never came back to me!

Calico Jam
The little Fish swam,
Over the syllabub sea,
He took off his hat,
To the Sole and the Sprat,
And the Willeby-wat,—
But he never came back to me!
He never came back!
He never came back!
He never came back to me!

Calico Ban
The little Mice ran,
To be ready in time for tea,
Flippity flup,
They drank it all up,
And danced in the cup,—
But they never came back to me!
They never came back!
They never came back!
They never came back to me!

Calico Drum,
The Grasshoppers come
The Butterfly, Beetle, and Bee,
Over the ground,
Around and around,
With a hop and a bound,—
But they never came back!
They never came back!
They never came back!
They never came back to me!

Pushing Up the Sky

ELLA E. CLARK

In the beginning, the Creator and Changer made the world. He created first in the East. Then he slowly came westward, creating as he came. With him he brought many languages. He gave a different language to each group of people he created. When he reached Puget Sound, he liked it so well that he decided that he would go no farther. But he had many languages left. These he scattered all around Puget Sound and to the north, along the waters there. That is why there are so many different languages spoken by the Indians in the Puget Sound country.

Even though these people could not talk together, they soon found that no one was pleased with the way the Creator had made the world. The sky was so low that the tall people bumped their heads against it. Also, sometimes people climbed up high in the trees and went into the Sky World. One time the wise men of the different tribes had a meeting to see what they could do about lifting the sky. They agreed that the people should try to push it up higher.

"We can do it," a very wise man of the council said, "if we will all push at the same time. We will need all the people and all the animals and all the birds when we push."

"How will we know when to push?" asked another of the wise men. "Some of us live in this part of the world, some in another. Some talk one language, and some another. We don't all talk the same language. How can we get everyone to push at the same time?"

That puzzled the men of the council, but at last one of them said, "Why don't we have a signal? When the time comes for us to push, when we have everything ready, let someone shout 'Ya-hoh.' That means 'Lift together' in all our languages."

So the wise men of the council sent that message to all the people and animals and birds and told them on what day they were to lift the sky. Everyone made poles from the giant fir trees, poles to push against the sky.

The day for the sky lifting came. All the people raised their poles and touched the sky with them. Then the wise men shouted, "Ya-hoh!" Everybody pushed, and the sky moved up a little. "Ya-hoh," the wise men shouted a second time, and the people pushed with all their strength. The sky lifted a little higher. "Ya-hoh," all shouted and pushed as hard as they could.

They kept shouting "Ya-hoh!" and pushing until the sky was up to the place where it now is. Since then no one has bumped against the sky, and no one has since been able to climb into the Sky World.

But a few people did not know about the sky pushing. Three were hunters who had been chasing four elk for several days. Just as the people and animals and birds were ready to push up the sky, the three hunters and the four elk came to the place where the earth nearly meets the sky. The elk jumped into the Sky World, and the hunters ran after them. When the sky was lifted, elk and hunters were lifted, too. In the Sky World they were changed to stars. At night, even now, you can see them. The three hunters form the handle of the Big Dipper. The middle hunter has his dog with him—now a tiny star. The four elk make the bowl of the Big Dipper.

Some other people were caught up in the sky in two canoes, three men in each of them. And a little fish also was on its way up into the Sky World when the people pushed. So all of them have had to stay there ever since. The hunters and the little dog, the elk, the little fish, and the men in the canoes are now stars, but they once lived on earth.

We may still shout "Ya-hoh!" when doing hard work together or lifting something heavy like a canoe. When we say "hoh," all of us use all the strength we have. Our voices have a higher pitch on that part of the word, and we make the *o* very long—"Ya-*hoh!*"

Reflections

1. In the beginning, what serious fault did the Indians find with the world?
2. How did the wise men get all the tribes and all the animals to work together to solve this problem?
3. What happened to the people and the animals who were caught in the sky?
4. Suppose that there hadn't even been one word that *all* the tribes understood. What little play could the wise men have invented and acted out so that everyone would get the meaning when they shouted "Ya-hoh"?
5. Choose one of the stars or constellations listed below and look up the legend about it in the encyclopedia. Write a summary of the legend.
   a. Cassiopeia
   b. The Pleiades
   c. Gemini
   d. Andromeda
   e. Orion

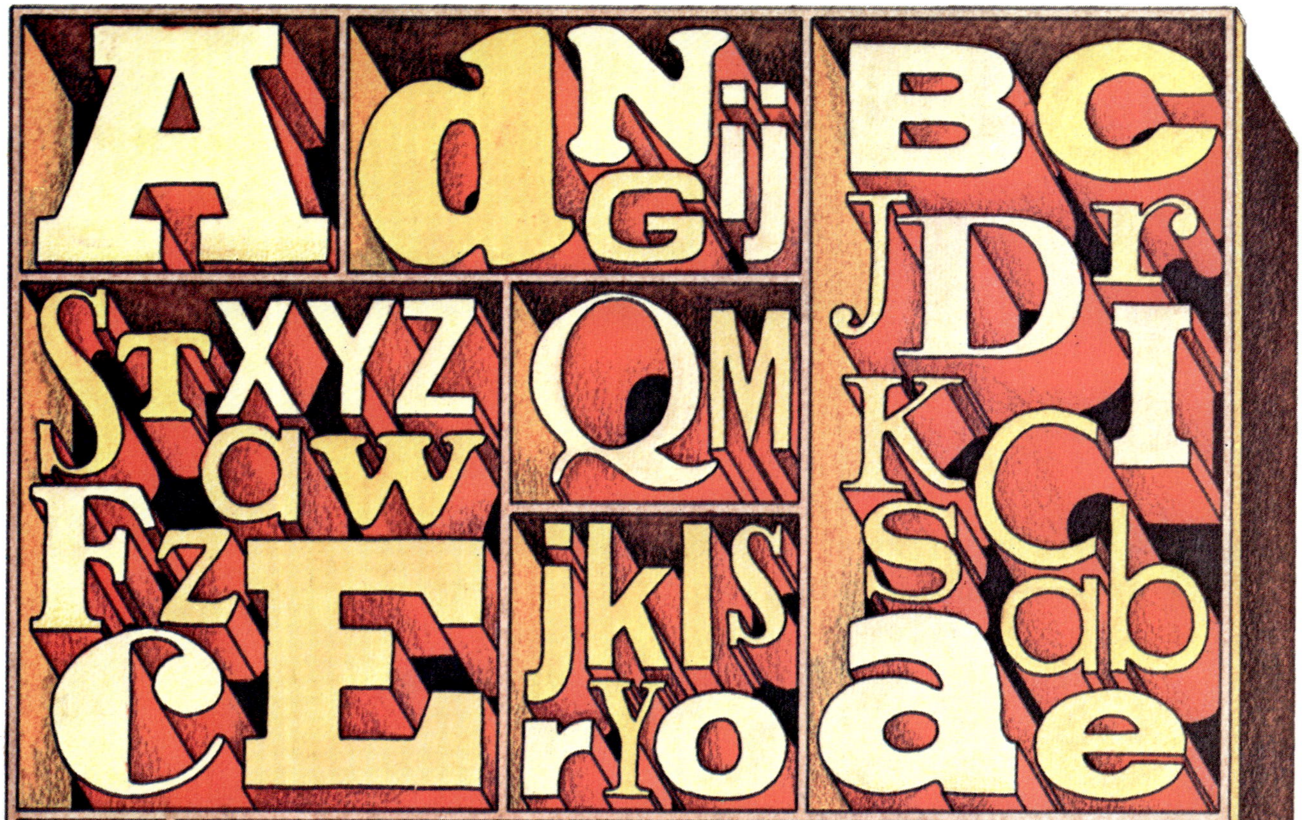

Handy Do-It-Yourself Word-Making Kit

FRANKLIN FOLSOM

Suppose you decided to dream up a language of your own and had to start from scratch. How would you go about it? You might start with sounds. Once you have chosen the sounds you want, you can go ahead and shape them into words. A word builder needs only a small kit of tools and a few plans to go by.

One plan is this: Just make some sounds and give them any meaning you like. Many English words were created in that way—*hunky-dory* and *flapdoodle,* for instance. Or take the word *googol.* This is the name for a huge number—1, followed by a hundred zeros. For a long time this number had no name. Then one day a famous mathematician asked his nine-year-old nephew what to call it. "Googol," the boy answered. And *googol* it became in all mathematics textbooks.

Perhaps you would like to make long words for long things and short words for short things. In English, of course, words seldom come in sizes that fit the things they go with. A *mile* is long. But a *millimeter* is only a tiny fraction of an inch. The *whale* is the biggest creature on earth. But you have to use a microscope to see a *paramecium!*

Or you might want to fit words to sounds—like *woof* and *tweet.* This kind of thing can be fun. Many languages do have a few words that match sounds in some special way. But most new words are built according to easier plans.

Lewis Carroll, who wrote *Alice's Adventures in Wonderland,* often used the trick of combining old words into new ones. He made *frumious* out of *fuming* and *furious.* He put *gallop* and *triumph* together and got *gallumph.* Navy divers invented *frogman.* Some other combinations are *loudspeaker; bookworm, jellyfish,* and *baseball.* On the day when millions of people watched John Glenn orbit the earth, they also heard a new word made from two old ones—*splashdown.*

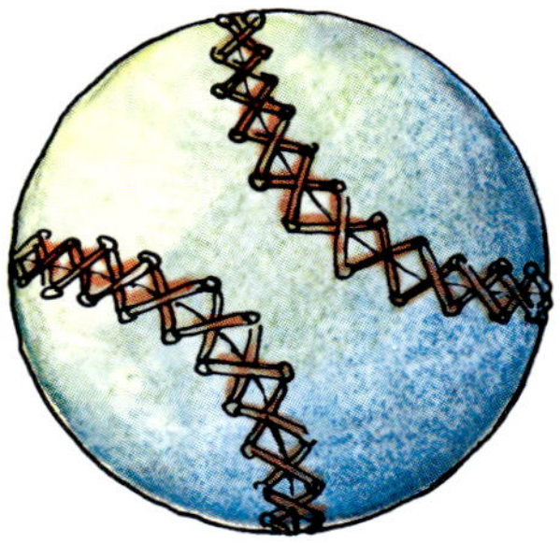

Another way you can create new words is by using old ones in new ways. For example, people thought that a fox was a clever animal, so they called a clever person *foxy*. Shining jewels are *brilliant*, and the word gets new meaning when people are called *brilliant*—that is, they seem to shine with intelligence. Your radio has a hidden *antenna* that picks up radio signals. This is a word that originally meant an insect's feeler.

One of the very good ways to get new words is to borrow them from other people. English is full of words that have been borrowed from other languages. The possibilities for borrowing words are endless. You can even take two at a time and combine them. Scientists do a lot of this. They made *dinosaur*, for instance, by combining two Greek words that mean "terrible" and "lizard." Many other words were made in the same way. *Democracy* is a combination of two Greek words that together mean "rule by the people." *Spelunker*, which means "cave explorer," was

made out of *spelaion*, the Greek word for "cave." The man who made *spelunker* said, "I added -*unker* because it reminded me of a man dunking himself in a cave."

You can also make new words by using the names of people or places or the characters in stories. For instance, a special kind of writing for blind people is called *Braille* because a man by that name invented it. The *saxophone* was named for its inventor, Sax. *Hygiene* comes from the name of the Greek goddess of health—Hygeia. Your *atlas* has that name because long ago on a famous collection of maps, there was a picture of the Greek god Atlas holding up the world.

You can make words by cutting big ones down into small ones. A *tarp* used to be a *tarpaulin*. When you say a mechanical person is a robot, you are using a cut-down form of *robotnik*, which means "worker" in several Slavic languages. You can cut down long phrases or sentences and make them into short words by joining together the first letters of each word. *UNESCO* comes from *United Nations Educational, Scientific, and Cultural Organization*. Scientists often shorten long terms by combining initials. Here is one science word that appeared in 1961: *avsep*. An *avsep* is a medical invention. Its full name is *Audio Visual Superimposed Electrocardiogram Presentation*. With long names like these, you cannot blame scientists for using so many shortcuts.

How many words must you actually make before you have a language? There are over 450,000 words in *Webster's Third New International Dictionary.* No one person knows all of them, but most grown people are able to understand about 35,000. Actually you use only about one-tenth as many words as you understand.

While we are counting, we might as well have one more figure. A famous mathematician has calculated that since the beginning of speech, people have used a total of ten million billion words. That's a heap of language.

Reflections

1. This selection gives at least eight ways of making new words. What are they?
2. Make up a word for each of the ideas in parentheses below.
   a. He was (having a good time).
   b. That is a (very tall) building.
   c. They are (collecting) stamps.
3. Make new words by combining each pair of words below.
   a. snow + sleet = (Example) sneet
   b. bananas + apples =
   c. huge + fierce =
4. Pretend that you went shopping for food and other things. Write a paragraph in which you tell about all the things you bought. Instead of giving the real name of the merchandise, make up an acronym for the item's name. Example: I always buy TRASH. (Terrifically Round And Sweet Honeydew)

A Time to Talk

ROBERT FROST

When a friend calls to me from the road
And slows his horse to a meaning walk,
I don't stand still and look around
On all the hills I haven't hoed,
And shout from where I am, "What is it?"
No, not as there is a time to talk.
I thrust my hoe in the mellow ground,
Blade-end up and five feet tall,
And plod: I go up to the stone wall
For a friendly visit.

Noah Webster: The Word Watcher

BERNARD WEISS

The Schoolmaster to America

The next time you use a dictionary, you may notice the name *Webster* on the cover. Noah Webster was the man who wrote the first American dictionary. He also wrote textbooks for American children. Because of this, Noah became known as the "schoolmaster to America."

Noah Webster was born in 1758 and died in 1843. As a boy, he lived on a small farm in the colony of Connecticut. There Noah went to the village school. When he was sixteen, he entered Yale College. At this time the colonies were getting impatient with their treatment by England. Noah and his friends held military drills so that they would be ready to fight if they had to. (Once, George Washington stopped at Yale to observe the young men in training.) Before Noah was graduated, he served as a volunteer in the American Revolution. After the Revolution he went back to finish college.

After leaving college, Noah began teaching. He loved to teach and was always eager to find better ways of helping children learn. He thought quite a lot about spelling and pronunciation; it seemed to him that the old rules and the old books should not be used. In his opinion, the new nation, which had just broken away from England, should have its own language and its own books. A properly written spelling book, he thought, could do more to spread the American language across the country than any other kind of book. It should help people learn the letters in the alphabet before they learned how to read. It should show the pronunciation people used daily, and it should give the spelling of words that reflected the way they were pronounced.

Finally Noah pulled all his ideas together, and in 1783 he published his speller, which soon became famous. It had a thin blue wrapper and was called *The American Spelling Book* or the *Blue-Backed Speller*. Included in it were abbreviations and the names of cities and countries. Later Noah added pictures and fables to the speller. Here is one of the fables.

Of the Boy That Stole Apples

An old man found a rude boy upon one of his trees stealing apples, and desired him to come down; but the young sauce-box told him plainly he would not. Won't you? said the old man, then I will fetch you down; so he pulled up some turf or grass and threw at him; but this only made the youngster laugh, to think the old man should pretend to beat him down from the tree with grass only.

Well, well, said the old man, if neither words nor grass will do, I must try what virtue there is in stones: so the old man pelted him heartily with stones; which soon made the young chap hasten down from the tree and beg the old man's pardon.

Moral

If good words and gentle means will not reclaim the wicked, they must be dealt with in a more severe manner.

Through such stories, Noah tried to give advice to boys and girls. He stressed manners, good habits, and success.

Even Noah was surprised at the welcome people gave his speller. It wasn't long before the book could be found in homes and schools all over America. People who could not get copies of it were disappointed.

Because of the speller, spelling bees became very popular. They were often held in schoolrooms and were attended by young and old alike. Schools would compete with each other. Or people often had them just for fun or to pass time. Sometimes a whole town might be so interested in a bee that everyone would stay up far into the night.

Many of Noah Webster's ideas about spelling and syllabication are still used. Words like *cluster, habit,* and *nation* are now broken into syllables like this: *clus-ter, hab-it, na-tion.* In Webster's time, these words were broken in this way: *clu-ster, ha-bit, na-ti-on.* Webster said that it would be easier to spell and pronounce words if words were divided as closely as possible to the way they were pronounced.

Webster also tried to take out extra letters when they seemed pointless. He took out the *u* from such words as *honor* and *favor.* Today the English still spell these words with a *u: honour, favour.* He also removed a letter from the words *music* and *logic,* which had been spelled *musick* and *logick.*

After Noah published his speller, he wrote other books. One of them was a reader that gave the history and described the geography of the American nation. The reader also contained stories and gave boys and girls advice to help them study and read better.

The Dictionaries

Noah Webster loved to work with words. He realized that American English and British English were different, and he wanted to write a dictionary of American English. His great knowledge of many subjects enabled him to write accurate definitions. For example, he knew much about medicine and law. His knowledge of foreign languages helped him find the sources of English words. Among the languages he knew were German, Old English, Greek, Latin, Italian, Spanish, French, Hebrew, and Arabic. By the end of his life, he had mastered twenty alphabets and twenty languages.

But Noah Webster had traits more important than his interest in words and his knowledge of many subjects. He had patience and determination. He continued his work even though people disagreed with him. At first he thought the job would take from three to five years, but he did not actually finish his work until about twenty years later! During that time he wrote three dictionaries. He completed and published the third and largest one in 1828.

Noah labored hard to complete his third dictionary. Finally the day came when his huge task was about to be completed. His own words tell how he felt:

> When I had come to the last word, I was seized with a trembling, which made it somewhat difficult to hold my pen steady for writing. The cause seems to have been the thought that I was so near the end of my labors. But I summoned strength to finish the last word, and then walking about the room a few minutes, I recovered.

Noah Webster's work gave America the first dictionaries of American English. He is thought of as our first *lexicographer,* or dictionary author. His word histories, his careful definitions, and his remarks about rules for spelling and for pronouncing words have added much to the science of lexicography.

A modern unabridged dictionary has far more words than the seventy thousand in Webster's dictionary of 1828. But Noah Webster worked alone. Today many people take part in the work of making a dictionary. We can almost trace the growth of our language in the growth of the dictionary started by Noah Webster.

Reflections

1. Noah Webster was called the "schoolmaster to America"—that is, schoolmaster to *the whole country.* Tell why.
2. Describe two spelling changes that Webster introduced in his spellers.
3. Why did Noah Webster feel a new dictionary was necessary?
4. Read the last two paragraphs again. From the context, what do you think is the meaning of *lexicography* and *unabridged?* Look these words up.
5. Do you think spelling books should teach people how to behave? Why or why not? Write a paragraph giving your opinion and the reasons for it.

WITHOUT WORDS

OCTOBER
VOL. 3
NO. 10

FROM THE EDITOR

Words . . . Words . . . Words . . . We say them, we hear them, we read them and write them. And telephones, radios, television sets, printing presses are all there to help carry our words to all parts of the world—and even to the moon and back.

But sometimes we must communicate without words. When people do not know each other's language, when it is too noisy for words to be heard, when someone has lost the power of speech, when there is no time for words—then there is sign language.

This is a magazine dedicated to all forms of wordless communication. Signs and symbols used in sports, in industry, on land and on sea, signs used by many different people in many different situations can be found in this issue. And more—photographs, filmstrips, and cartoons. Read Without Words *every month.*

Many different Indian tribes lived on the Great Plains before the eastern settlers moved west. And each tribe had its own language.

They moved from place to place hunting the buffalo. They didn't stay together long enough to learn each other's languages. But still for hundreds of years Crow, Sioux, Kiowa, Blackfeet, and Arapaho could meet and understand each other because they had developed a sign language that was used and understood by all of the tribes. One of these signs is on page 193. You will find many more in our next issue.

WITHOUT WORDS

VOL. 3 NO. 10

PUBLISHER
Joan Lexiconi

EDITOR
Max Mot

MANAGING EDITOR
Alice Sordine

ON THE COVER What are these people saying? You can say it with music. You can say it with flowers. You can say it with a hug.

CONTENTS

LETTERS TO THE EDITOR

Dear Editor,

We want to congratulate *Without Words* for the important part it is playing in fighting noise pollution. Remember our motto: No noise is good noise. Keep up the good work!

Golden Silence Assn

Dear Editor,

I have no words to describe how great I think your magazine is!

Dick Shunary

SIGNS AND SYMBOLS. WHO USES THEM? WHY? WHAT DO THEY MEAN?

Answers appear on page 199.

Photographing the World

GORDON PARKS (1912–   )
American photographer Gordon Parks says what he has to say with many voices, among them prose, poetry, and music. But in his photography—his documentaries and films—he combines something of them all. To government, to industry, to *Life* magazine, to Hollywood, among others, Parks has lent his poet's eye. His work, though often stark, has an artist's sense of fitness and beauty.

MARGARET BOURKE-WHITE (1904–1971)
Margaret Bourke-White was a picture-reporter who always got her story. Traveling the globe on assignment, this world-famous American photographer captured with her camera not only her subject but its context. Her sensitive eye saw what lay beneath each person or event. And this made her pictures what she wanted them to be—a record of our history.

DOROTHEA LANGE (1895–1965)
This is a picture taken by the famous photographer, Dorothea Lange. What can you tell about this scene? What are the children watching? What makes you think so? Was the picture taken a long time ago, or recently? How can you tell?

FILMSTRIP MAKERS

They say a picture is worth a thousand words. A filmstrip is a series of still pictures made to be shown on a screen. First, an **author** thinks up a story. An **artist** draws the pictures. And an **editor** makes sure the pictures flow smoothly together.

(*above*) An artist, an author, and an editor are discussing the art for the filmstrip *John Henry,* the story about the legendary American folk hero.

When the author, artist, and editor are satisfied, the art boards are sent to a plant where the film-strip will be produced. When the **photographer** (*left*) finishes his work, the negatives will go to a room filled with machines and tanks for developing the film.

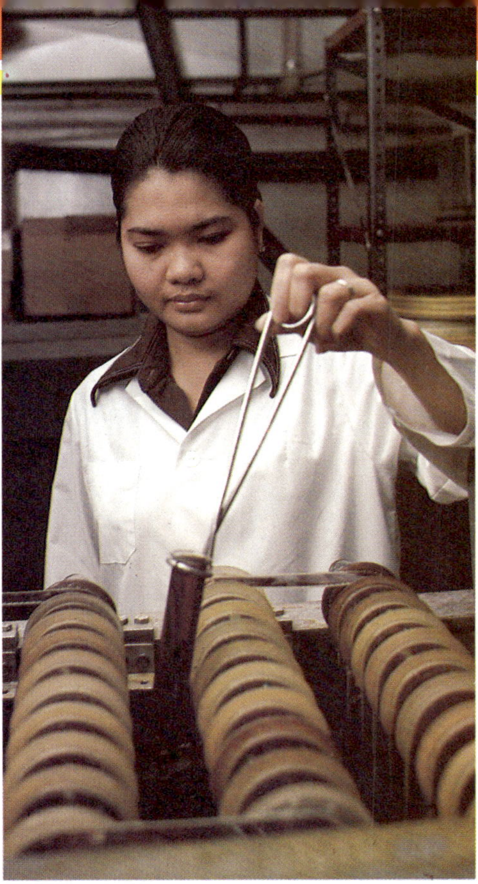

(*top left*) Here, a **chemist** checks the chemicals in one of the film baths. If the filmstrip is in color, she will also check to see how deep and true the colors are.

(*below*) Before the filmstrip is finished, the customer looks at it to make sure that it is just the way she wants it.

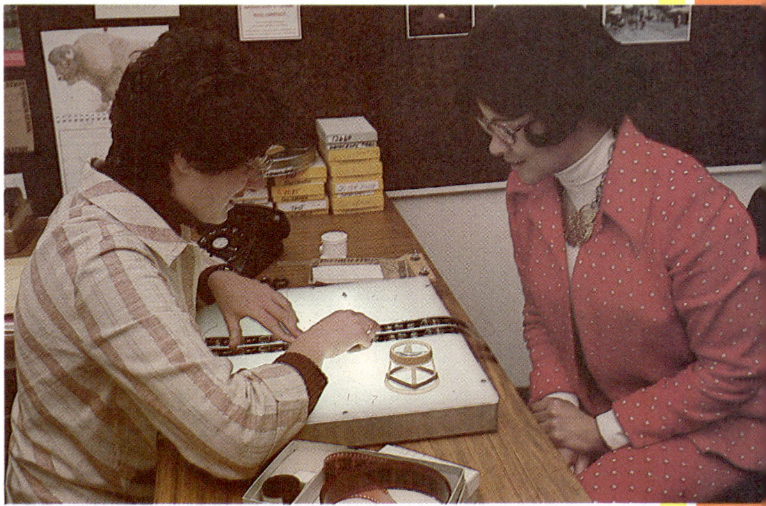

(*bottom left*) If there are any mistakes, several prints of the strip are lined up on a "sync" wheel, and the correction is made.

The last stop for the filmstrip is the packaging room. Here, the film is cut, rolled, put in small cans, and labeled. It is ready for you to watch.

JOHN HENRY

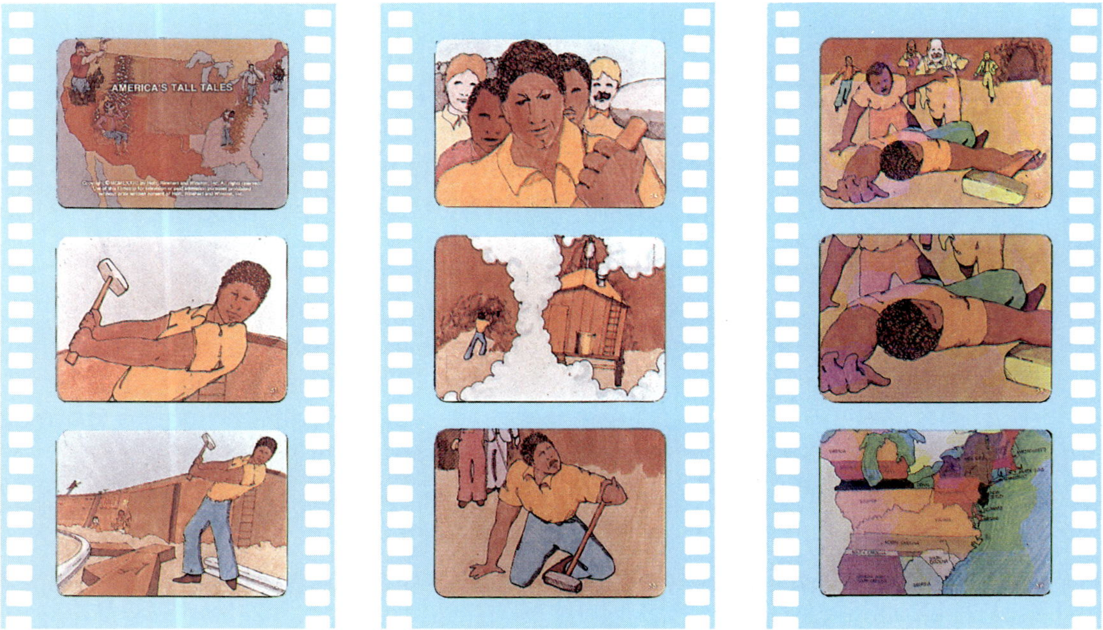
AMERICA'S TALL TALES

OUT OF GAS?
Fill Up With Air.
Let Pedal Power
Get You There.

SIGNS AND SYMBOLS (ANSWERS)

1. Scientist uses mathematical symbols to solve a complicated problem.
2. Railroad worker swings a lamp in a low arc, signaling a moving train to stop.
3. Singer reads musical notes and sings the melody they represent.
4. Signal landing officer on an aircraft carrier waves a pair of red and yellow paddles to tell an incoming plane to make another run and try again.
5. Sailboat owner signals that her boat is in trouble by putting up a square flag with a round ball beneath it.
6. Construction worker signals a crane operator to raise a load of steel.
7. Before the telegraph was invented, Indians used a blanket to control the smoke rising from a fire to send a signal to someone too far away to hear.
8. Football referee signals an incomplete forward pass when the receiver drops the ball, and the timekeeper stops the clock.
9. Red cross on the building tells an injured person that help can be found inside.
10. Police officer raises her hand as a signal for traffic to stop.
11. Girl Scout uses a flashlight after dark to send a message for help in Morse Code. In daylight, she uses a mirror to send the same message.
12. Member of the Kiowa tribe asks a Sioux how many miles he has traveled. First he makes the sign for question. Then he makes the sign for *how many* by striking the right index finger against each finger of the left hand, closing the fingers of the left hand as they are struck.

LEFT-HAND COLUMN

International Flag Code—*Letter B*

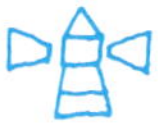
Lighthouse—*Fog lights*

Indian written sign language, broken arrow—*Peace*

Skull and Crossbones—*Poison*

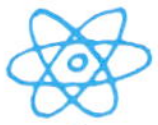
Science—*Atom*

Music—*G clef*

Road sign—*Curve*

Mathematics—*Divide*

RIGHT-HAND COLUMN

Automobile racing flag—*Finish*

Map Legends—*Fence line*
Railroad line

Coast Guard Flag—*Hurricane warning*

Money—*Dollar sign*

Olympic Games

Morse Code—*SOS (help)*

Manual Alphabet—*Letter C*

Railroad semaphore—*Proceed*

SPRING

A Commercial for Spring

EVE MERRIAM

Tired of slush and snow and sleet?
Then try this dandy calendar treat!

You'll like the longer, king-size days;
You, too, will sing this season's praise.

It's the scientific sunshine pill
(Without that bitter winter chill).

It's naturally warmer, it's toasted through,
Exclusively mild for you and *you*.

It comes in the handy three-month pack:
March, April, May—or your money back.

So ask for S–P–R–I–N–
G, you'll never regret it;
Remember the name, it's headed for fame:
Be the first on your block to get it!

Word Travelers

DONALD LLOYD

When the first settlers came to America, they brought with them their clothing and their tools, their religions and their customs. And they also brought their languages. Around the time that the first English-speaking settlers set sail for America, the English language was made up of about 150,000 words. Today, more than 350 years later, an unabridged dictionary of the English language has about 450,000 words. Where did all these new words come from?

There are several ways that speakers of a language get new words. One of the ways is by borrowing words from other languages. This is most likely to happen when people who speak different languages live and work side by side. In early America the English-speaking settlers came in contact with people speaking French, Spanish, Dutch, and Indian languages. During this period the English-speaking settlers began to use many words from these languages. The vocabulary of American English began to grow. Let us see how and why this happened.

Indian Words

The first English settlers in America saw plants and animals in their new home that they had never seen before. They had no names for them, but the Indians did. The settlers heard these Indian name-words and tried to repeat them. If they could, they said the words exactly as the Indians did. But if it was too hard for the settlers to pronounce some of the Indian words, they changed them a little. In 1608 Captain John Smith reported seeing a strange new animal about the size of a large cat. He first wrote its Indian name as a *rahaugcum.* By 1672 the word was written and pronounced in English as *raccoon,* just as we know it today.

Woodchuck, chipmunk, moose, opossum, and *skunk* were made from some other Indian names for animals the settlers had never seen before. *Hickory, pecan, squash,* and *succotash* were Indian names for trees and vegetables that did not grow in England. Because there were no English words to describe these things, the settlers simply borrowed the Indian names for them.

As the settlers and Indians continued to live and work together, the settlers learned much about Indian life and customs. They saw clothing, tools, and dwelling places they had never seen before. *Moccasins, wigwams, tepees, totems, tomahawks,* and *canoes* were new things for the settlers, and their names became new words in English.

Dutch, French, and Spanish Words

By 1664 the Dutch had settled in sections of New England and in the area that is now New York State. They mixed with the English-speaking settlers who borrowed many of their words. Many of the foods the Dutch people cooked were new words to the English. *Coleslaw, cookie, waffle,* and *cruller* soon became part of the language spoken by the English settlers.

The word *Yankee,* which came from the Dutch, has an interesting history. Some reference books tell us that the Dutch people in New York used a nickname for a typical English settler in their area. They called such a person *Jan Kee*—"John Cheese." After a while the English settlers began to use this name, but it became *Yankee,* meaning exactly what it means today. *Santa Claus* came from the Dutch name *Sinterklaas. Spook, snoop,* and *stoop* were also borrowed from the Dutch during this period.

By 1700 French explorers had settled the area around the Great Lakes and along the Mississippi River. At the same time English settlers were moving westward into these areas. When the two groups came into contact, our English vocabulary grew even more.

The French people in the north-central part of America were hunters and explorers. Many of the French words that the English settlers borrowed have to do with the land they explored and settled. *Prairie* is a French word that describes the large areas of flat, grass-covered land of the Midwest. The swift-moving currents of the Mississippi were called *rapids* by the French. *Levees* were built to prevent flooding along the Mississippi. The English settlers learned these French words, and they, along with many others, are still a part of our language.

The Spanish people settled chiefly in what is now the southwestern part of our country. They lived very differently from the way the settlers on the eastern coast lived. They raised cattle on *ranchos*. They used *lariats* and *lassos*. They kept their horses in *corrals*. They wore *sombreros* and cloaks called *ponchos*. The large, open area in the center of a Spanish settlement was called a *plaza*. Buildings were made of *adobe*. As the English-speaking pioneers moved into the Southwest, they continued to borrow words, and the English vocabulary continued to grow.

Modern Word-Borrowing

Immigration to America did not stop when the country was completely explored and settled. And word-borrowing did not stop either. People continued to come to America from countries where English is not the native language. They came from such countries as China and Japan, Germany and Hungary, Greece and Russia, Italy and France, and from some African nations.

Many of the words we borrowed from the languages of immigrants are names of foods they ate in their homelands. In America immigrants still cooked many of these foods, and the names for them have become part of our language.

Suppose that for your next meal you could choose from a menu that listed the names for many kinds of foods. Part of the menu might look like this.

Menu

POLYGLOT RESTAURANT

Appetizers

Hors d'Oeuvre (French)
Caviar (Turkish)
Olives (Greek)
Gefilte Fish (Yiddish)

Soups

Borscht (Russian)
Minestrone (Italian)
Gumbo (African)

Main Dishes

Pizza (Italian)
Omelette (French)
Soufflé (French)
Chow Mein (Chinese)
Frankfurters (German)
Shish Kebab (Turkish)
Goulash (Hungarian)
Tortillas (Spanish)
Smorgasbord (Swedish)

Breads

Bagels (Yiddish)
Muffins (German)
Matzoth (Hebrew)

Side Dishes

Spaghetti (Italian)
Yams (African)
Okra (African)

Desserts

Apricots (Arabic)
Lingons (Swedish)
Almonds (Greek)
Petits Fours (French)
Eclair (French)
Sherbet (Arabic)
Candy (Arabic)

Beverages

Coffee (Arabic)
Tea (Chinese)
Cola (African)

The next list contains some words that have come into English because of contact between English speakers and non-English speakers in America and elsewhere. The words we have borrowed from the non-English speakers tell us about their countries, achievements, and ways of life. For example, many Italian words that are now part of English have to do with music. This is no accident. For hundreds of years, Italian musicians have been among the most famous in the world. Let's look at some borrowed words and see what they tell us about non-English speakers.

French	**Italian**	**Indian Languages**	**Arabic**
blouse	opera	bungalow	algebra
cinema	piano	calico	camphor
coiffure	solo	jungle	gazelle
culotte	soprano	sari	safari
jacket	stanza	sitar	sofa

Persian	**African Languages**	**Japanese**
bazaar	banjo	haiku
caravan	chimpanzee	hibachi
pajamas	impala	karate
shawl	marimba	kimono
tiger	okapi	obi

So you see, when people of different countries who spoke different languages met, they borrowed words from each other. English-speaking Americans borrowed words from immigrants who spoke other languages. Americans who traveled to other countries brought back with them more words from foreign languages. Today people are still borrowing words from each other. In our age of communications satellites, television, and radio, we can come in contact with foreign languages right in our own homes. As long as word-borrowing continues, our language will continue to grow.

Reflections

1. When are people who speak different languages most likely to borrow words from each other?
2. How did the word *Yankee* come into the English language? What does the word mean to you?
3. Look at the African words in the last list in this selection. Why did English borrow these names from African languages?
4. The words we have borrowed from non-English speakers often tell about an important part of their lives. Choose one of the following groups of people. Skim the story to find the words we have borrowed from that group. Then write a short essay telling what these words show about the way of life or special interests of the group.
   a. American Indian
   b. Spanish
   c. modern French
   d. Dutch

WAYS TO DEFINE WORDS

Because our alphabet is used by people in many countries of the world, we can "read" many words of foreign languages. Try these sentences:

German:	Ja, Mutter, ich habe drei.
Danish:	Ja, Mor, jeg har tre.
Dutch:	Ja, Moeder, ik heb drie.
French:	Oui, ma mère, j'en ai trois.
Spanish:	Sí, Madre, yo tengo tres.
Italian:	Si, madre, ce n'ho tre.

All of these sentences mean the same thing. Can you guess the meaning of the first word? What word in English sounds like *Mutter, Moeder, madre?* What about *drei? tre? drie?* In English we would write this sentence as "Yes, Mother, I have three."

As we read or listen, we sometimes meet a word we do not know. It might as well be a foreign word as far as its meaning goes, because it may mean almost nothing to us, although we may be able to guess its meaning. Following are some ways we have of defining words.

Definition by Demonstration

Perhaps the easiest way to define many words is to demonstrate, or show, the thing that the word names. For example, if we have a small child in the family just learning to speak, we hold a pencil and say, "This is a pencil." We call this a demonstrative definition. Beginning pupils often learn to use pictures in their books as clues to word meaning. This way of defining words is also used in nearly all dictionaries, and it is often used in newspapers and magazines. We find it in many advertisements.

Toucan

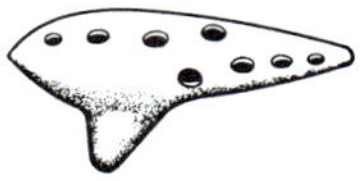

Ocarina

Cruet

Churn

Let the dictionary illustrations help you get the meaning of these words.

But we may not have an illustration handy, and, of course, for words like *large, beautiful, mention,* and *very,* a picture often cannot work.

Definition by Context

Many words take their meaning from the words near them in a sentence. When we read the whole sentence, one word may make the meaning of an unknown word clear. For example:

1. My friend, the *cryptographer,* broke the code.
2. These are the bones of a *brontosaurus,* one of many kinds of dinosaurs.

Some words have several meanings. Tell what *head* means in each of these sentences.

1. The pillow is by the *head* of the bed.
2. The *head* of the school is the principal.
3. *Head* the ship into the wind.
4. President Lincoln's *head* is on the penny.
5. The *head* of the river is a spring.
6. My *head* aches.

In each of the sentences above, all the words in the sentence are woven together to give us the proper meaning of *head*. This is called definition by context. Context is one of the most valuable clues we use when we read.

Dictionary Meanings

In a dictionary we find words defined by other words. We call this a dictionary definition. Here is an example from a dictionary.

> **knell** (nel), *n.* **1,** the sound of a bell, especially when tolled for a death or at a funeral; **2,** hence; a sign of the ending or extinction of something; as, "The curfew tolls the *knell* of parting day":—*v.i.* to toll dolefully.

In any dictionary definition, we need to know each of the words that explain, or define, the entry word. If we do not know the meaning of *dolefully* or *extinction,* we need to look up their definitions before we can understand the definition of *knell.* A dictionary gives the pronunciation of a word. Often the word is used in a sentence. Many dictionaries give synonyms for the word being defined. What does *n.* mean in the definition above?

Historical Definition

Another way to define a word is to find out about its history. Often the original meaning of the word is helpful. For example, *brontosaurus* is from two Greek words, *bronté,* meaning "thunder," and *sauros,* meaning "lizard." The historical definition, in this case, does not give you a scientific definition of *brontosaurus.* It suggests that the big lizard thunders. Knowing the history of the word *democracy,* from *dēmos,* Greek meaning "people," and *-kratia,* Greek meaning "power," helps us know its meaning today.

A large dictionary gives word origins. These are good to know because many English words often come from one foreign root. For example, our word *meter* is from the Greek word *metron,* meaning "measure." This is a clue to the meaning of *thermometer, altimeter, centimeter, telemetry, metronome, barometer, kilometer,* and other words we make from the Greek root *metron.* See if you can find these words in a large dictionary. Find out what *thermo–, alti–, centi–, tele–, –onome* (from *–onym*), *baro–,* and *kilo–* mean.

Definition by Synonym and Antonym

We often define a word by telling how closely it resembles other words. The meaning of *colossal, enormous, tremendous,* or *gigantic* can be explained by easier words, such as *big, huge,* and *large*. This is an example of definition by synonym.

Use a dictionary and find synonyms for *vanish, hilarious,* and *appropriate.*

Sometimes we define a word by telling what is opposite to it. We call this definition by antonym. For example, *hubbub, ruckus, din, clamor,* and *uproar* are opposites of *calm* or *quiet* or *peacefulness.*

Because words are essential to reading, we cannot break the reading code without ways to define them. Improve in reading by learning to define words in all of the ways you have just studied. You will need to use these ways whenever you read.

3 RIDING HIGH

Earth, Moon, and Sun

While the earth spins on,
Turning, turning
Toward the sun,

The moon floats by
In its circle
In our sky.

And while it floats,
Earth and moon, two in one,
Rush on
With the bright planets
In a ring
Around the sun.

And as they rush
And swing
And turn
The gases of the sun
Swirl
And burn.

And all the while these three,
Swirling sun
And moon
And earth,
Spiral in the galaxy.

Spiral in that great wheel turning
With its billion stars
Sparkling,
Burning;

That starry wheel
Where you and I
Night and day
Are riding high,
Riding high!

Claudia Lewis

Many Moons

JAMES THURBER

Once upon a time, in a kingdom by the sea, there lived a little princess named Lenore. She was ten years old going on eleven. One day Lenore fell ill of a surfeit of raspberry tarts and took to her bed.

The Royal Physician came to see her and took her temperature and felt her pulse and made her stick out her tongue. The Royal Physician was worried. He sent for the King, Lenore's father, and the King came to see her.

"I will get you anything your heart desires," the King said. "Is there anything your heart desires?"

"Yes," said the Princess. "I want the moon. If I can have the moon, I will be well again."

Now, the King had a great many wise men who always got for him anything he wanted, so he told his daughter that she could have the moon. Then he went to the throne room and pulled a bell cord, three long pulls and a short pull, and presently the Lord High Chamberlain came into the room.

The Lord High Chamberlain was a large, fat man who wore thick glasses which made his eyes seem twice as big as they really were. This made the Lord High Chamberlain seem twice as wise as he really was.

"I want you to get the moon," said the King. "The Princess Lenore wants the moon. If she can have the moon, she will get well again."

"The moon?" exclaimed the Lord High Chamberlain, his eyes widening. This made him look four times as wise as he really was.

"Yes, the moon," said the King. "M-o-o-n, moon. Get it tonight, tomorrow at the latest."

The Lord High Chamberlain wiped his forehead with a handkerchief and then blew his nose loudly. "I have got a great many things for you in my time, your Majesty," he said. "It just happens that I have with me a list of the things I have got for you in my time." He pulled a long scroll of parchment out of his pocket. "Let me see, now." He glanced at the list, frowning. "I have got ivory, apes, and peacocks, rubies, opals, and emeralds, black orchids, pink elephants, and blue poodles, gold bugs, scarabs, and flies in amber, hummingbirds' tongues, angels' feathers, and unicorns' horns, giants, midgets, and mermaids, frankincense, ambergris, and myrrh, troubadours, minstrels, and dancing women, a pound of butter, two dozen eggs, and a sack of sugar—sorry, my wife wrote that in there."

"I don't remember any blue poodles," said the King.

"It says blue poodles right here on the list, and they are checked off with a little check mark," said the Lord High Chamberlain. "So there must have been blue poodles. You just forget."

"Never mind the blue poodles," said the King. "What I want now is the moon."

"I have sent as far as Samarkand and Araby and Zanzibar to get things for you, your Majesty," said the Lord High Chamberlain. "But the moon is out of the question. It is 35,000 miles away and it is bigger than the room the Princess lies in. Furthermore, it is made of molten copper. I cannot get the moon for you. Blue poodles, yes; the moon, no."

The King flew into a rage and told the Lord High Chamberlain to leave the room and to send the Royal Wizard to the throne room.

The Royal Wizard was a little, thin man with a long face. He wore a high red peaked hat covered with silver stars, and a long blue robe covered with golden owls. His face grew very pale when the King told him that he wanted the moon for his little daughter, and that he expected the Royal Wizard to get it.

"I have worked a great deal of magic for you in my time, your Majesty," said the Royal Wizard. "As a matter of fact, I just happen to have in my pocket a list of the wizardries I have performed for you." He drew a paper from a deep pocket of his robe. "It begins: 'Dear Royal Wizard: I am returning herewith the so-called philosopher's stone which you claimed—' no, that isn't it." The Royal Wizard brought a long scroll of parchment from another pocket of his robe. "Here it is," he said. "Now, let's see. I have squeezed blood out of turnips for you, and turnips out of blood. I have produced rabbits out of silk hats, and silk hats out of rabbits. I have conjured up flowers, tambourines, and doves out of nowhere and nowhere out of flowers, tambourines, and doves. I

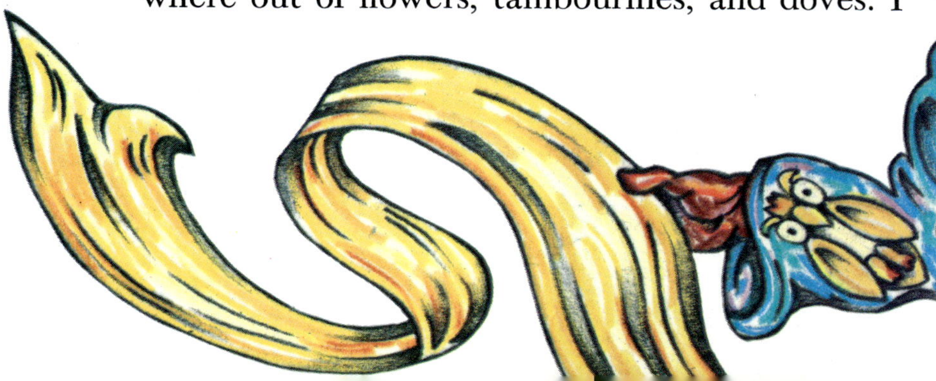

have brought you divining rods, magic wands, and crystal spheres in which to behold the future. I have compounded philters, unguents, and potions, to cure heartbreak, surfeit, and ringing in the ears. I have made you my own special mixture of wolfsbane, nightshade, and eagles' tears, to ward off witches, demons, and things that go bump in the night. I have given you seven-league boots, the golden touch, and a cloak of invisibility—"

"It didn't work," said the King. "The cloak of invisibility didn't work."

"Yes, it did," said the Royal Wizard.

"No, it didn't," said the King. "I kept bumping into things, the same as ever."

"The cloak is supposed to make you invisible," said the Royal Wizard. "It is not supposed to keep you from bumping into things."

"All I know is, I kept bumping into things," said the King. The Royal Wizard looked at his list again. "I got you," he said, "horns from Elfland, sand from the Sandman, and gold from the rainbow. Also a spool of thread, a paper of needles, and a lump of beeswax—sorry, those are things my wife wrote down for me to get her."

"What I want you to do now," said the King, "is to get me the moon. The Princess Lenore wants the moon, and when she gets it, she will be well again."

“Nobody can get the moon,” said the Royal Wizard. “It is 150,000 miles away, and it is made of green cheese, and it is twice as big as this palace.”

The King flew into another rage and sent the Royal Wizard back to his cave. Then he rang a gong and summoned the Royal Mathematician.

The Royal Mathematician was a bald-headed, nearsighted man, with a skullcap on his head and a pencil behind his ear. He wore a black suit with white numbers on it.

“I don’t want to hear a long list of all the things you have figured out for me since 1907,” the King said to him. “I want you to figure out right now how to get the moon for the Princess Lenore. When she gets the moon, she will be well again.”

"I am glad you mentioned all the things I have figured out for you since 1907," said the Royal Mathematician. "It so happens that I have a list of them with me."

He pulled a long scroll of parchment out of a pocket and looked at it. "Now, let me see. I have figured out for you the distance between the horns of a dilemma, night and day, and A and Z. I have computed how far is Up, how long it takes to get to Away, and what becomes of Gone. I have discovered the length of the sea serpent, the price of the priceless, and the square of the hippopotamus. I know where you are when you are at Sixes and Sevens, how much Is you have to have to make an Are, and how many birds you can catch with the salt in the ocean—187,796,132, if it would interest you to know."

"There aren't that many birds," said the King.

"I didn't say there were," said the Royal Mathematician. "I said *if* there were."

"I don't want to hear about seven hundred million imaginary birds," said the King. "I want you to get the moon for the Princess Lenore."

"The moon is 300,000 miles away," said the Royal Mathematician. "It is round and flat like a

coin, only it is made of asbestos and it is half the size of this kingdom. Furthermore, it is pasted on the sky. Nobody can get the moon."

The King flew into still another rage and sent the Royal Mathematician away. Then he rang for the Court Jester. The Jester came bounding into the throne room in his motley and his cap and bells, and sat at the foot of the throne.

"What can I do for you, your Majesty?" asked the Court Jester.

"Nobody can do anything for me," said the King mournfully. "The Princess Lenore wants the moon, and she cannot be well till she gets it, but nobody can get it for her. Every time I ask anybody for the moon, it gets larger and farther away. There is nothing you can do for me except play on your lute. Something sad."

"How big do they say the moon is," asked the Court Jester, "and how far away?"

"The Lord High Chamberlain says it is 35,000 miles away, and bigger than the Princess Lenore's room," said the King. "The Royal Wizard says it is 150,000 miles away, and twice as big as this palace. The Royal Mathematician says it is 300,000 miles away, and half the size of this kingdom."

The Court Jester strummed on his lute for a little while. "They are all wise men," he said, "and so they must all be right. If they are all right, then the moon must be just as large and as far away as each person thinks it is. The thing to do is find out how big the Princess Lenore thinks it is, and how far away."

"I never thought of that," said the King.

"I will go and ask her, your Majesty," said the Court Jester. And he crept softly into the little girl's room.

The Princess Lenore was awake, and she was glad to see the Court Jester, but her face was very pale and her voice very weak.

"Have you brought the moon to me?" she asked.

"Not yet," said the Court Jester, "but I will get it for you right away. How big do you think it is?"

"It is just a little smaller than my thumbnail," she said, "for when I hold my thumbnail up at the moon, it just covers it."

“And how far away is it?” asked the Court Jester.

“It is not as high as the big tree outside my window,” said the Princess, “for sometimes it gets caught in the top branches.”

“It will be very easy to get the moon for you,” said the Court Jester. “I will climb the tree tonight when it gets caught in the top branches and bring it to you.”

Then he thought of something else. “What is the moon made of, Princess?” he asked.

“Oh,” she said, “it’s made of gold, of course, silly.”

The Court Jester left the Princess Lenore’s room and went to see the Royal Goldsmith. He had the Royal Goldsmith make a tiny round golden moon just a little smaller than the thumbnail of the Princess Lenore. Then he had him string it on a golden chain so the Princess could wear it around her neck.

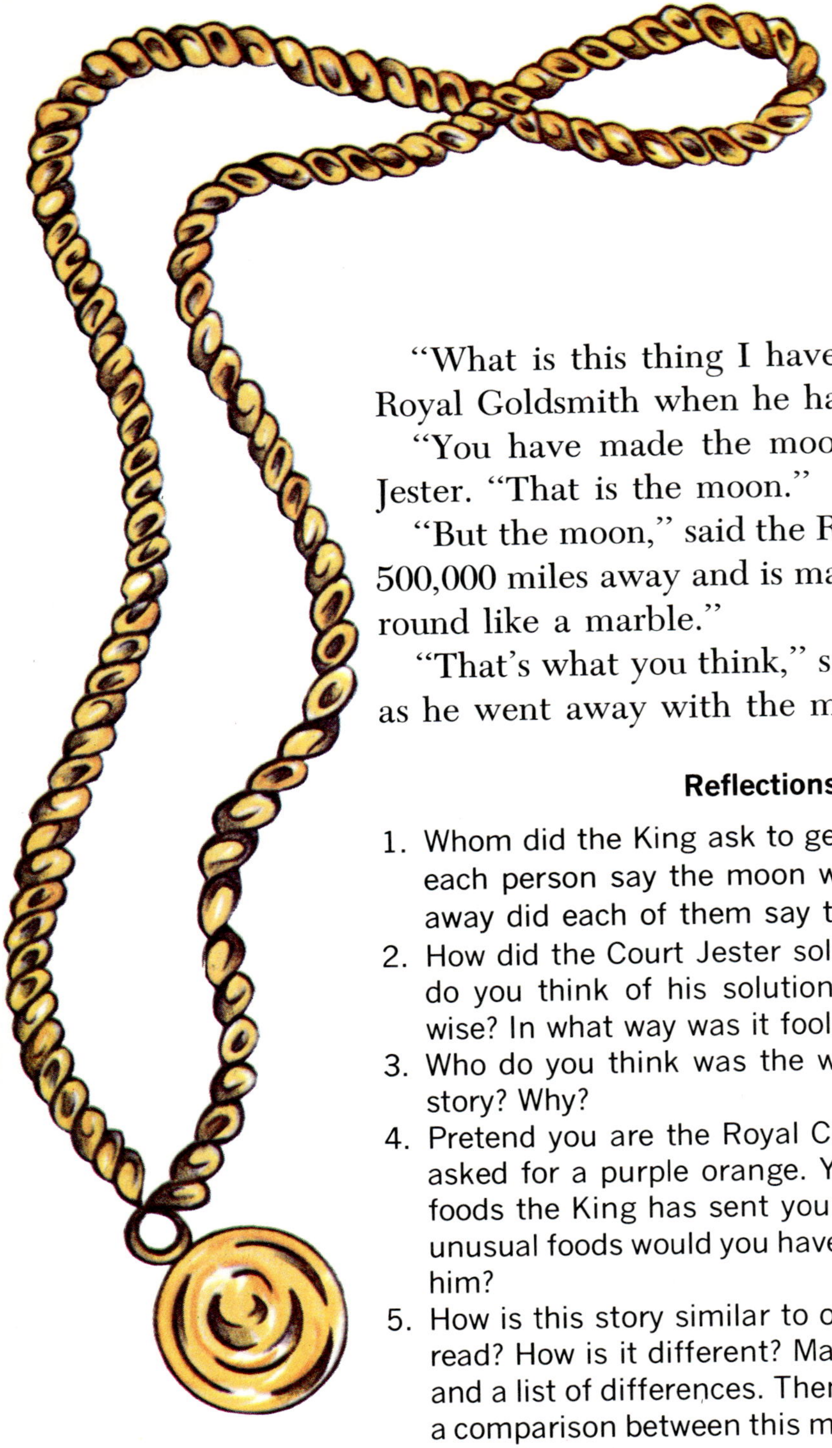

"What is this thing I have made?" asked the Royal Goldsmith when he had finished it.

"You have made the moon," said the Court Jester. "That is the moon."

"But the moon," said the Royal Goldsmith, "is 500,000 miles away and is made of bronze and is round like a marble."

"That's what you think," said the Court Jester as he went away with the moon.

Reflections

1. Whom did the King ask to get the moon? What did each person say the moon was made of? How far away did each of them say the moon was?
2. How did the Court Jester solve the problem? What do you think of his solution? In what way was it wise? In what way was it foolish?
3. Who do you think was the wisest character in the story? Why?
4. Pretend you are the Royal Cook. The princess has asked for a purple orange. You, too, have a list of foods the King has sent you to find for him. What unusual foods would you have on the list you read to him?
5. How is this story similar to old fairy tales you have read? How is it different? Make a list of similarities and a list of differences. Then use your lists to write a comparison between this modern fairy tale and an old-fashioned one.

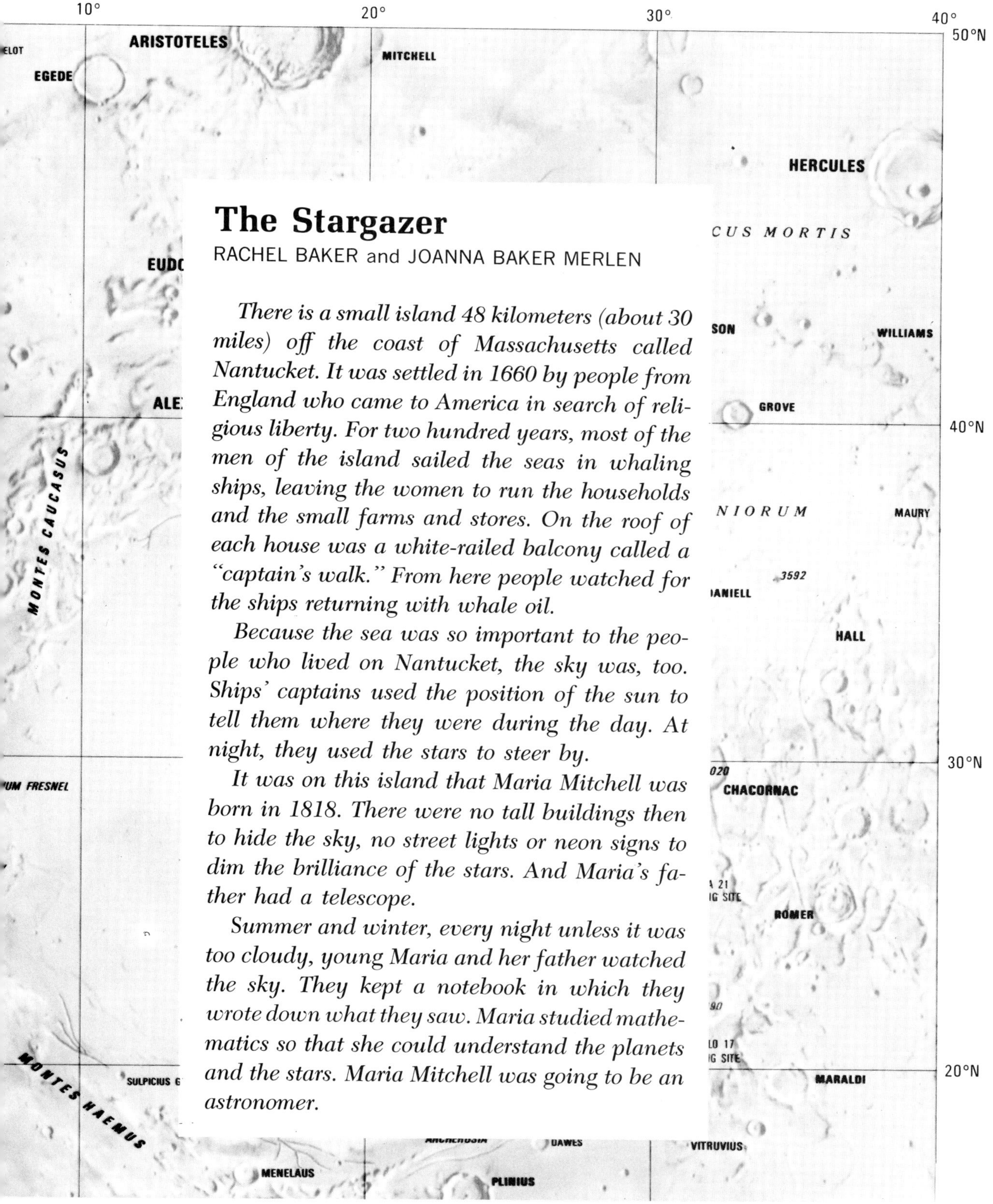

The Stargazer

RACHEL BAKER and JOANNA BAKER MERLEN

There is a small island 48 kilometers (about 30 miles) off the coast of Massachusetts called Nantucket. It was settled in 1660 by people from England who came to America in search of religious liberty. For two hundred years, most of the men of the island sailed the seas in whaling ships, leaving the women to run the households and the small farms and stores. On the roof of each house was a white-railed balcony called a "captain's walk." From here people watched for the ships returning with whale oil.

Because the sea was so important to the people who lived on Nantucket, the sky was, too. Ships' captains used the position of the sun to tell them where they were during the day. At night, they used the stars to steer by.

It was on this island that Maria Mitchell was born in 1818. There were no tall buildings then to hide the sky, no street lights or neon signs to dim the brilliance of the stars. And Maria's father had a telescope.

Summer and winter, every night unless it was too cloudy, young Maria and her father watched the sky. They kept a notebook in which they wrote down what they saw. Maria studied mathematics so that she could understand the planets and the stars. Maria Mitchell was going to be an astronomer.

The Eclipse

On windless nights Maria helped her father take the telescope from the attic to the captain's walk on the roof. She liked to look at the colors of the stars. The hottest star glowed blue-white. The cooler ones shone golden. And those still cooler were ruby-red.

In the summer her father sometimes took the telescope down into the yard. Then the neighbors came to look at the moon. Maria's sister Sally passed out glasses of lemonade, while Mrs. Mitchell and Mrs. Woodbridge talked about the slugs in the garden.

At the telescope twelve-year-old Maria showed the craters of the moon named after famous astronomers. And when Mr. Woodbridge wanted to know when the next eclipse would take place, she told him promptly, "Next February." Maria had never seen an annular eclipse, but she knew that the moon, passing between the sun and the earth, would blot out the sun in a particular way.

Later, with a penny and a candle, she tried to show Sally how the shadow of the moon cuts off our view of the sun.

"At this distance," said Maria as she held up the penny before the candle, "only part of the light is cut off. That is a partial eclipse." She moved the penny a little away from the candle. "Over here it shuts off all the light. That's a total eclipse." Now Maria moved the penny slightly closer to the candle. "But here thee can see a circle of light around the penny. That's an annular eclipse," she said. "The kind of eclipse depends on the distance of the moon from the earth."

When Sally went to sleep, Maria sat at the window looking out at the round yellow moon.

She could hardly wait for autumn to come. And when the first snow fell, she joyfully counted the days to the eclipse. On the night before, she prayed, "Please, Lord, no clouds tomorrow."

The next morning, the pale February sun rose in a cold sky without a cloud. "We will be able to see the eclipse!" cried Maria.

PARTIAL ECLIPSE TOTAL ECLIPSE ANNULAR ECLIPSE

She went up to the attic with her father. But when they tried to take the telescope up to the roof, such a wind was blowing that they had to come down again.

"What will we do, Father?" she asked in despair.

"We could never hold the telescope steady in the back yard with this wind," he said. Then he thought for a moment. "But from the parlor we could sight the sun."

"What!" cried Mrs. Mitchell. "Take out the parlor window in February?"

"How else will we see the eclipse?" cried Maria. And she helped her father remove the glass panes.

The twins, Eliza and Henry, were only a few months old. They were bundled into quilts until only their noses showed. The others, wrapped in coats and shawls, blew on their fingers to keep warm.

Mr. Mitchell set up the telescope pointing at the pale, faintly glowing sun. In the sky a little shadow appeared. It moved closer and closer to the sun. Maria passed out pieces of smoked glass. The twins, who had been screaming, grew still. A strange twilight filled the room.

"Now!" Mr. Mitchell cried.

Maria began to count off the seconds.

"Mark!" he called.

The shadow of the moon hung like a black penny before the sun. And all around the black penny a rim of light glowed. No one breathed. In the yard the roosters crowed. Then the black penny slipped away. The eerie light passed.

Mrs. Mitchell drew her shawl round her shoulders. "William, get that window back before we all catch a death of cold," she said.

In the icy room Maria drew a deep breath. Her fingers tingled, but not from the chill.

"Wasn't it beautiful?" she said.

"Beautiful," replied her father.

All during the years of Maria's growing up, she and her father continued their observations. Maria was a young woman when Nantucket opened a library and Maria became its librarian. Since the library was open only a few hours a day, it was an ideal job for Maria. It gave her many hours to study.

If the sky was clear when she returned home in the evening, Maria climbed to the roof to "sweep the sky." It was on such a clear night in October, 1847 that Maria discovered a comet. For this she received a gold medal from the King of Denmark and world-wide fame. When Vassar College opened its doors in 1865, Maria Mitchell became its first Professor of Astronomy.

Professor Mitchell

In the autumn of 1873, when leaves were starting to fall, students again bent over their books at Vassar College.

On a day of blue haze filled with the drift of falling leaves, an old woman stood before a class of bright-cheeked girls. She wore a gown of by-gone days. Round her face fell old-fashioned curls.

"The satellites of the planet Jupiter were discovered by Galileo," she said. And she described the creamy disk of Jupiter veiled by smoky brown belts.

On a clear, cold winter evening she watched with her students as the first satellite of Jupiter passed "in all its dazzling whiteness." For a long

time she had been watching the four satellites of Jupiter, appearing, disappearing, casting shadows.

Maria Mitchell studied the sun as the center of our solar system and she took the first daily photographs of the sun. Eagerly she waited for the total eclipse of the sun. It would not be seen in the East, but only from the plains of Colorado. And, though frail of health, she set out in the summer of 1878 with a group of her students.

As the train rolled westward, she told the girls that the last total eclipse to be seen in the East had occurred many years before.

"How fortunate I am to be spared to this day so that I may see the corona of the sun." Only during a total eclipse, she explained, at the instant when the moon blots out the sun, could the great streaming arms of light be seen.

In Denver the streets were filled with boys selling bits of smoked glass. Foreign scientists were looking for choice spots from which to view the eclipse.

Professor Mitchell drove with her students beyond the city. They went out into the open country where the golden grasslands stretched to the distant mountains.

On the slope of a hill, a mile above sea level, they pitched their tents. On the morning of the eclipse they all rose early. Each student was given her task. One girl was told to tend the chronometer. "We must note the exact second when the moon touches the sun." Another, with charcoal in hand, stood ready to sketch the phases of the eclipse. Professor Mitchell and her two assistants pointed their telescopes.

"There it is!" someone cried.

In the bright blue sky, near the golden sun, floated the pale, round, ghostly moon. As it approached the sun, the moon became invisible in the bright light.

A hush fell on the watchers. The girl at the chronometer began her count. As they waited, a rim like that of a black penny touched the sun.

"Mark!" Maria whispered.

The count went on for over an hour as the black penny slowly slipped over the sun. The plain grew dark; the chill of night filled the air. Then as the moon obliterated the sun, huge streamers of light burst out, shooting across the sky. It was the corona.

Reflections

1. Maria Mitchell was an astronomer. What do astronomers study? What special equipment do they use?
2. Describe what happens during a total eclipse of the sun. Have you ever seen one? What was it like?
3. Have you ever been as excited about something in nature as young Maria was about seeing the eclipse? Explain.
4. Would Maria Mitchell have had an easier time becoming a famous astronomer if she had been a man? Write an essay considering this question, using whatever evidence you can find in the story to support your opinion. Check the dates to find out how old she was before she actually got a job as an astronomer. And remember, at that time Vassar College was a college for women.

COUNTING THE STARS

ANNIE JUMP CANNON (1863–1941)
(*right*) Annie Jump Cannon, an astronomer at the Harvard Observatory, was for forty-five years a census-taker of the stars. The methods she used to examine and list the stars were not new. But she made these methods simpler and easier. Then she used them to classify nearly 300,000 stars.

HARLOW SHAPLEY (1885–1972)
(*left*) Astronomer Harlow Shapley was a mapmaker of the stars. He calculated the length and breadth of our galaxy. All his measurements proved that our galaxy, the Milky Way, was far greater in size than was ever imagined. He compared the Milky Way to a giant pinwheel 100,000 light years across. Then he placed our sun at its outer edge. Shapley numbered the stars that keep our sun company at 160 billion.

on-off-off-on-off-on

DANIEL PAUL

The numbering system that you know and use is built on a base of ten. The base number, ten, is the number of symbols, or digits, in the system. Here they are: 0,1,2,3,4,5,6,7,8, and 9. But number systems can be built on any base. You would use the digits 0,1,2,3 in base four, 0,1,2 in base three, 0,1 in base two. And if you made up ten single digits to replace 10 through 19, you could make up a way to count in base twenty.

In base ten, the value of a digit in any place is *ten* times the value of that digit if it were one place to the right. So you have a one's column, a ten's column, a hundred's column, a thousand's column, and so forth. But base two uses only two digits, 0 and 1. Therefore, in base two, each place has a value only *two* times that of the place to its right. So you have a one's column, a two's column, a four's column, an eight's column, and so forth.

Just as there is no single digit for the number ten in base ten, there is no single digit for the number two in base two. Two in base two is written 1 0. That is, we write 1 in the two's

PLACE VALUES						
Places	6	5	4	3	2	1
Base Ten	1000000 (10 × 10000)	10000 (10 × 1000)	1000 (10 × 100)	100 (10 × 10)	10 (10 × 1)	1
Base Two	32 (2 × 16)	16 (2 × 8)	8 (2 × 4)	4 (2 × 2)	2 (2 × 1)	1

place; and, since there are no ones, we hold that place with a zero. Three is then written as 1 1 (one in the two's column and one in the one's column). Four is written 1 0 0. Can you explain why? Five, written 5 in base ten, is written as 1 0 1 in base two (one in the four's place, zero in the two's place, and one in the one's place).

As you can see, a number written in base two is much longer than a number with the same value written in base ten. Then why do we bother with base two? Base two is of special importance because computers often use it.

A computer is just a series of electrical circuits. These circuits either have current flowing through them, or they don't. If each circuit is controlled by a switch, that switch can be either "on" or "off." There is no in between.

In base two, there are only two digits, 0 and 1. A switch which is "off" is easily represented by a zero, and an "on" switch is then a one.

A six-place number, like 100101 base two, is represented by six switches which are, in order, on-off-off-on-off-on. Current is either on or off, a switch is either open or closed, a punch card has a hole in it, or it doesn't. This is why many computers use base two.

Base Two	Base Ten
1	1
10	2
11	3
100	4
101	5
110	6
111	7
1000	8
1001	9
1010	10
1011	11
1100	12
1101	13
1110	14
1111	15
10000	16

Reflections

The title of this article is written 1 0 0 1 0 1 in base two. What numerals represent its value in base ten?

One for the Computer

ETHELYN M. PARKINSON

A Second Einstein

We might never have had a computer if we had not met Albert Einstein Smedley. Albert came to visit in Wakefield during the teachers' meeting vacation.

I first heard about him at breakfast Thursday morning.

"Rupert," my mother said, "what in the world are you dreaming about?"

"Oh, not much," I said. "I was thinking about something that is in Miss Smithwick's alley."

"Oh, dear!" Mom said. "I might have known!"

"What's in the alley, Rupert?" Dad asked.

"Well," I said, "Miss Smithwick's good old piano box is in the alley."

Ma looked at Dad and shook her head. "Why *is* it?" she said. "We are as smart as Don and

Irene Smedley. Why would their child be a second Einstein, while ours dreams great dreams about a piano box in an alley? *Why?*"

"That," Dad said, "is one for the computer."

This was a very good answer. A computer is an electric machine that can answer almost anything. You just feed the question into it, and it buzzes and whirs, and little lights blink, and after a while out pops the answer.

I ate my Pop-O's and drank my milk. "Excuse me," I said.

Mom said, "Where are you going?"

"Well, to find the guys."

"Naturally! And then where?"

"Ma," I said, "that's a toughie. That is one for the computer."

Mom looked at Dad. "Now!" she said. "See what you started, Mr. Piper! Rupert, if you have any notion of bringing that piano box home, you get it right out of your head—while the Smedleys are in town. I won't have Mrs. Smedley saying that our son is a trash picker!"

I hated to tell the fellows. So I waited until afternoon when we were sitting out back of our garage, on the piano box.

"How did your mom know what we were going to do?" Milt said.

I said, "That's one for the computer. Mothers are funny. It would take a brain machine to figure them out."

“Well,” Clayte said, “we will not take up any of her yard. All her troubles will be over as soon as we get this good old piano box up in this tree.”

“Right!” Dood said. “But how are we going to do it?”

Just then a car came down our drive. It was Opal’s father, Mr. Duncan. “Hello, gentlemen!” he said. “Rupert, your dad said he’d leave some plumbing tools in the garage where a good amateur master plumber could borrow them. Hey! What’s this?” He looked at the piano box. Next he looked up in the tree and smiled a very big smile. “A very good idea!” he said. “If you’ll wait until tomorrow, I’ll help you put it up there.”

He got the tools and drove away.

“How did he know?” Milt said.

“Well,” I said, “he is an electrical engineer. Maybe he has a computer.”

Right then Mom called me. “Rupert? Rupert Piper! Come here!”

“Oh-oh!” Clayte said. “I just knew this would happen!”

But Mom was not mad. She was standing on the back porch with my basketball in her hands, and Annabelle and Albert were with her. Their mothers had come to call.

"Now you can have a lot of fun throwing baskets," Mom said.

"Mom," I said, "it's cold."

"It's a nice, mild February day," Mom said. "You've been outside all day, and you can enjoy it a bit longer."

"Well," Dood said, "I think I will be going."

"Me, too," said Milt and Clayte.

Mom smiled very sweetly. "Your mothers are dropping in, boys. They expect to find you here playing with Albert and Annabelle." She shut the door.

Albert was taking a little stroll in the yard, looking at things.

Annabelle said, "Albert simply has to get away by himself, to dream great dreams. His mother says so. She wishes he would share his great thoughts with other people. But she says someday the world will know, when Albert has his private little chain of satellites around the sun."

Well, we did not want a little chain of satellites around the sun. All we wanted was a house in a tree.

Albert came back, looking excited. "Rupert," he said, "what is that big box doing back of your garage?"

"Well," I said, "I suppose that is one for the computer."

"Computer?" Albert said. "You can't make a computer out of a piano box!"

Milt poked me. "Oh, indeed you can!" Milt said. "You can, Albert, if you know enough science. And we do!" Milt put his hands in his pockets and kind of rocked on his heels and smacked. He said, "Our computer will be just about the best computer in the U.S.A. It will answer all questions correctly within five minutes—or your money back."

My teeth almost dropped out. So did Dood's and Clayte's. We weren't *that* sure about making the computer.

Albert's face was very red. He said, "I have a fine laboratory at home. It cost hundreds of dollars! But I cannot make a computer."

"You do not need a laboratory to build a computer," Milt said. "You just need to know how!" he smacked. "And we do!"

So the next morning we were working very hard in my backyard when Annabelle came along with Sylvia and Opal and Albert.

The girls stopped to ask a few very personal questions. "What in the world are you boys doing with that old sweeper and that old beat-up fan and that old dog clipper?" Opal said.

"Or is it a secret?" Sylvia said.

"Oh, no," I said. "We are willing to share our great thoughts with the whole world. But you'll have to wait."

Annabelle flipped her eyelashes at me. "Come on, Albert," she said.

But Albert stood still. "Excuse me," he said. "I think I shall stay here and learn how to build a computer."

Computer, Inc.

So we worked on the computer all day. Mr. Duncan helped us.

"I do not want all the boys in town to get fatal electric shocks and die," Mr. Duncan said. "Especially all you boys in Opal's room. Why, Opal tells me her class is sure to win the School Spellarama this year. I imagine some of you boys are terrific spellers. Right?"

Nobody said much to that. Even if you like spelling, it isn't the kind of thing I wanted to admit to Mr. Duncan.

He fixed all the Christmas tree lights in the computer. He worked on the old sweeper, the fan, and the old dog clipper. Then he tested all the cords and connections so that no one would get a shock.

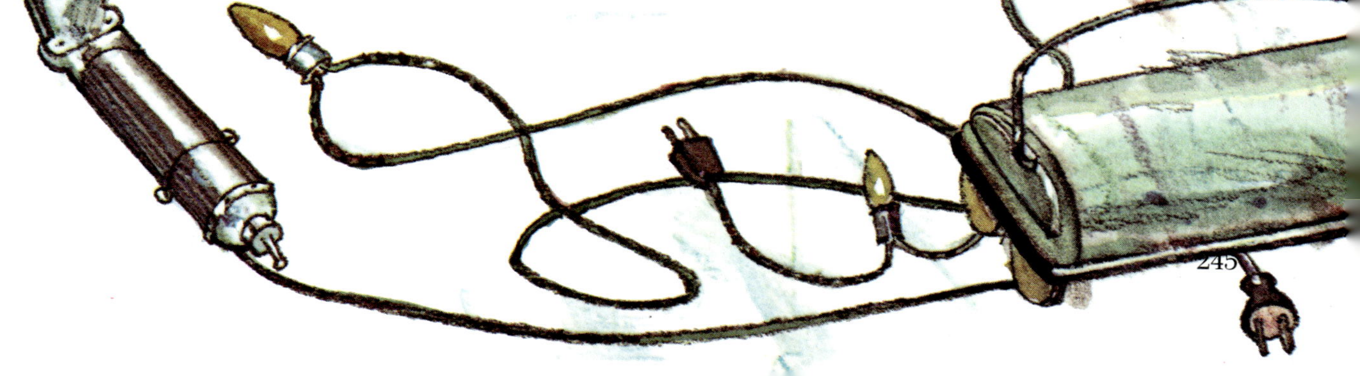

We painted the computer a very keen green color. Then we moved it onto our front lawn.

After a while Mom walked home from her club meeting with Albert's mother and all the other mothers, and you should have heard Mom scream.

"What is this horrible thing on my lawn? It looks like a prospector's hut or an ice fisherman's shanty!"

"No, ma'am," I said. "Please read the sign, ma'am."

"I give up!" Mom said. "What did I ever do to deserve this?"

"Do you wish to ask the computer?" I said. "Write it on this piece of paper and slip it in here, with a nickel."

So Mom put her question in the computer. All the little lights began to wink and blink. The sweeper motor ran. The fan whirred. The dog clipper whined. Everything made a terrible noise. After a while the noise slowed down, and another slot opened, and out came the answer.

The answer was: "Don't worry, Mrs. Piper. This will make a lot of money."

Mom laughed. "Well, well! That's different Do any of you ladies care to try the computer?"

"It's amusing," Mrs. Smedley said. "However, Albert would be bored with any toy as childish as this."

Mom's cheeks got kind of pink. So did the other mothers'.

"I'll ask it something," Clayte's mother said, quite loud. So she found a nickel and wrote, "What can I fix quick for supper?"

The lights blinked, and the machines all roared, and the answer came out: "Bake some frozen chicken pies. Clayte can eat two."

"An excellent idea!" Mrs. Snow said.

Dood's mother said, "I'll ask it something, to see if it's honest." So she wrote a note: "Who is the smartest boy I know?"

The computer almost shook to pieces, and then the answer came: "He is the boy who likes you best."

"How sweet!" Mrs. Hall said. "Thank you so much!" She patted the computer.

Mrs. Willman dug a nickel out of her purse. She wrote: "Is Annabelle going to do the dishes tonight?"

This was a toughie. But the answer was good. Very good. "The prettiest and smartest girl at your house is going to do the dishes. Tell this to Annabelle."

"I'll try it, computer," Mrs. Willman said. "If it doesn't work, I might try something else." She slapped her hands together and then laughed.

The Dad's Club carnival was the next night in Legion Hall. Mr. Duncan came around to my house at four o'clock.

"Rupert," he said, "how about moving the computer down to the carnival? We can pick up some extra cash."

The cash was for our camp fund.

"A very keen idea," I said.

"Bring your crew of great scientists," Mr. Duncan said. "They will get some free ice cream and pop."

Well, the computer was so busy that our crew of great scientists had to take turns working and eating.

After a while Mrs. Smedley came along. "Where on earth is Albert?" she said. "I haven't seen that boy since I got here!"

Right then Mr. Duncan came up, smiling. "Hello there, Mrs. Smedley," he said. "What do you think of the computer?"

"It's very silly," she said.

Mr. Duncan laughed. "Come, now. It's a lot of fun. You ask Albert."

Mrs. Smedley kind of sniffed. "Albert wouldn't be interested in it. He's going to be a brilliant scientist."

"Well!" Mr. Duncan said. "What has he made?"

"Why, nothing—yet. He's learning."

"Then," Mr. Duncan said, "you'll be proud to know he helped make this computer."

"I don't believe it!" Mrs. Smedley said.

Mr. Duncan winked at me. "Rupert," he said, "I'll risk a nickel on Albert. Ask the computer where he is."

So I wrote: "Where is Albert?"

The poor old computer almost blew a fuse. It shivered and shook, and after a while the answer came: "I am very busy. Don't worry about me!"

Mrs. Smedley screamed. "Is my Albert in that contraption?"

"He sure is!" Mr. Duncan said. "My old typewriter is in there, and Albert is writing up these answers and having himself a ball. Of course, it's all a very scientific secret."

"That's right, Mrs. Smedley," I said. "Next it's Albert's turn to run the sweeper and the fan."

"And if you want to break his heart—you stop him!" Mr. Duncan said.

Mrs. Smedley stood and watched the computer a long time. It was very busy.

At last Mrs. Smedley said, "Rupert, please give me a piece of paper." She wrote a question. "Would the computer like a hamburger?"

The computer shook, and the lights blinked. The answer came: "The computer would like five hamburgers."

The hamburgers were very good, and Mrs. Smedley did not have to ask the good old computer how many bottles of pop to order.

Reflections

1. Why do you think the Smedleys named their son Albert Einstein Smedley? Who was the "first" Albert Einstein? (If you don't know, look up his name in an encyclopedia.)
2. The boys used each of the following things in their invention. What do you think was the purpose of each item?
   a. Christmas lights
   b. A sweeper motor
   c. An old electric fan
   d. An old dog clipper
   e. An old typewriter
3. When Albert asked for five hamburgers, what do you think he did with them? What does this show about him?
4. Choose the best ending for the sentence below, and explain your choice.
   To judge from this story, Albert Einstein Smedley
   a. really was a genius.
   b. was about as bright as the other boys.
   c. was stupid.
5. How does Rupert first describe a computer? How would you describe a computer? Compare your description and Rupert's with one in a reference book.
6. Write a dialogue between two characters in the story. Select one of the following topics:
   a. Annabelle and her mother discuss doing dishes.
   b. Mrs. Smedley and Albert talk about the computer after the carnival.
   c. Rupert and Milt try to decide what to do with the computer after the carnival.
   d. Rupert's mother describes the computer to Rupert's father.

Computers Today and Tomorrow

CONTROL DATA EDUCATION COMPANY

Exploring Space

Long before our sun began to burn, there were huge starlike forms. These starlike forms were brighter than a million suns. They gave out more energy than anything else in space. They raced toward the edges of the universe nearly as fast as a beam of light can travel.

These starlike forms are called "quasars." Quasars are so far from earth that no one knew about them until 1963. That year, scientists heard high-energy waves on powerful new equipment. They knew than that they had discovered something new.

A special explorer was sent into space to learn more about quasars. The explorer wasn't a person. It was a computer. Aboard a satellite with powerful telescopes, the computer circled the earth for months. It carefully looked at each bit of sky and remembered what it saw. Then it sent the information to people on earth. The computer never made a mistake. It never got bored. When it finished mapping the universe, it started over. No person could have done this job even once.

How Computers Are Used

Today, computers help people do many things they couldn't do alone. Bankers use them to keep track of money. Telephone operators use them to put calls through. Without computers, weather forecasters would make more mistakes. The list of uses is long. Computers help companies keep records, doctors treat sick people, and scientists solve problems.

People depend on computers so much that they sometimes think the machines are giant brains. Compared to people, however, computers aren't at all smart. Computers are machines that will do only what they are told to do. If one is told a wrong fact, like "Abraham Lincoln was the first president," the computer will use that false fact as though it were true.

Why then is this machine so important? It is because the computer is a very useful tool. Like any tool, it helps people to do things better. Because computers can add very fast, they can solve math problems that would take a person a lifetime to figure out. Because computers are accurate and never forget, they can keep more complete records than any man or woman. Since computers don't get bored or tired, they can be worked around the clock. People would have to rest and eat.

Types of Computer Jobs

Computer jobs are of two types: *data processing* and *process control.*

In data processing, the computer keeps track of many facts and figures. It adds, subtracts, multiplies, and divides numbers. If asked, it can remember any fact it was told.

In process control, the computer watches how some activity is being done. For example, it might watch a person landing on the moon. The computer has been told how the process or activity should work. If something goes wrong, the computer will help to correct the problem. It might call a person, or it might take an action by itself.

The person who tells a computer what to do is called a *programmer*. Programmers learn a special language. Then they use the language to tell the computer every step it must take in doing a task. If the programmer's directions are wrong or incomplete, the computer won't work correctly.

Why Computer Use Is Growing

When computers were first built in the 1950s, they were huge. They filled entire rooms and cost millions of dollars. The earliest computers solved less than a thousand problems each second. Since then, computers have become smaller, cheaper, and faster. Today, the world's fastest computers can solve a hundred million problems in a second. Scientists are working to make them even faster. The computer that looked for quasars is so small it would fit in a shoebox. Still, computers are being made even smaller. Most important of all, computers are costing less. Very small computers cost only a few hundred dollars.

When computers were big and expensive, they were only used for very special purposes. Now, they are being used in many ways. One way is to help teachers and students. Programmers can tell a computer how to score tests, how to give drill-and-practice problems, and how to play games that teach new facts and skills. Another new place to use computers is in the home. Computers are being used to help plan dinner, keep track of how much money is in the checkbook, and even play checkers with their owners.

Someday, if you haven't already, you probably will work with a computer. You may use this tool in school, at home, or on the job. You may even discover a new use for this machine that allows people to do things they could never do alone.

Reflections

1. What are quasars? When did scientists first learn about them? How did scientists learn about them?
2. Why was it better for a computer to map the universe than for a person to do this job?
3. Are computers really giant brains? Explain. Why are computers important?
4. What does a data-processing computer do? What does a process-control computer do? What does a programmer do? Explain why the programmer's job is so important.
5. Name three reasons why computer use is growing.
6. Write a paragraph that explains some of the ways computers are being used today.

Space Programmer

MARGARET HAMILTON
"The Eagle has landed!" That was the shout heard 'round the world as the first astronauts put down on the moon. Margaret Hamilton had good reason to be excited. She headed the group of engineers and mathematicians who designed many of the computer programs that guided Apollo 11 to the moon. And the landing had been on target!

Margaret Hamilton's job for each Apollo flight was to program her computers to be ready for any emergency. In a mockup of the Apollo command module (*top*), Dr. Hamilton shows how a pinpoint landing on the moon was programmed right into the spacecraft. *(left)* Here she is checking each stage of the astronauts' journey.

COMPUTER WORKERS

Computers are machines. They are fast. They are accurate. And they have wonderful memories. But people have to decide which facts to put into the computer. People have to plan the program that tells it what to do with the facts. And people have to interpret and use the information that comes out of it.

(above) **Data entry clerks** put information into the computer. Sometimes they punch holes on cards. The holes stand for the information that the computer will put into its memory bank. At other times, data entry clerks type information directly into the computer memory banks.

(left) **Programmers** prepare step-by-step instructions that tell the computer what to do with the facts. Programmers also interpret the information that comes out of the computer on a *printout.*

(*below*) **Field engineers** are important to everyone working with computers. They keep the machines running well and they repair them if something goes wrong.

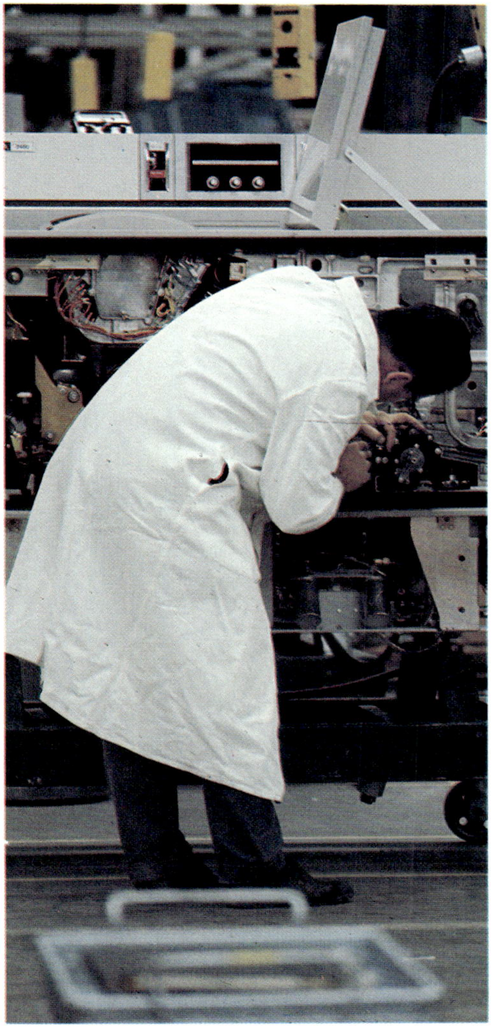

(*top right*) A **console operator** loads the computer with tapes. He starts the computer and watches it work. Blinking lights may signal trouble.

(*bottom right*) A **computer analyst** makes up ways for the computer to solve problems. With a light pen, this analyst is marking places on a display screen. She is planning a program that will enable a computer to recognize Corn Leaf Disease in farm areas.

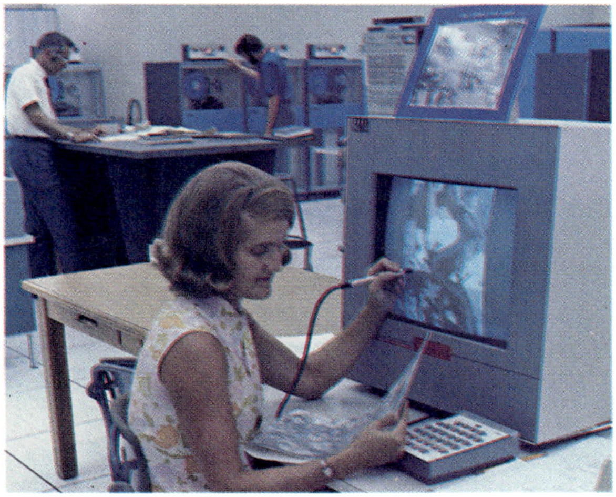

The Cloud-Mobile

MAY SWENSON

Above my face is a map.
Continents form and fade.
Blue countries, made
on a white sea, are erased,
and white countries traced
on a blue sea.

It is a map that moves,
faster than real,
but so slow.
Only my watching proves
that island has being,
or that bay.

It is a model of time.
Mountains are wearing away,
coasts cracking,
the ocean spills over,
then new hills
heap into view
with river-cuts of blue
between them.

It is a map of change.
This is the way things are
with a stone or a star.
This is the way things go,
hard or soft,
fast or slow.

Robert H. Goddard: Father of the Space Age

CLYDE B. MOORE

Ever since he was a young boy, Robert Goddard was interested in anything that zoomed through the air. He learned all he could about the planets and outer space. By the time he was a professor of physics at Clark University in Worcester, Massachusetts, he dreamed of making a many-staged, liquid-fueled rocket. He did the first experiments at his Aunt Effie's nearby farm. But they angered the neighbors because of the noise and the threat of fire. If he was to continue with his experiments, he would need a better place to work—and more money.

Goddard's good friend, Charles Lindbergh, was able to get him a grant of $50,000 from the Guggenheim Foundation. Roswell, New Mexico, was picked as the perfect site for his work because of its warm climate and dry air, its light rainfall and no snow. And it was far from any neighbors who might complain.

The crew Goddard took with him included Mrs. Goddard, his official photographer; Henry Sachs, his instrument maker; and Albert Kisk and Larry Mansur, his close assistants. In the summer of 1930, Dr. and Mrs. Goddard set out for New Mexico by car. The equipment they would need—enough to fill a freight car—was sent by rail.

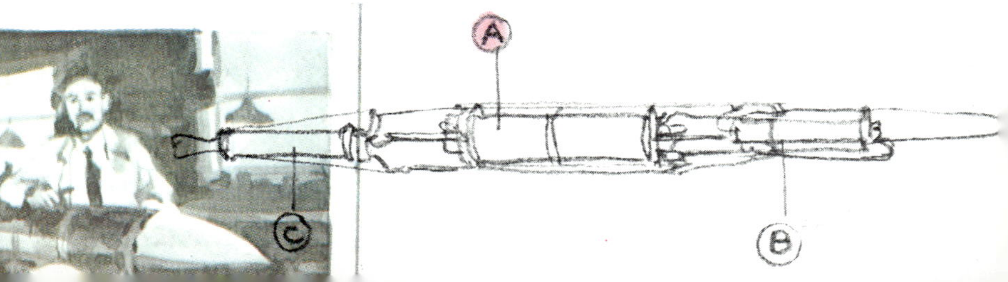

Through the friendly help of the Roswell people, the Goddards were soon settled. They would live five kilometers (3 miles) from town in an old house on the Mescalero Ranch. Eden Valley, where the launching tower was to be built, was more than nineteen kilometers (12 miles) away.

The Goddards drove out to see it. It was a desolate place, but the crew went to work with a will. Each of them was eager for success in the experiment. Each felt it was a pioneer adventure.

The workshop was started before the freight car loaded with tools and materials had arrived. It was to be eighteen meters (about 60 feet) long. This is the distance from the pitcher's box to home plate on a baseball diamond.

The climate was mild. There would be no New England ice and snow during the coming winter. The crew would have constant good weather for working.

Dr. Goddard and his crew planned to build and test a small model of a rocket as soon as possible. They wanted to learn if a large rocket could be made on such a pattern. Every point needed to be tested and retested. Dr. Goddard was eager to have a real test before the year ended. He asked the crew if it could be done.

Every member of the crew thought they should try it. They corrected flaws in the motor and tried not to overlook anything. By late December they had checked and rechecked every point. All agreed that the test must be made immediately and eagerly awaited the result.

The rocket, nicknamed Nell, had to be moved from the shop to the launching tower, which was nineteen kilometers (12 miles) away. It was wrapped in blankets and lifted like a piece of delicate china. Then it was set on a smaller trailer and tied in place. A truck carefully pulled the trailer over the trail to the launching site.

The flight tower, which would guide the rocket in its takeoff, could be seen in the distance. At first glance it looked much like the steel tower of a windmill. But no turning wheel could be seen. The tower was open at the top to let the rocket escape. The four steel supports were firmly anchored in concrete.

The rocket, looking like a giant dart, was about three meters (11 feet) long. That is twice the height of the average person. It was twenty-two centimeters (11 inches) around, about that of a lunch plate. Its nose was a smooth, shiny cone, shaped to pierce the atmosphere easily. At the other end were balancing vanes, formed like the tail of a fish. These vanes were to keep the rocket on its course. They must hold firm and not be swished about as a fish's tail is flipped.

Inside the cylinder were many delicate parts. There were pipes, small tanks to hold gasoline and liquid oxygen, and a powerful motor. The weight was less than 23 kilograms (50 pounds).

Near the base of the tower was a dugout with a heavy trapdoor. From this safe place Albert Kisk could touch off the flight. Farther away was a shelter of sheet iron. Dr. Goddard and two crew members would wait there.

All members of the crew were busy putting the rocket into perfect shape in the tower. Early in the afternoon Mrs. Goddard drove out in her car. As the photographer, she was ready with her camera. Larry Mansur, with telescope and stop-watch, was at a safe distance to measure time and distance.

The valves and containers for gasoline and liquid oxygen were given a final check. Then the igniter was fired. (Think of a big person weighing 90 kilograms (about 200 pounds) resting on one leg of a chair.) The rocket was allowed to rise five centimeters (2 inches). The pressure rose to one hundred two kilograms (225 pounds). Then Dr. Goddard gave the signal. And Albert Kisk, from the dugout, released the rocket.

With a mighty roar the rocket moved up through the eighteen-meter (60-foot) tower. Up it went, faster and faster, shrieking as it rose. In seven seconds it was 120 meters (400 feet) above the tower. According to Larry Mansur's measurements, it reached a height of six hundred meters (about 2,000 feet). An important part of Dr. Goddard's dream had come true. He had used liquid fuel to shoot a rocket into the air.

Many years slipped by. Test after test was made. Some experiments failed and others succeeded. Goddard's test rockets soared less than three kilometers (2 miles) into space, but his genius, experiments, and dreams provided the principles on which the mighty program of space rocketry is founded today.

At Greenbelt, Maryland, the National Aeronautics and Space Administration has developed a large space center. In 1961 a ceremony was held to dedicate this space center to Dr. Goddard. It is now called the Goddard Space Center.

Reflections

1. What is meant by a "many-staged, liquid-fueled" rocket?
2. Why was Roswell, New Mexico, chosen for Goddard's experiments? Give as many reasons as you can.
3. How long ago did Dr. Goddard perform his first experiments near Roswell?
4. The introductory note says that Charles Lindbergh helped Goddard get money for his experiments. For what is Charles Lindbergh famous? Why does it seem natural that Lindbergh and Goddard were good friends? (Think of some ways in which they were probably much alike.)
5. Pretend that you are a NASA official. Write a letter to the Goddard family announcing the naming of the Goddard Space Center. In your letter, explain why NASA chose Dr. Goddard for this honor.

By the Light of the Moon

ALFRED SLOTE

Good Luck, Bad Luck

Today most of us are pretty used to the moon. There it is up in the sky—crescent or half or full. . . .

Years ago people lived by the changing phases of the moon. They kept calendars and holidays by the moon. They planted seed in the spring's new moon and harvested in the autumn's full moon. And fishermen all over the world told the morrow's weather by the moon.

For many people the moon long remained a mysterious heavenly body that could bring good fortune or ill.

It could bring good luck if it was a new moon and you had silver coins in your pocket to jingle.

A new moon was also the time to make a wish, take a trip, go a-courtin', or cut your hair.

But the moon could bring bad luck, too. If you saw a woman combing her hair in the light of the full moon, or if you planted seed during the full moon, you would have bad luck. Almost everyone believed that if you slept with moonlight on your face, you'd go crazy. Indeed, so many people believed this that we get our word *lunatic* from the Latin word for moon, *luna.*

Today, of course, we know that none of these things is true. You can sleep in the moonlight and wake up as normal as you were yesterday. You might harvest your crops in the full moon with poor results or harvest in a sickle moon and do well. You might start your vacation during the new moon and have a flat tire right away.

Nevertheless, there it is . . . the moon, hanging up there in the sky, seeming to change its shape before our very eyes. No wonder people continue to be fascinated by it. Since the beginning of time, they have tried to explain how it got there and why it behaves the way it does.

The first people to try to explain the creation and behavior of the moon were tribal poets and storytellers. There are hundreds of folktales about the moon. One story, told by the Ekoi people of East Africa, not only tries to explain the origin and phases of the moon, but tells us why we see only one side of the moon.

A Gift from the Python

Now all this took place long, long ago. Mbui, a kindhearted sheep, and Etuk, a hardhearted antelope were hardworking farmers. Mbui grew banana trees, and Etuk grew cocoyams. When the two friends got tired of eating the same foods, they would exchange and eat each other's food. When the bananas got too soft, Etuk the antelope would demand angrily that Mbui fetch him some fresher bananas, and kindhearted Mbui always did so.

One day while Mbui was fetching fresh bananas, he met a crowd of apes. Being hungry, they begged Mbui for some bananas, and the kindhearted Mbui gave them some.

The apes ate their fill and went their way. Soon they met a herd of wild pigs, who saw how well fed the apes looked.

Being hungry themselves, they asked the apes where they got their food.

"From Mbui the sheep," said the apes.

Whereupon the pigs went to Mbui and begged for some bananas, and the kindhearted Mbui gave them some.

The pigs ate their fill and went their way. Soon they met an elephant, who saw how well fed the wild pigs looked, and, being hungry himself, he asked the pigs where they got their food.

"From Mbui the sheep," said the pigs.

Whereupon the elephant went to Mbui and begged for food, and, of course, kindhearted Mbui gave him some, too.

And so, in time, all the bush beasts, even the bush cow, came to the two farmers, but especially to Mbui, and received food.

Now, not far from the farms of Mbui and Etuk was the great river called Akarram. In the midst of this river, deep down, dwelt the crocodile. One day the bush cow went to drink by the river.

"You look well fed, Cow." said the crocodile.

"I am," said the bush cow.

"Where do you get your food?"

"From those two busy farmers—Mbui the sheep and Etuk the antelope."

Well, no sooner did the crocodile hear this than, naturally enough, he crawled out of the water and went to Mbui and Etuk and said, "I am dying of hunger. Please give me food."

Etuk the antelope drew himself up. "To the animals who are my friends, I may give food, but to you I will give nothing, for you are no friend of mine."

But Mbui the sheep, who was kindhearted, shook his head. "It is true I do not like you either, Crocodile, but I will give you one bunch of bananas."

The crocodile took the bananas and said, "Tonight, farmers, I will return and buy more food from you at a great price."

Then the crocodile returned to the river with his bananas and sought out the great python who lived there. The python had something very precious, and the crocodile knew about it.

"I have found two farmers who have much food," the crocodile said to the python.

"I am also very hungry," said the python. "Will you give me something to eat?"

The crocodile gave him a few bananas. When the python had tasted them, he sighed and said, "How sweet they are. Will you go back and bring me some more?"

"Yes," said the crocodile, "but will you give me something to buy bananas with?"

The python hesitated, and then he nodded, "Yes, I will give you something so valuable you can buy the whole farm with it."

And so the python took from his head a great shining stone and gave it to the crocodile. Night fell and the road grew dark, but the crocodile held in his jaws the shining stone, and it made a light on his path, and the way before him was bright. When he came near the farm, he hid the stone beneath his claws and called out.

"Come out, Mbui the sheep. Come out, Etuk. I have something very valuable for you."

It was dark when the two farmers came out to speak with the crocodile, but slowly the crocodile opened his claws, and he held up the stone. It began to gleam, and when he held it up high, the whole land became so bright that you could see a needle or a pebble or any small thing. The crocodile then said, "The price of this that I bring from the python is one farm."

Etuk the antelope frowned and said, "It would be stupid of me to sell my cocoyam farm for a great shining stone like that. What good will that shining stone be to me if I starve to death?"

But Mbui the sheep loved the stone. "I will buy the python's stone," he said. "I will give you my whole farm of bananas for that stone." And so the exchange was made. Mbui went to his house and placed the stone over the doorway so that it might shine for the whole world.

Well, in the morning Mbui was hungry, and he had nothing to eat. He was hungry at night and hungry the next day. He had nothing to eat, for he had sold his farm for that great white stone.

On the third day of his hunger, Mbui asked Etuk the antelope for a single cocoyam, but Etuk said coldly, "I will give you nothing, Mbui, for you have nothing to give me in exchange. Did I tell you to buy that shining thing?"

Poor Mbui was bewildered and upset. "I have done nothing bad," he thought. "Before, no one could see in the night. But now the stone shines so that everyone can see the path at night."

That very night, weak with hunger, Mbui dragged himself down to the riverbank to drink. By the riverbank he saw one of the sky men—those lords of the sky who came down to earth to gather food. This sky man was up in a tree trying to gather palm kernels, but he was having a hard time because it was so dark.

Mbui called out to him. "It is useless to do such a thing in the dark, O Lord of the Sky. Are you blind?"

The sky man answered, "I am not blind. Why do you ask such a thing?"

"If you are not blind, I beg you to throw me only one or two palm kernels, and in return I will show you a thing more bright and glorious than any you have seen before."

The sky man threw down three palm kernels, which Mbui quickly ate. Then the sky man climbed down with great difficulty since it was dark, and together he and Mbui went to Mbui's house.

Mbui said, "Will you wait there a little while, Lord of the Sky, while I question my friends?"

"I will wait," said the sky man.

Mbui the sheep went to his friend Etuk the antelope and asked, "Will you not give me a single cocoyam to eat? The great python stone which I bought at the price of all that I had turns darkness to light for you, but as for me—I die of hunger."

Etuk said, "I will give you nothing. Take away your python stone for which you foolishly sold everything, and we will stay in our darkness as we did before."

Then Mbui asked all the other animals if they would give him just a little food in return for the light he had bought for them, but they all refused.

So Mbui went to his house and took the great shining stone down from the doorway and gave it to the sky man.

"I love the animals, but they do not love me," Mbui said. "Take the shining thing and go back from where you came. I know that you are one of the sky people. When you arrive home in the heavens, hang up my stone in a place where all of the animals on earth may see it shining and be glad."

The sky man took the stone and went back to the palm tree. He climbed the tree, higher and higher, pointing to the sky, and the tree lifted its branches and lifted him till, from its very top, he could climb into heaven.

When he reached his home, the sky man called all the other men of the sky and spoke to them.

"With me I have something very precious and beautiful. It can shine so that all the earth will be light. From now on everyone on earth or in heaven will be able to see at the darkest hour of the night."

The sky lords marveled at the stone, and they decided that such a precious stone needed a box. But when they put the great shining stone in the box, it could only shine out from one side.

The sky man who had got it from Mbui took the box and said, "Behold. This stone is mine. From this time on, all the sky people must bring me food. I will no longer have to look for any myself."

Because he was the owner of the great shining stone, they brought him food. But sometimes they got tired and didn't bring him any. Then the sky man would cover the side of the box so that the stone could not shine until they brought him some. He would cover it just a little, and then a bit more, and then he would cover it all until they brought him food.

That is why the moon is sometimes dark, and then people on earth say, "It is the end of the month. The sky people have grown tired of bringing food to the owner of the great shining stone, and he will not let the stone shine out till they bring him a fresh supply."

The old African folktale is as much about hunger as it is about the moon. But the Ekoi storyteller, in trying to explain the universe to his people, was doing, in a sense, what scientists do today: seeking to explain the universe.

Reflections

1. The Ekoi people of East Africa believed that once, long ago, animals ruled the earth. But did these animals behave like animals you know? Support your answer with examples from the legend retold here.
2. Give two reasons why primitive people might have more myths about the moon than about the sun.
3. What do we know about the moon today? In what ways did people get this knowledge?
4. Think about the two statements below. In what ways might each of them be true? Choose one as the topic of an essay.
   a. Legends and myths were the first step toward knowledge.
   b. Legends and myths tended to keep people from learning the facts.

Moonflight

The suited-up astronauts—Neil A. Armstrong, Edwin E. Aldrin, and Michael Collins—prepare to enter the van that will take them to the launchpad.

The *Apollo II* spacecraft lifts off at 9:32 A.M., July 16, 1969.

The flight is watched carefully by the Operations Director and the staff at the Goddard Space Center.

FACING PAGE: The Lunar Module is seen behind Edwin Aldrin, who is setting up an experiment on the moon.

Earth can be seen rising above the moon's horizon.

The three astronauts relax in a life raft after their safe splashdown in the Pacific Ocean.

SKY
of
Sea
High
Deep
As the
A blue
So bright
So new
So old
No other blue
To you
What is the bluest blue?

CLAUDIA LEWIS

Blue

What is the bluest blue?
To the astronaut ace
Afloat
In space,
Ringing,
Swinging,
Rocket-hurled,
No other blue
So new
So bright
A blue
As the
Great
Blue
Ball
of the
WORLD

FINDING PATTERNS IN WORDS

There are many ways of putting words together in English. Sometimes we combine two or more words to make one word. Sometimes we add prefixes and suffixes borrowed from Greek, Latin, or Old English. The exercises below will show you some of the ways of putting words together.

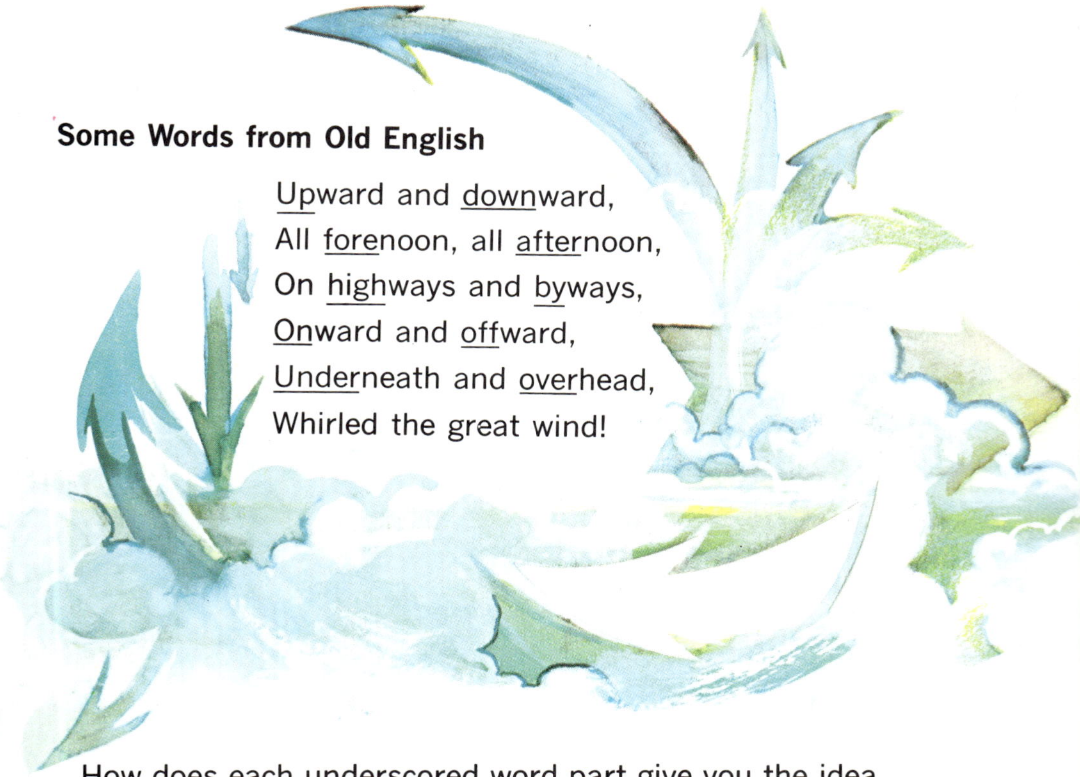

Some Words from Old English

Upward and downward,
All forenoon, all afternoon,
On highways and byways,
Onward and offward,
Underneath and overhead,
Whirled the great wind!

How does each underscored word part give you the idea of time or place or direction? On a sheet of paper, copy each underscored word part on a separate line. Then add a different second part to each word. For example, you could write *upstairs.* Add as many words as you can to each line. Use a dictionary if you need one. All the underlined word parts are from Old English.

From Latin

English has borrowed from Latin a number of prefixes that show time, direction, or place. First, study the chart; then read each sentence below and tell how the italicized word makes use of one of the prefixes in the chart.

trans- "across"	**super-** "over"	**pre-** "before"	**in-** "in" or "into"
sub- "under"	**post-** "after"	**ante-** "before"	**re-** "backward" or "again"
per- "through"	**ex-** "from" or "outward"	**circum-** "around"	**ab-** "from" or "away"

1. We sailed on a *transoceanic* liner.
2. John's father is a *supersalesman.*
3. He arrived on a *predawn* flight.
4. *Insert* a coin in the parking meter.
5. We take the *subway* to school.
6. Do you mind if we *postpone* the ball game?
7. Meet me in the *anteroom* after lunch.
8. *Refresh* yourself with lemonade.
9. We watched the bears *perform* in the circus.
10. Maria is an *exchange* student from Mexico.
11. Sir Francis Chichester *circumnavigated* the globe.
12. We may be *absent* on Monday.

Now write twelve sentences, using words with the prefixes in the chart above. Do not use the italicized words in the preceding sentences. Check your dictionary if you need help.

From Greek

English has also borrowed prefixes which show direction or place from Greek. Among them are the following:

meta-	"along with" or "after"
hyper-	"over," "above," or "beyond"
peri-	"all around"
sym-	"with"

Which word in each of the sentences below uses one of the prefixes defined above?

1. Since I share your sorrow, you have my sympathy.
2. When we measure the four sides of a square, we find its perimeter.
3. The change from a caterpillar to a butterfly is called metamorphosis.
4. If you find fault with everything, you are hypercritical.

Oh, No!

Perhaps the quickest way to say "no" is simply to say "no." But here are some other ways that we use to change a word from a "yes" to a "no" or negative meaning.

a- "no, not"	anti-, ant- "against"	counter- "against"	in- "not"
mis- "wrong"	non- "not"	ob- "against"	un- "not"

Now write the numbers from 1 to 10 in a column on a sheet of paper. In each of the following sentences, find the word that uses one of the above prefixes. Copy it on your paper after the proper number. Underline the prefix.

1. Marsha is able to sing, but Jan is unable.
2. Although Mike is quite capable, Jerry is incapable.
3. If you do not favor going, tell me your objection.
4. *Tall* is the antonym of *short*.
5. After I dictated my plans, he contradicted them.
6. With all those claims and counterclaims, who is right?
7. With winter coming on, Dad filled the car with some antifreeze.
8. Water conducts electricity, but glass is considered a nonconductor.
9. I have no feelings about that; I am apathetic.
10. Judy behaves, whereas Sandy misbehaves.

Good readers increase their vocabulary when they learn how word patterns operate. You have learned how word parts can help you to know direction and place and how words parts can say "no." You will learn to read better if you work to master word meanings.

4 FOR YOU AND ME

This Land Is Your Land

Words and Music by *Woody Guthrie*

The Mud Ponies

LACE KENDALL

A Sign

The wind was cold and hard and shook the thick walls of the earth lodges. A young Indian boy stood at a safe distance from the village. Running Star was the boy's name; for when he was born, a large star had fallen from its place in the sky. In his lodge it had been a sign that some day Running Star would become a great leader of his tribe.

But now he stood cold, hungry, and alone under the spring moon, with the wind stinging his bare legs and lifting his black hair. He had no lodge of his own, no father and mother, not even a grandmother or a great-grandmother whom he could remember. They had all gone into the world above the sky.

A very old, wrinkled squaw had told him the reason for this. "The star was evil; for when you were born, a great sickness came down upon the tribe. It took away your mother and father and even strong warriors into the sky. If we were to let you into our villages, the sickness may come again."

For a time Running Star had believed the squaw. Ashamed, he had crept off by himself to live on berries and roots.

Then one day a wise Pawnee priest found him. "It was not the star," the priest said. "The sickness came out of the air. This was not your doing. Only, many of our people believe it is so. Therefore, Running Star, you must walk alone until you can find a great deed to do. A star did fall for you. But it was a clean, strong star."

Running Star breathed deeply of the night air, his face turned toward the sky. He knew that the wise man's words were true. And the star—clean and strong—had chosen to fall. Stars had once been human beings and had been given great powers. Evening Star was the chief power in the west even now, and Morning Star in the east. But even mightier than they was the Sky Father, Tirawa.

Beyond the stake fences that protected the village cornfield from wild animals, the prairie grass grew high. Running Star went to the grass and lay down in it and pulled the long, bright, green-smelling stems over him like a blanket. He put his hands under his head for a pillow and slept.

Sometime in the middle of his sleep, he had a strange and wonderful dream. All the stars in the heavens seemed to cluster together, and then, suddenly, they began to fall. As they fell, they separated into two remarkable animal figures. The figures had four long, slender legs with hooves at the tips. They had graceful necks and glossy manes flying from them, and their noses had round, pinkish-colored nostrils. Each strange animal had a flowing tail and a broad back wide enough and strong-looking enough to carry bundles far heavier than any dog could carry.

Never, asleep or awake, had Running Star seen such beautiful creatures. How elegant their pointed ears were, standing up above their star-bright foreheads! How fleet and noble and shining they looked! In his dream he saw every detail of the animals. Even more amazing, Running Star knew what they were. They were ponies, fallen from the sky. And they were meant for him!

He woke with the new day's sun glowing in his face and the prairie grass making a rustling, spinning sound in his ears. He sat up, rubbing his eyes, looking around him, searching for the two ponies. He got to his feet, not caring that dead grass clung to his hair or that his old robe hung from his shoulders like tattered bark.

"I am here!" he called, but nothing moved or answered. He saw only the empty prairie land, stretching away from one edge of the sky to the other, and the round, blue shadows of the lodges in front of him. Running Star looked up at the sky, thinking that the ponies had gone back to their home there and that he could see them still. There was only the blue sky with one small, white cloud going across it slowly and a crow flying beneath the cloud.

Downcast and hungry, Running Star walked toward the small, green river that ran past the lodges. He walked alongside the stream and out of sight of the village. Wild rose thorns scratched at his legs. A chokecherry branch whipped across his face. A rattlesnake buzzed between two rocks. Soon Running Star sat down by the green river.

He took off his ragged moccasins and rested his tired feet against the cool, blue mud at the water's edge. He worked his toes in the mud, making patterns and shapes, and he thought about the ponies. He remembered just how their heads had looked and how their bodies were shaped. He remembered their flowing tails and their legs, slender as the willow's branches.

He stared at the mud where his feet had been making designs and saw that he had drawn a picture of a pony. He stood up. Excitement sparkled in him like a bright cloud of fireflies. He stooped down and began working in the mud with his hands. He scooped up handful after handful of mud until he had a mound of the gleaming, damp stuff. The blue clay squeezed through his fingers and covered his palms. He felt joy in handling the moist earth and making it into something new, something that had never been in the world before.

The sun moved higher overhead. An eagle drifted so close to Running Star, it almost grazed his shoulder. Running Star did not notice. Now he was shaping the mud into a figure with slim,

strong legs and a lovely arched neck, nostrils round as hoops, and a tail like flowing rushes. He forgot all else except the mud figure in front of him. He forgot even his hunger.

When he had finished, a small mud pony stood at the stream's edge. So perfectly had Running Star remembered his dream that the pony looked almost alive. One hoof was lifted in the air, and the arched neck was so real, it seemed the pony would turn and whinny.

"You are a Horse of Horses!" Running Star said. "And you are mine. Your name shall be Blue-Wind-Fallen-from-the-Sky."

Maker of Ponies

For a long time Running Star stood looking at the mud stallion drying and hardening in the sunlight. Then he frowned. There had been two ponies. He must make another. But the second pony in the dream had not been quite the same as this one. The second pony had been a reddish color and smaller. Since it was smaller, it must be a mare. Female foxes were smaller than male foxes, buffalo cows were smaller than buffalo bulls, and so it must be with horses.

Running Star waited until Blue-Wind was dry and as firm as a clay pot. Then he picked the pony up, put him carefully inside his robe, and walked until he came to a part of the river where the mud was a rich red color. Then he stopped, put his mud pony down, and began making another. Again he knew deep joy as he shaped the cool clay and felt it turn warm in his hands.

When he had finished, another mud pony stood before him, her reddish neck arched as the stallion's, her round nostrils so real, they seemed to quiver.

"You are a Mare of Mares!" Running Star said. "And you are mine. Your name shall be Red-Wind-Fallen-from-the-Sky."

Red-Wind was beautiful, he saw, but it was Blue-Wind he loved the most. He stroked Blue-Wind's forehead before he put the pony into a fold of his robe. Then, so that Red-Wind should not be jealous, he touched her back tenderly before he put her beside the stallion.

Running Star walked on, carrying the ponies with him. In late afternoon he came to another village, Village-Leaning-by-the-Pond. Next to the pond's edge, Running Star took the ponies from his robe. He stretched himself on his stomach and drank from the clear water, for he was thirsty. When he had drunk all he wanted and had wiped the clear drops from his chin, he thought of Blue-Wind and Red-Wind. They, too, would be thirsty.

He set the two mud ponies side by side at the edge of the water.

"Drink," he said in a lordly tone. "I give you the right."

Leaving them there to drink as long as they wished, he walked toward the lodges.

"I am a maker of ponies," he announced to the first Indian man he met.

The man asked, "What are ponies?"

"Follow your eyes, and I will show you," said Running Star, leading the man toward the pond.

Others who had heard followed: braves and squaws, children and dogs. Even the chief came. When they saw the ponies, they ran forward, their hands reaching out.

Running Star moved in front of the ponies. "They are drinking. No one but me must touch them."

The crowd hung back, staring at the strange animals of mud. Then a fierce-looking warrior grunted.

"They are not breathing."

Another said, "They are earth without life."

"They are Horses of Horses," Running Star said proudly, "and they are mine. They will carry great burdens and run faster than wild rivers."

The chief took a step forward. He folded his arms in thought and studied the mud ponies. At last he said, "They are the wind on four still legs. They are worth food for their owner. Come," he said to Running Star.

Running Star and the crowd followed the chief back to the lodge. There Running Star ate until he could hold no more. He thanked the chief and returned to the pond.

"You have drunk enough water," he told the ponies.

The ponies stood as they had been, motionless. Their muzzles were dry. The manes on their necks did not move.

Nevertheless, Running Star patted each gently as he picked them up and put them once again into his robe.

Running Star's heart was torn. He closed his eyes, listening to the sky and the wind, waiting for a voice to speak or a song to come to him. He heard only the dry whisper of a fly's wing close to his ear. The world was so still, he thought he heard an ant crawling slowly and painfully up a thin steeple of grass. He heard his own heart, and it seemed to be saying:

"They come from your hands.
In your hands you hold them.
Out of your dream you made them.
They are yours. Your hands shaped them
Out of stars and mud.
You must carry the dream
Across many sunsets."

A Gift to the World

Through all the summer, Running Star wandered over the land, begging food from whoever would give it to him. Autumn came. He grew hungrier. Many times he was so weary that he could scarcely lift one foot after the other.

After the first frost Running Star headed toward the village where he was born. It was important that he be there before winter came, for it was there that all the tribes gathered in the cold winter months.

For three suns and three moons he traveled, until at last he came within sight of his village. He was almost too tired to move, but he carried the mud ponies to a stream that rippled at a distance from the village. There he set them down.

"Drink," he ordered.

After he rested, he found a few currants on bushes along the shore. These gave him the strength to go on toward the village.

The people looked at him as if they had never seen him before, although he had been born among them. The dogs barked at him as if they had never seen a Pawnee boy before. Nobody offered him food.

Because he was weak from hunger, Running Star felt dizzy. He scarcely knew where he was or who he was. He stumbled. Darkness floated across his eyes, and for a moment he thought he

was going to fall. Straightening, he saw the mocking faces of the tribe through a cloud, and then he heard himself talking and shouting, but it was as if the voice belonged to somebody else.

"Horses of Men!" he cried out, talking wildly and not knowing what he was saying. "Men of Horses! They are mine. I have left them to drink, but I cannot carry them forever around the sun. I am faint and hungry, but they are mine and a gift to the world!"

He fell.

One warrior, kinder than the others, picked the boy up and carried him to his own lodge. "Feed him buffalo meat," he said.

Running Star lay with his eyes closed, too tired even to eat. At last he was able to nibble the food brought to him. Almost before he had finished, he fell into a deep sleep.

The wind rose in the night. It walked over the round roof of the lodge and stamped its heels. It pried at the log walls with long, chilly fingers and fluttered the willow-mat curtains. Running Star did not hear. He slept on.

Morning Star was almost up over the rim of the earth when Running Star had a strange dream. He dreamed that Tirawa made a long slit in the sky and dropped two ponies through it, a blue pony and a red one. Then he heard a voice, the voice of Tirawa.

"You shall become a leader," the voice said. "Listen closely, Running Star," Tirawa continued. "Go this night to where your mud ponies are standing, and there you will find two live ponies."

Running Star woke. He rubbed his eyes. Quietly he pulled his tattered robe around him and left the lodge. He ran through the center of the village, his torn robe flapping behind him like ragged leather wings.

He raced on, on toward the stream, straining to see through the darkness.

"Blue-Wind!" he cried out. "I am here."

He puckered his mouth and whistled. "Red-Wind, I have come!"

An owl fluttered past. Far off a coyote lifted its nose toward the rising moon and howled. There was no other sound in the night. Nothing moved in the spot where the two mud ponies had been.

Running Star stood still, his heart pounding, waiting.

Then he heard it—a strange, high nickering sound—followed by a softer sound, as of air going in and out a doorway covered with reeds.

He whirled. There stood Blue-Wind and Red-Wind, side by side. But they were no longer toy mud ponies. They stood great and tall in the moonlight, higher than any fox or coyote, higher than the biggest dog in any village. The moonlight flashed against their moving eyes. The wind lifted the dark-blue mane and tossed the reddish tail. Blue-Wind made the nickering sound again. One front hoof was still raised. Now, with a silken motion, he set it down, and Running Star heard the hoof click against a pebble.

For an instant Running Star felt fear.

There was a noise of quick footsteps and voices behind him. All the village people were moving toward him. Only the dogs stood back, their heads down and their tails pressed up against their bellies.

"You will become a leader," the voice in his dream had said.

Running Star walked toward Blue-Wind. "You are mine," he whispered. He reached up and closed one hand on the coarse, shining, blue mane. He took a deep breath, crouched down, and with one spring leaped onto Blue-Wind's back.

Running Star faced the chiefs and warriors as they stretched themselves full length on the ground in fear and awe.

He raised one hand. "Return to the village and prepare a lodge for me and my horses."

Then the people got up and hurried to do as he said.

Running Star kicked his heels once against Blue-Wind's sides.

Blue-Wind reared up, front hooves scraping the air, seeming to paw at the stars. He gave a little snort and tossed his head. Red-Wind reared up at the stallion's side.

Then, swifter than lightning shot from the bent bow of the sky, the ponies raced to the village. Running Star felt himself carried as by a wave of blue wind. Grass and trees and rocks rushed past so swiftly, he could not tell one from another. At the stallion's side the mare seemed a streak of fire.

On they galloped. Wind rushed against Running Star's face. It tore his ragged buffalo-skin robe from him. It tore his ragged moccasins from his feet. He smiled, riding on through the star-shot night.

When he came to the lodges, he leaped down from Blue-Wind's back. He stood between Blue-Wind and Red-Wind, waiting for the villagers to catch up.

Tomorrow he would have the finest robe in the tribe. Tomorrow he would wear his hair like a warrior's. He had done his great deed.

Reflections

1. At the beginning of this story, do you think the Pawnees knew about horses? Give evidence from the story to support your opinion.
2. Why was it important that Running Star "saw every detail of the animals" in his dream?
3. Suppose the mud ponies had not come alive. Do you think they would then have been worth all the hardships Running Star had to bear? Give reasons for your answer.
4. What have you made that has never been in the world before? How did you happen to make it? Think carefully of everything you have made—from sounds to sentences, from doodles to pictures, from cutouts to birdhouses or dresses.
5. Use an encyclopedia to find out how Indians first got horses. Then write an essay comparing these facts with the legend you have just read.

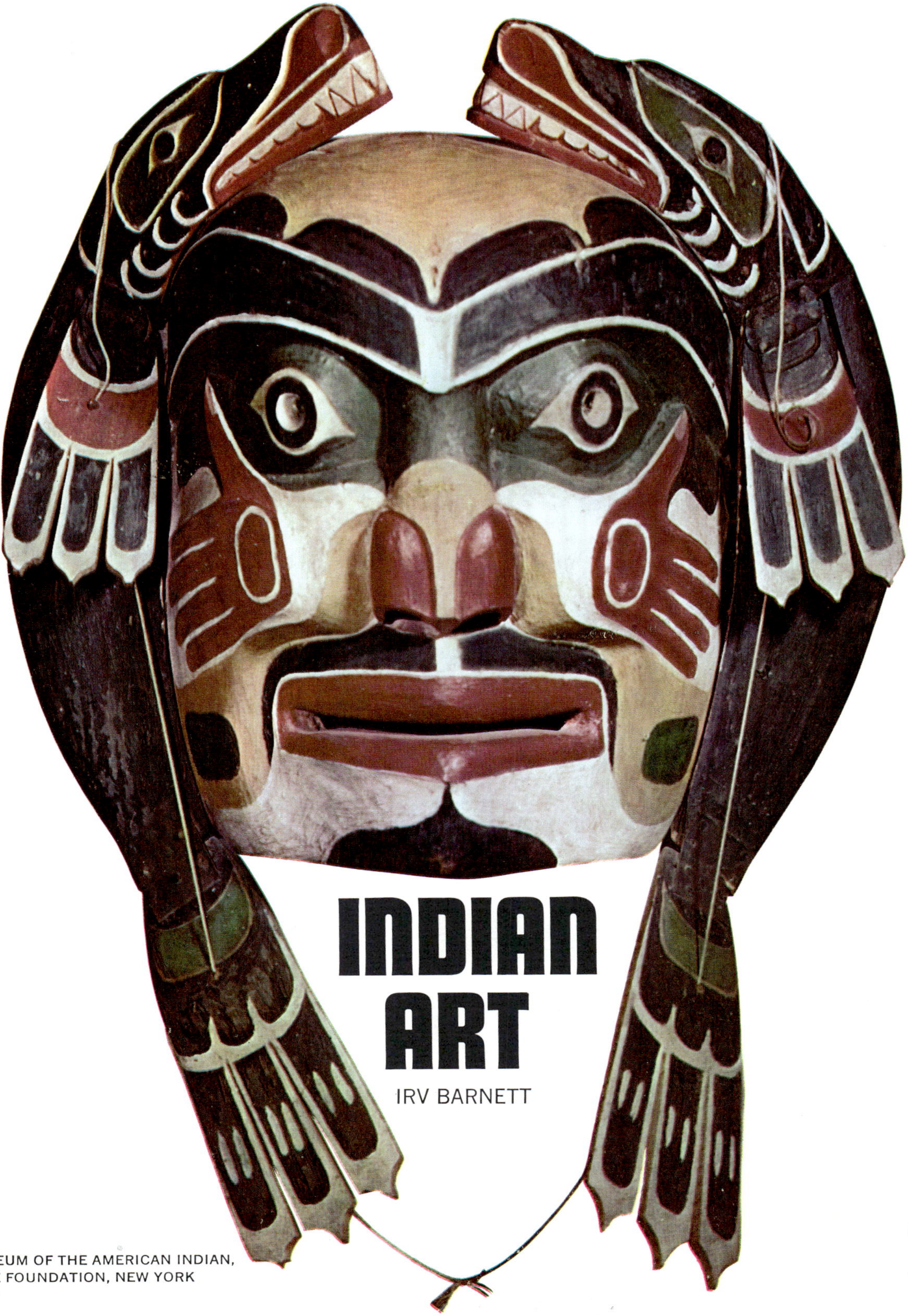

INDIAN ART

IRV BARNETT

MUSEUM OF THE AMERICAN INDIAN,
HEYE FOUNDATION, NEW YORK

THE DENVER ART MUSEUM

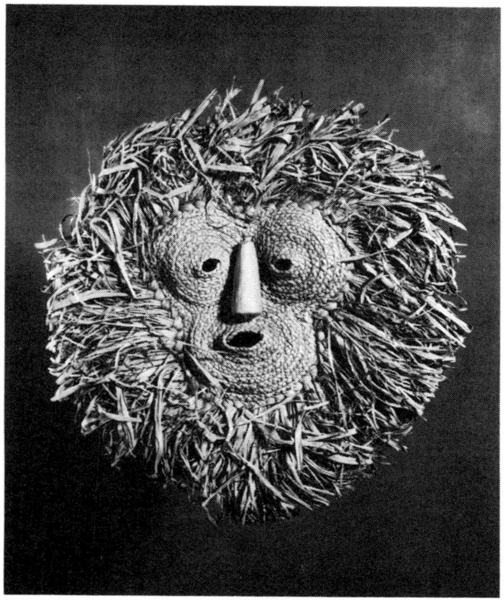

MUSEUM OF THE AMERICAN INDIAN, HEYE FOUNDATION, NEW YORK

Long ago American Indians had many ideas about religion and nature. They made up stories about these ideas. Indians also were proud of their history. Because they had no written language, they passed on their history to their children by telling stories. As they told the stories again and again, the Indians often added dancing, drama, and art forms to them. They acted out their past in dramatic ceremonies.

Masks like those on pages 305 and 306 and the ones above are often used in these ceremonies. Such masks are carved from wood. Sometimes they also have shells, fur, feathers, human hair, or small stones on them. The masks add a sense of excitement and mystery. Many kinds of art go into one of these Indian ceremonies. Storytelling, music, dancing, costumes, history, and religion all come into play.

THE MUSEUM OF PRIMITIVE ART, NEW YORK

COURTESY, THE AMERICAN MUSEUM OF NATURAL HISTORY, NEW YORK
PHOTO: CURTISS, 1915

This photograph shows a potlatch festival held by the Kwakiutl Indians of the Northwest coast. These fall festivals are exciting parties. Each host tries to make his party the most exciting. Gifts are often given to guests.

Here the dancers, dressed as animal spirits, wear movable masks. They are posed before the totem poles elaborately carved from wood. The totem pole represents important events in the family history of a clan.

BOTH BELOW: COURTESY, THE AMERICAN MUSEUM OF NATURAL HISTORY, NEW YORK

On this page you see the beginning of a Navaho sand-painting ceremony. On the next page you see a finished sand painting. A sand "painting" isn't really a painting at all. It is made by carefully gathering grains of sand of different colors. It often has a religious meaning. A sand painting may be made to heal the sick, to bring rain, or in other ways to control nature. A sand-painting ceremony includes singing or chanting, dancing, and storytelling. Each color, each line, each detail in the painting has a special meaning.

The Navaho Indians not only make beautiful sand paintings. They also weave blankets, rugs, and baskets. They make pottery and jewelry that are of rare and high quality, as well.

MUSEUM OF NAVAHO CEREMONIAL ART, SANTA FE, NEW MEXICO
PHOTO: LAURA GILPIN

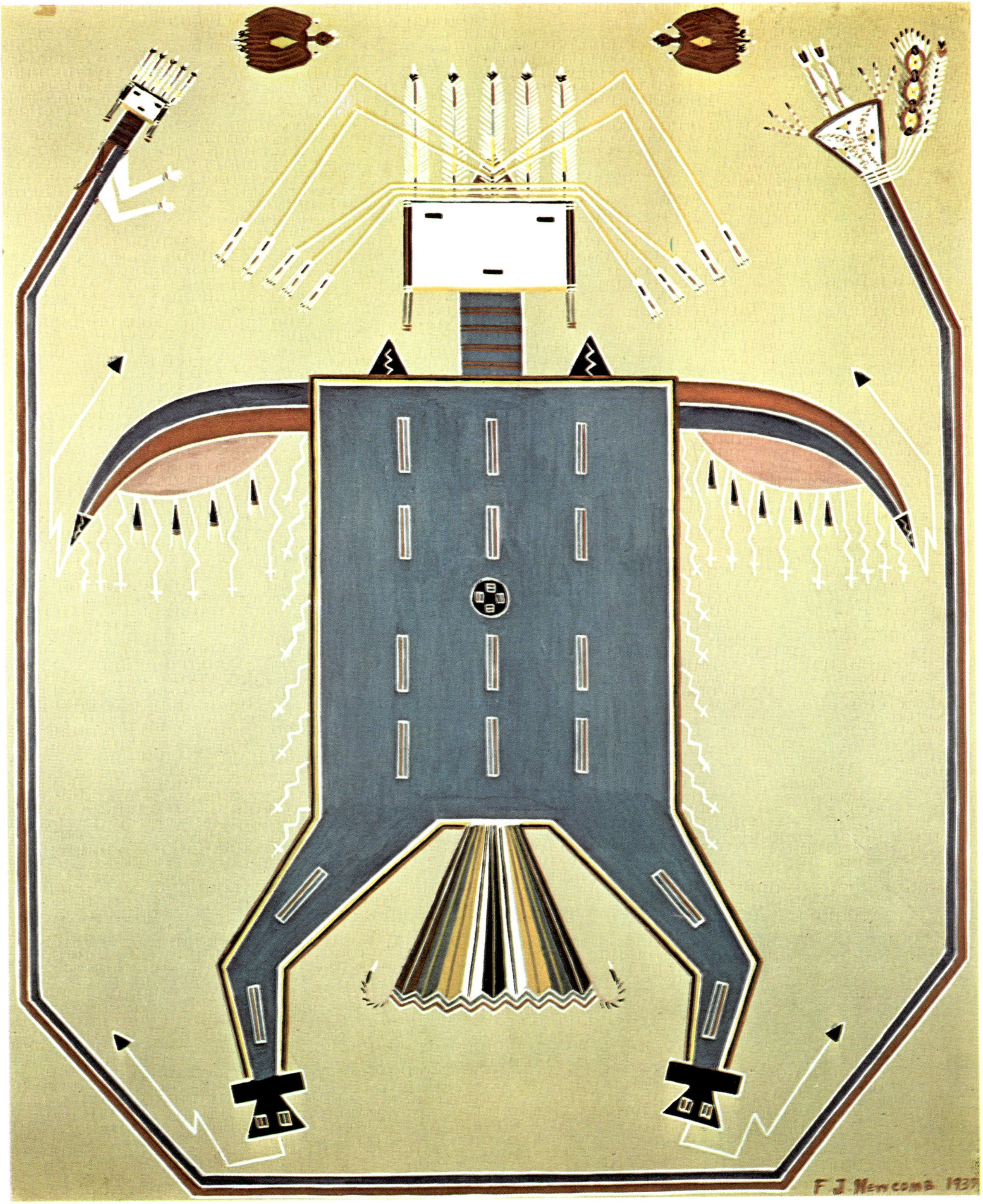
F. J. Newcomb 1937

PHILBROOK ART CENTER, TULSA, OKLAHOMA

In this modern painting by Quincy Tahoma, the artist has chosen an event from the past. He shows an Indian killing a buffalo.

The Indian art you have seen on these pages makes clear the close feeling the Indian peoples have with nature. Each piece shows how Indians made wise and beautiful use of materials they found in nature. Their contribution to the art of the Americas is both great and unique.

American Paintings

by Shirley Glubok

THE TRUSTEES OF THE BRITISH MUSEUM

A CHIEF (about 1587)
JOHN WHITE

Some of the earliest settlers in America were artists. John White was sent from England in 1587 to be governor of the first English settlement in America. This settlement was on Roanoke Island, off the coast of North Carolina. White made many watercolor sketches of the Indians such as this one. They showed people in England how the first Americans looked and lived.

THE RAPALJE CHILDREN (about 1768)
JOHN DURAND

The children of Garret Rapalje grew up in Brooklyn, New York, in the 1760s. John Durand, who painted this portrait, was a self-trained artist.

PAUL REVERE
JOHN SINGLETON COPLEY (1738–1815)

Paul Revere, a silversmith, is about to carve a design on a teapot he has just made. He is best known for his midnight ride during the Revolutionary War, when he warned people that the British were coming.

MUSEUM OF FINE ARTS, BOSTON. GIFT OF J. W. REVERE, W. B. REVERE, AND E. H. R. REVERE

THE NEW-YORK HISTORICAL SOCIETY, NEW YORK CITY

NATIONAL GALLERY OF ART, WASHINGTON, D. C. GIFT OF EDGAR WILLIAM AND BERNICE CHRYSLER GARBISCH

GENERAL WASHINGTON ON A WHITE CHARGER

UNKNOWN ARTIST (about 1830)

The name of the painter of George Washington, shown riding a white horse, is not known. In early America painters of houses, barns, wagons, and signs sometimes painted portraits. Often these painters did not sign their names to their work.

THE COTTER'S SATURDAY NIGHT

EUNICE PINNEY (1770–1849)

A wide range of subjects was chosen by Eunice Pinney for her art. She painted her family, neighbors, and even a jail. This family group is spending Saturday night together in their cottage. The week's work is over. The father is reading the Bible by candlelight. The painting is based on a poem by the Scottish poet Robert Burns.

NATIONAL GALLERY OF ART, WASHINGTON, D. C. GIFT OF EDGAR WILLIAM AND BERNICE CHRYSLER GARBISCH

PEACEABLE KINGDOM

EDWARD HICKS (1780–1849)

A prophecy in the Bible tells that there will be a peaceable kingdom in the world. In this kingdom the fierce lion will lie down with the gentle lamb. Edward Hicks painted many versions of this prophecy. In the background of this painting, William Penn makes a peace treaty with the Indians. Penn, who founded the colony of Pennsylvania, was a Quaker. He worked for peace between the settlers and the Indians.

ALBRIGHT-KNOX ART GALLERY, BUFFALO, NEW YORK

IVORY-BILLED WOODPECKER

JOHN JAMES AUDUBON (1785–1851)

Audubon traveled through fields and woods. He painted and described hundreds of birds and animals. This painting records the ivory-billed woodpecker. Even at the time Audubon painted it, this bird was rare. Now it is almost extinct.

THE NEW-YORK HISTORICAL SOCIETY, NEW YORK CITY

ARRANGEMENT IN GRAY AND BLACK

JAMES McNEILL WHISTLER
(1834–1903)

The artist did not expect that people would be interested in just a portrait of his mother. So he made the forms and shapes in the painting more important.

THE LOUVRE, PARIS. PHOTO: SEGALAT

PHILADELPHIA MUSEUM OF ART. PHOTO: A. J. WYATT

HOME RANCH

THOMAS EAKINS
(1844–1916)

It was the aim of Thomas Eakins to look deeply into American life. He painted people in everyday scenes. A friend of his posed in the costume of a western rancher for this portrait.

CHILDREN ROLLER SKATING

WILLIAM GLACKENS (1870–1938)

City children at play were a favorite subject of William Glackens. He painted them roller-skating on the sidewalks and sledding in the snow in the park. This lively painting of girls on skates is filled with joyful movement.

THE BROOKLYN MUSEUM

THE METROPOLITAN MUSEUM OF ART, NEW YORK CITY, WOLFE FUND, 1906

THE GULF STREAM

WINSLOW HOMER (1836–1910)

The artist liked an outdoor life of hunting and fishing, and even more he loved the sea. In this painting, the small boat has been severely damaged by a storm. The unfortunate sailor on the boat is looking into the distance while sharks swim around him. One hopes the ship on the horizon will see and rescue him.

THE BATH

MARY CASSATT (1845–1926)

Mary Cassatt was born in Pennsylvania but lived most of her life in Paris, France. Cassatt never married, but she was most interested in women and their children. She painted many mother-and-child portraits.

THE ART INSTITUTE OF CHICAGO. ROBERT A. WALLER FUND

PHILADELPHIA MUSEUM OF ART. LOUIS E. STERN COLLECTION. PHOTO: A. J. WYATT

ROCHESTER MEMORIAL ART GALLERY

NEARLY EVERYBODY READS THE BULLETIN

BEN SHAHN (1898–1969)

Ben Shahn grew up in Brooklyn, New York. He was a poor boy from Lithuania, which is now part of Russia. Shahn believed that the world could be made a better place in which to live. He painted life as he saw it—such as these women on a park bench in a big city. The figures are strangely shaped. One sees their forms rather than their faces.

BOOM TOWN

THOMAS HART BENTON (1889–1975)

The Middle West has produced some of America's outstanding artists. Thomas Benton, who was born in Missouri, was proud of his native land and painted the things he knew best. *Boom Town* shows a small city where oil was discovered, and the city is suddenly booming. The new oil fields pour ugly black clouds of smoke over the city.

STREET SHADOWS

JACOB LAWRENCE (1917–   )

Jacob Lawrence was brought up in Harlem, a section of New York City. He painted the people and places where he lived. This painting shows the streets of Harlem on a summer night. Some people are sitting on crates, playing games, while others watch or talk to each other.

COLLECTION OF MR. AND MRS. LEWIS GARLICK, NEW YORK CITY. PHOTO: JOHN KING

FARAWAY

ANDREW WYETH (1917-   )

The background is simple in this painting. The main point of interest is the boy in a fur hat. Andrew Wyeth painted the boy, his son, as if he were recording him through a camera lens. We see him as if we were looking down on him.

COURTESY OF MRS. ANDREW WYETH

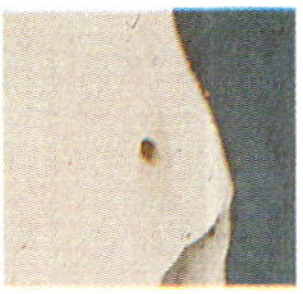

COW'S SKULL, RED, WHITE AND BLUE

GEORGIA O'KEEFFE (1887–   )

Georgia O'Keeffe lives in the beautiful desert country of New Mexico. She searches for animal bones bleached white by the sun and worn thin by the wind. Then she brings them home and paints them. A cow's skull becomes an important object when painted by O'Keeffe.

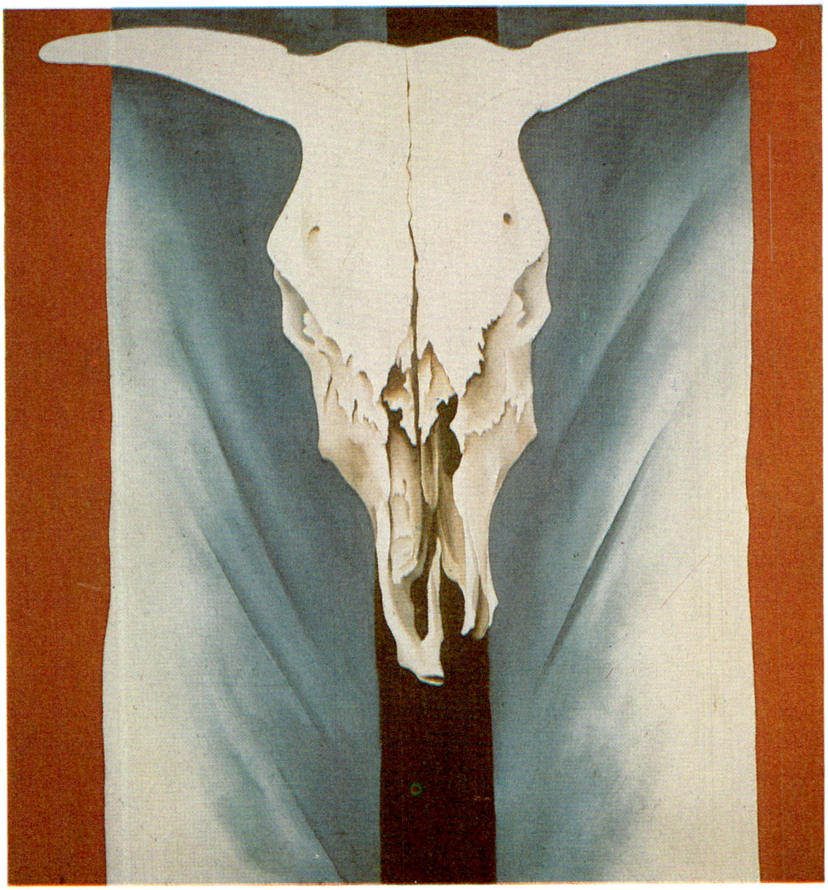

THE METROPOLITAN MUSEUM OF ART, THE ALFRED STIEGLITZ COLLECTION, 1949

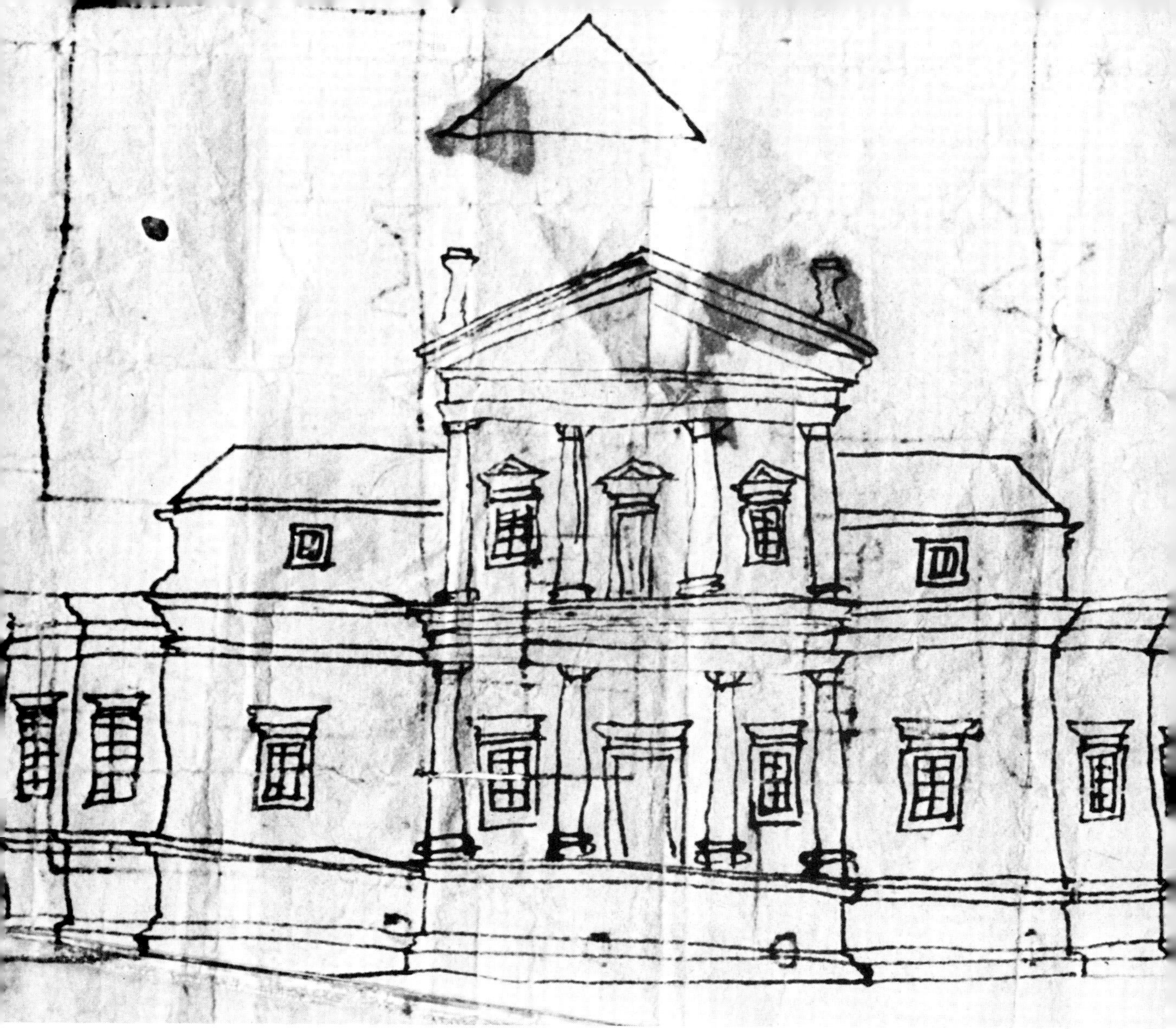

Thomas Jefferson, Architect

SARAH ELLIOTT

You probably know that Thomas Jefferson was one of our early Presidents. Do you also know that he was the first American architect to become world famous?

E PLURIBUS UNUM
MONTICELLO
FIVE CENTS
UNITED STATES OF AMERICA

When Jefferson was young, there were no architects in the colonies. The settlers built their own houses, which were mostly box-shaped and considered ugly by Jefferson. Pictures of ancient Greek and Roman buildings in Europe fascinated him. He began to study the writings of European architects, especially those of Andrea Palladio.

After finishing college, Jefferson became a lawyer. When he was not practicing law, he was working on the design of the house he planned to build for himself. He had already chosen the site. It was called Monticello, which is an Italian word meaning "little mountain."

In 1768 he began to level the mountaintop. He cut trees to clear a road and saved the timber to use as beams in the house. He made bricks from the hard red clay dug up for the foundation. The first part of the house was a small, one-room, brick building. Jefferson and his wife moved into this room shortly after their marriage. But Monticello was not completed until after Jefferson left the Presidency in 1809.

In 1784 Jefferson was sent to Europe to set up trade agreements with European countries. The next year he became America's minister to France. He studied the buildings of Paris and traveled to see other buildings in other European cities. These travels changed some of his ideas about architecture.

Before going to Europe, Jefferson had begun the design for a building that was to be the State Capitol in Richmond, Virginia. While in France, he was asked to send home plans for the new building. Jefferson imagined a building that would look like the ancient Roman temple in the French city of Nimes. While still in the United States, he had worked from pictures of the temple. On arriving in France, Jefferson went to see the temple for himself. He worked with a French architect. Then he sent finished plans and a plaster model to Richmond.

The State Capitol was completed in 1792. It was the first building in the United States modeled after an ancient Roman temple. Later this style became very popular.

Jefferson spent most of his last years creating the University of Virginia. He urged the state to start a public university and to pay for its construction. His work at the university enabled him to combine his love of education with his love of architecture. He designed all the buildings. He planned the courses. He hired the teachers and bought the books. The university opened in March, 1825. Jefferson was its first head.

On July 4, 1826, Thomas Jefferson died. He is best remembered as a great President and the author of the Declaration of Independence. But he is also famous for being the foremost American architect of his time.

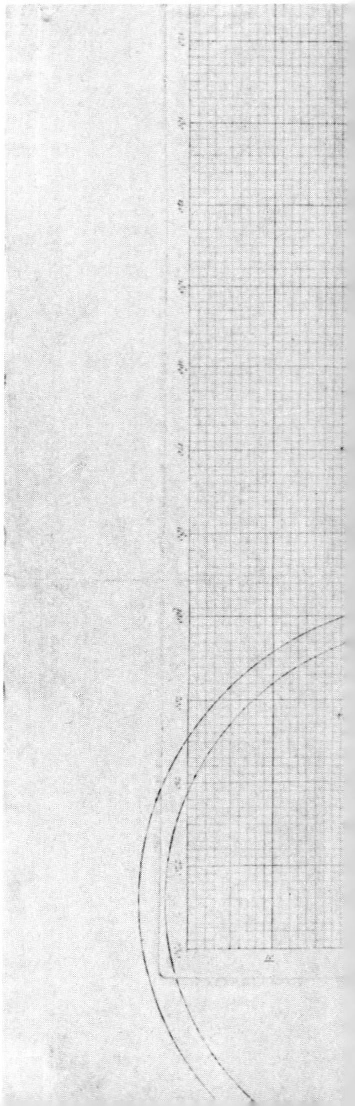

Fig. 1.

Opera Star

LEONTYNE PRICE

Leontyne Price once said, "Since I first began to train as a singer, my special goal and ambition has been to sing at the Metropolitan Opera in New York." She fulfilled this goal when she made her debut there in 1961. Her performance was called "one of the greatest operatic triumphs of recent years."

Leontyne Price had come a long way from Laurel, Mississippi, where she was born February 10, 1927. After graduating from college in 1948 and from the Juilliard School of Music in 1952, Ms. Price spent two years playing Bess in George Gershwin's *Porgy and Bess,* both on Broadway and around the world.

She made her grand opera stage debut on September 20, 1957, with the San Francisco Opera. Then followed appearances in Vienna, Verona, Brussels, Salzburg, and Milan, where she played Aida at La Scala.

When the new Metropolitan Opera opened at Lincoln Center in 1966, Leontyne Price was chosen to star as Cleopatra in its first production, Samuel Barber's opera *Antony and Cleopatra.*

The Reluctant Dragon

dramatized from a story by KENNETH GRAHAME

Characters

Boy
His Mother
His Father
Dragon
  His Head
  His Left Paw
  His Right Paw
  His Tail
Eight Villagers
St. George

The part that the dragon plays is so long and so much fun that it has been divided among four actors.

(The play takes place long ago in the shepherd country of England. At the back right corner of the stage is a screen painted to look like rough boards. This is the cottage where the Boy *lives. Later in the play, it is the Village Inn. The rest of the stage is open countryside with blue sky, a few bushes and rocks, a wind-blown tree. At stage left is the rocky entrance to an enormous cave. This side of the stage is very dim, but there is bright light on the cottage, where the* Boy *sits on a little stool reading a big book and his* Mother *sits on a little stool sewing. After a bit of homey quiet, the* Father *rushes onto the stage from the right.)*

FATHER (*shaking with fear*). It's all up with me, Maria! Never no more can I go up on them there Downs, be it ever so!

MOTHER (*calmly*). Now don't you take on like that. Tell us all about it first, whatever it is as has given you this shake-up. Then me and you and the son here, between us, we ought to be able to get to the bottom of it!

FATHER. It began some nights ago. You know that cave up there—I never liked it somehow, and the sheep never liked it neither; and when sheep don't like a thing, there is generally some reason for it. Well, for some time past there's been faint noises coming from that cave—noises like heavy sighings, with grunts mixed up in them; and sometimes a snoring, faraway down—*real* snoring, yet somehow not *honest* snoring, like you and me o' nights, you know!

BOY (*quietly*). *I* know.

FATHER. Of course, I was terrible frightened; yet somehow I couldn't keep away. So this very evening, before I come down, I took a cast around by the cave, quietly. And there—oh my, there I saw him at last, as plain as I see you!

MOTHER. Saw *who?*

FATHER. Why *him*, I'm a-telling you! He was sticking halfway out o' the cave and seemed to be enjoying o' the cool o' the evening in a poetical sort o' way. He was big as four cart horses and all covered with shiny scales. He had his chin on his paws, and I should say he was meditating about things.

MOTHER. Peaceful, was he?

FATHER. Oh, yes, a peaceable sort o' beast enough, and not ramping or carrying on or doing anything but what was quite right and proper. I admit all that. And yet, what am I to do? *Scales*, you know, and claws and a tail for certain, though I didn't see that end o' him—I ain't *used* to 'em, and I don't *hold* with 'em and that's a fact!

BOY (*closes his book, yawns, clasps his hands behind his head*). It's all right, Father. Don't worry. It's only a dragon.

FATHER. Only a dragon? What do you mean, sitting there, you and your dragons? *Only* a dragon indeed! And what do *you* know about it?

BOY (*quietly*). 'Cos it *is*, and 'cos I *do* know. Look here, Father, you know we've each of us got our line. *You* know about sheep and weather and things; *I* know about dragons. I always said, you know, that that cave up there was a dragon-cave. Now, please, just leave this all to me. I'll go up and have a talk with him, and you'll find it'll be all right. Only, please, don't you go worrying round there without me. You don't understand 'em a bit, and they're very sensitive, you know!

MOTHER. He's quite right, Father. As he says, dragons is his line and not ours. He's wonderful knowing about book-beasts, as everyone allows. And to tell the truth, I'm not half happy in my own mind, thinking o' that poor animal lying alone up there, without a bit o' hot supper or anyone to 'change the news with; and if he ain't quite respectable, our Boy'll find it out quick enough. He's got a pleasant sort o' way with him that makes everybody tell him everything. Now, you two come along to bed now! (*She leads the* BOY *off right, followed by the* FATHER.)

(*The lights dim on the cottage and brighten on the cave entrance. The* DRAGON *emerges from his cave, looks happily about him, puts his chin on his paws, and purrs blissfully. The* BOY *enters from stage right.*)

BOY. Well we live and learn! None of my books ever told me that dragons purred! (*Goes nearer.*) Hullo, Dragon!

DRAGON HEAD (*severely*). Now don't you hit me or bung stones or squirt water or anything. I won't have it, I tell you!

BOY (*calmly*). I've simply looked in to ask you how you were and all that sort of thing; but if I'm in the way, I can easily clear out.

DRAGON LEFT PAW. No, no, don't go off in a huff. Fact is—I'm as happy up here as the day's long; never without an occupation, dear fellow, I am never without an occupation! And yet, between ourselves, it *is* a trifle dull at times.

BOY (*politely*). Going to make a long stay here?

DRAGON RIGHT PAW. Can't hardly say at present. It seems a nice enough place; but I've only been here a short time, and one must look about and reflect and consider before settling down. Fact is, I'm such a confoundedly lazy beggar, I hate to think of stirring.

BOY. You surprise me.

DRAGON TAIL. It's the sad truth, and I fancy that's really how I came to be here. You see, all the other dragons were so active and *earnest* and all that sort of thing. They were always rampaging and skirmishing and scouring the desert sands and pacing the margin of the sea and chasing knights all over the place and devouring damsels. But as for me, I liked to get my meals regular and then prop my back against a rock and snooze a bit. Then I'd wake up and think of things going on and how they kept going on just the same, you know! So when it happened, I got fairly caught.

BOY. When *what* happened, please?

DRAGON HEAD. That's just what I don't precisely know. I suppose the earth sneezed or shook itself, or the bottom dropped out of something. Anyhow, there was a shake and a roar and a general stramash, and I found myself miles away, in a hole underground and wedged in as tight as tight.

BOY. That must have been awful!

DRAGON TAIL. Well, thank goodness, my wants are few, and I had peace and quiet. But time went on, and there was a certain sameness about the life. At last I began to think it would be fun to work my way upstairs and see what the other fellows were doing. So I scratched and clawed, and at last I came out through this cave. On the whole, I feel inclined to settle down here.

BOY. What's your mind always occupied about?

DRAGON LEFT PAW (*bashfully*). Did you ever—just for fun—try to make up poetry—verses, you know?

BOY. Course I have. Heaps of it. And some of it's quite good, I feel sure; only there's no one here cares about it . . .

DRAGON RIGHT PAW. Exactly, my own case exactly. Now you've got culture, you have. I could tell it on you at once. I'm awfully pleased to have met you, and I'm hoping the other neighbors will be equally agreeable. There was a very nice old gentleman up here only last night, but he didn't seem to want to intrude.

BOY. That was my father, and he *is* a nice old gentleman. I'll introduce you if you like.

DRAGON TAIL (*eagerly*). Can't you two come up here and dine tomorrow?

BOY. Thanks awfully, but we don't go out anywhere without my mother, and, to tell you the truth, I'm afraid she mightn't quite approve of you. You see, there's no getting over the hard fact that you're a dragon, is there? And when you talk of settling down, I can't help feeling that you don't quite realize your position. To anybody else but me, you're an enemy of the human race, you see!

DRAGON HEAD (*cheerfully*). Haven't got an enemy in the world. Too lazy to make 'em, to begin with.

BOY. Oh, dear! I wish you'd try and grasp the situation properly. When the other people in the village find you out, they'll come after you with spears and swords and all sorts of things. You'll have to be exterminated, according to their way of looking at it. They'll think you're a scourge and a pest and a baneful monster!

DRAGON LEFT PAW. Not a word of truth in it. I assure you, my character'll bear the strictest investigation. And now, there's a little sonnet thing I was working on. . . .

BOY. I can't stop for sonnets. Do, for goodness' sake, try and realize that you're regarded as a pestilential scourge, or you'll find yourself in a most awful fix. Good night! (*The* BOY *waves good-by as he goes off the stage. The* DRAGON *waves, yawns, and backs carefully into his cave as the lights dim.*)

(*After a few moments of quiet, which means the night has passed, the right side of the stage brightens. From different parts of the audience, the* VILLAGERS *hurry anxiously onto the stage. They carry small stools. After greeting each other, they settle themselves on their stools in a half circle at stage right.*)

FIRST VILLAGER. Fancy! A real live dragon in the cave on our Downs!

SECOND VILLAGER. I say he's a pestilential scourge!

THIRD VILLAGER. Just where the family was a-picnicking, peaceful as could be, along he comes only last Sunday!

FOURTH VILLAGER. As big as four cart horses!

FIFTH VILLAGER. And covered from tip to tail with *scales!*

SIXTH VILLAGER. But in a way it's a distinction for a village to have a dragon of its very own!

SEVENTH VILLAGER. Not many a village can say the same, that's sure!

EIGHTH VILLAGER. He sits there so quiet, he don't behave like a dragon. . . .

FIRST VILLAGER. Well, that's his own lookout! He *is* a dragon, and no denying it!

SECOND VILLAGER. They do say there's a princess in the cave waiting to be freed!

THIRD VILLAGER. And I hear tell many a sheep's been stolen o' nights!

FOURTH VILLAGER. Not only *sheep!* Children, too, who have wandered on the Downs alone, have not come back . . .

FIFTH VILLAGER. Who's telling you this?

SIXTH VILLAGER. Never mind, who's a-telling! Anyone knows what a dragon does!

SEVENTH VILLAGER. My great-grampa had tales enough in *his* time. Anyone knows what a dragon does!

EIGHTH VILLAGER. This sort of thing can't go on!

FIRST VILLAGER. The dreadful beast must be *exterminated!*

SECOND VILLAGER. The countryside must be freed from this pest!

THIRD VILLAGER. This terror! This destroying scourge!

FOURTH VILLAGER. (*rises*). Who will take sword and spear and free our suffering village?

FIFTH VILLAGER (*rises*). And rescue the captive princess?

SIXTH VILLAGER (*rises*). And win deathless fame?

SEVENTH VILLAGER (*rises*). Who?

EIGHTH VILLAGER (*rises*). Who? Who?

(*They look at each other in silence. There is a pause, and then they all sit down again.*)

FOURTH VILLAGER (*looks straight out at the audience and then rises in great excitement*). It's all right! He's a-coming!

ALL OTHERS. *Who's* a-coming?

FOURTH VILLAGER. Why, St. George, of course!

(*The* VILLAGERS *see* ST. GEORGE *striding through the audience. They stand on their stools and cheer.*)

ALL. St. George! St. George!! St. George!!!

FIRST VILLAGER. He's heard tell of our dragon . . .

SECOND VILLAGER. He's coming on purpose to slay the deadly beast . . .

THIRD VILLAGER. And free us from his horrid yoke!

FOURTH VILLAGER. Oh, my! Won't there be a jolly fight!

FIFTH VILLAGER. It's all up, Dragon! He's coming! He's coming!

SIXTH VILLAGER. Now we'll have a real fight!

SEVENTH VILLAGER. Who'll give me odds on St. George?

EIGHTH VILLAGER. Let's have a good look at him first!

ALL (*making a path for* ST. GEORGE, *as they continue to cheer and wave*). Hail, St. George!

ST. GEORGE (*striding through the* VILLAGERS, *goes to the stool at the center of the half circle and mounts it. He silences the* VILLAGERS *with a wave of his hands*). Dear friends, I have come to rid your village of the dreadful dragon. (*The* VILLAGERS *all cheer.*)

ST. GEORGE. Tell me the wrongs which you have suffered and which I am here to avenge.

(*There is an awkward silence, in which the* VILLAGERS *prod each other.*)

FIRST VILLAGER. Well, our sheep have been disappearing . . .

SECOND VILLAGER. And children . . .

THIRD VILLAGER. And crops ravaged . . .

FOURTH VILLAGER. And a princess bound in the cave . . .

FIFTH VILLAGER. And folk being murdered all over the place . . .

SIXTH VILLAGER. And thieving and wrongdoing such as would shame your ears to hear and shame my lips to speak.

SEVENTH VILLAGER. We daren't even go out of doors for fear of being snatched alive . . .

EIGHTH VILLAGER. Or burned to a crisp because of his scorching breath a-blowing on us—and a-making waste our countryside.

ST. GEORGE. All will be well now. Sleep tonight, and tomorrow I will slay your foe. But now, good night!

(*The* VILLAGERS *bow to him and go off in groups. As they go, they look back at him, making bets on the fight.* ST. GEORGE *watches them go. Then he sits wearily on a stool and puts his head in his hands.*)

BOY (*entering politely*). May I come in, St. George?

ST. GEORGE (*kindly*). Yes, come in, Boy. Another tale of misery and wrong, I fear me. Well, it shall soon be avenged.

BOY. Nothing of the sort. There's a misunderstanding somewhere, and I want to put it right. (*He moves a stool close to* ST. GEORGE *and sits beside him.*) The fact is, this is a *good* dragon and a friend of mine. Nobody can help liking him when once they know him.

ST. GEORGE (*smiling*). I like a fellow who sticks up for his friends. But that's not the question. I've been listening to tales of murder, theft, and wrong. This dragon has to be exterminated speedily.

BOY (*impatiently*). Oh, you've been taking in all the yarns those fellows have been telling you. Our villagers are the biggest storytellers in all the country round. All they want is a *fight*. I came down the street just now, and they were betting six to four on the dragon!

ST. GEORGE (*sadly*). Six to four on the dragon! This is an evil world, and sometimes I begin to think that all the wickedness is not entirely bottled up inside the dragons. And yet—may there not be, at this very moment, some princess within yonder gloomy cavern?

BOY (*earnestly*). I assure you, St. George, there's nothing of the sort at all. The dragon's a real gentleman, every inch of him.

ST. GEORGE. Well, perhaps I've misjudged the animal. But what are we to do? Here is this dragon, and here am I, almost face to face, each supposed to be thirsting for the other's blood. I don't see any way of our getting out of it, exactly.

BOY. I suppose you couldn't be persuaded to go away quietly, could you?

ST. GEORGE. Impossible, I fear. Quite against the rules. *You* know that.

BOY. Well then, look here, would you mind strolling up with me and seeing the dragon and talking it over?

ST. GEORGE (*rising*). Well, it's *irregular*, but really it seems about the most sensible thing to do. Perhaps there won't have to be any fight after all.

BOY (*follows him off the stage*). Or perhaps there will have to be a fight. Who knows? There's nothing more enjoyable than a good fight.

(*They circle through the audience and come onto the stage again. The lights grow dim on the Inn side of stage and become brighter on the cave.*)

BOY (*calling out*). I've brought a friend to see you, Dragon!

DRAGON HEAD (*coming out from the cave*). Very pleased to make your acquaintance, sir. Charming weather we're having!

BOY. This is St. George. We've come up to talk things over quietly, Dragon. You know what a hue and cry the villagers have raised against you. Do let us have a little straight common sense.

DRAGON LEFT PAW (*nervously*). So glad to meet you, St. George. You've been a great traveler, I hear. I've always been rather a stay-at-home. But if you're stopping here for any length of time, I'd love to hear . . .

ST. GEORGE (*shakes hands with the* DRAGON). I think first we'd better try to come to some understanding about this little affair of ours. We're supposed to be enemies, and the villagers want me to fight you.

DRAGON HEAD. Don't think I'm going to stir myself for these people. I'm a perfectly peaceful person.

ST. GEORGE. But don't you think that the simplest plan would be just to fight it out and let the best one win? They're betting on you down in the village, but I don't mind that!

BOY. Oh, *do* consider it, Dragon. It'll save such a lot of bother!

DRAGON RIGHT PAW. Believe me, St. George, there's nobody in the world I'd sooner oblige than you and this young gentleman here. But the whole thing's nonsense and conventionality and popular thick-headedness. There's absolutely nothing to fight about, from beginning to end. And anyhow, I'm not going to, so that settles it!

ST. GEORGE. But suppose I make you?

DRAGON TAIL. You can't. I should only go into my cave and retire for a time down the hole I came up. And as soon as you'd gone away, why I'd come up again. For I tell you frankly, I like this place, and I'm going to stay here!

ST. GEORGE (*looking around him*). This would make a beautiful place for a fight. These great rolling Downs, and me in my golden armor showing up against your big, blue, scaly coils! Think what a picture it would make!

DRAGON HEAD. Now you're trying to get at me through my artistic sensibilities. But it won't work. Not but what it would make a very pretty picture, as you say.

BOY. You must see, Dragon, that there's got to be a fight of some sort, 'cause you can't want to have to go down that dirty old hole again and stop there till goodness knows when.

ST. GEORGE (*thoughtfully*). The fight might be arranged—in other words, fixed. I *must* spear you somewhere, of course, but I'm not bound to hurt you very much. (*He walks the length of the* DRAGON, *looking him over.*) There's such a lot of you that there must be a few places where it wouldn't matter. (*He prods the* DRAGON *with his spear in several spots. Each time the* DRAGON *giggles.*) Here, for instance. Or here! Or here!

DRAGON LEFT PAW. You're tickling, George! Those places won't do at all.

ST. GEORGE. Let's try somewhere else, then. Here! (*Points his spear at the back folds of the* DRAGON'*s neck.*) All these folds of thick skin. If I speared you here, you'd never even know I'd done it!

DRAGON RIGHT PAW (*anxiously*). But are you sure you can hit the right place?

ST. GEORGE. Of course, I am. You leave that to me!

DRAGON TAIL. It's just because I've *got* to leave it to you that I'm asking.

BOY. Look here, Dragon, I don't see quite where your opinion counts! There's to be a fight, apparently, and you're to be licked. But what happens after the fight? What are you going to get out of it?

DRAGON HEAD. St. George, just tell him, please—what will happen after I'm vanquished in the deadly combat?

ST. GEORGE. Well, according to the rules, there'll be speeches and things, and I shall explain that you're converted and see the error of your ways and so on.

DRAGON LEFT PAW. Quite so. And then what will happen?

ST. GEORGE. Oh, and then—why, and then there will be the usual banquet, I suppose.

DRAGON RIGHT PAW. Exactly. And that's where I come in. I'm bored to death up here, and no one really appreciates my talents. This little episode will open doors for me. I'll be able to go into Society. You'll find I've got all the qualities to endear me to people! So now that's all settled. . . .

ST. GEORGE. Remember, you'll have to do your proper share of the fighting, Dragon! I mean ramping and breathing fire and so on!

DRAGON TAIL. I'll do the best I can. (*Yawns.*) And now, good night! (*He backs into his cave as the lights grow dim.*)

ST. GEORGE (*as he and the* BOY *leave*). I knew I had forgotten something. There ought to be a princess, terror stricken and chained to a rock, and all that sort of thing. Boy, can't you arrange a princess?

BOY (*yawning*). I'm tired to death, and I can't arrange a princess or anything more at this time of night. And my mother's sitting up, and *do* stop asking me to arrange things.

(*They are now off the stage, and the lights have dimmed until the stage is in blackness, for the night has come. After a few moments the light brightens. The* VILLAGERS *enter from different places in the audience. They are calling out to each other as they come to the stage in a holiday mood of festivity. They get the stools from the Inn and line them up across the back of the stage. Then they stand on them to watch the fight.*)

FIRST VILLAGER. Six to four on the dragon!
SECOND VILLAGER. Wait till we collect from you!
THIRD VILLAGER. Taken—and glad to!
FOURTH VILLAGER. I'll raise that!
FIFTH VILLAGER. Don't get too near that cave!
SIXTH VILLAGER. If the dragon wins, he'll take us on next!
SEVENTH VILLAGER. *If* he wins! Sure he'll win!
EIGHTH VILLAGER. Anyway, keep your distance from the cave!

(*The* BOY, *with his* MOTHER and FATHER, *joins the crowd at the right side of the stage.* MOTHER and FATHER *carry baskets of food.*)

BOY. He's coming! He's coming!
ALL (*cheer*). St. George! St. George!

(ST. GEORGE, *in all his splendor, strides down the center aisle of the audience. He comes to center stage and bows to the cheering crowd. Then he walks magnificently to stage right and poses.*)

ALL. Now then, Dragon!!

(*The* DRAGON, *with great snorts and bellows, comes from his cave. He lashes his tail, claws the ground, and gives a good show of fierceness.*)

ALL. Oh, well done, Dragon! Well done!

(*The* Dragon *bows and poses at stage left.*)

First Villager (*waving a banner*). Round One!
All. Round One!

(St. George *lowers his spear and rushes at the* Dragon. *The crowd is breathless. The* Dragon *snorts, roars, squeals, and dodges.*)

All. Missed! Missed!

(St. George *strides back to his place at stage right. He wipes his brow and winks at the* Boy.)

All. End of Round One!

(*The* Dragon *gives a ramping exhibit, which terrifies the crowd. Then he bows and poses.* St. George *nods that he is ready.*)

All. Time! Round Two!

(St. George *rushes at the* Dragon, *who leaps from side to side, bellowing and snorting.*)

ALL. Missed! End of Round Two!

(ST. GEORGE *returns to stage right, sighing heavily. He pats the* BOY *on the shoulder and gives him his spear to hold while the* DRAGON *entertains the crowd with a little dance.*)

ALL. Time! Round Three!

(ST. GEORGE, *with spear lowered, advances carefully. The* DRAGON *circles. They spar while the crowd is silent and breathless. Then a quick movement of* ST. GEORGE'*s spear pins the* DRAGON *to the earth.* ST. GEORGE *stands astride the* DRAGON.)

ALL (*cheering and clapping wildly*). St. George! St. George!! St. George!!!

FIRST VILLAGER (*above the cheers*). Aren't you going to cut his head off, master?

ST. GEORGE (*commands silence with a gesture*). There's no hurry about that, you know. I have a few words to say first. (*The crowd listens.*) My friends! I have removed your direful scourge. Now I want to ask the dragon a few questions. Do you, Dragon, see that there are two sides to everything? (*The* DRAGON *nods.*) Are you going to be bad any more? (*The* DRAGON *shakes his head.*) Would you like to stay and settle down here in a peaceful sort of way? (*The* DRAGON *nods vigorously.* ST. GEORGE *draws the*

spear out of the DRAGON*'s neck. The* DRAGON *sits up and shakes hands with* ST. GEORGE, *who then turns to the* VILLAGERS.) Now, my friends, I do not want you to be prejudiced any more. You are never to go around grumbling and fancying that you have grievances. And you should not be so fond of fights, because next time you might have to do the fighting yourselves, which is not at all the same thing. And now I think we should have some refreshments!

ALL. Refreshments! Celebration! Party! Food! Drink! That's what we'll have!

(MOTHER *and* FATHER *start passing out food and drink. When everyone's cup has been filled,* ST. GEORGE *pats the happy* DRAGON *on the head.*)

ST. GEORGE (*lifting a cup*). And now I give you—your friend from now on—the dragon!

ALL. Our friend—the dragon!

(The DRAGON *bows courteously as they all drink to him. The* BOY *runs to the* DRAGON *and hugs him as the curtain closes.)*

Reflections

1. Do you think the Villagers were more interested in eliminating the dragon or in watching a good fight? Give reasons for your opinion.
2. Do you think the Boy always kept the dragon's best interests in mind? Why or why not?
3. Have you ever wanted to have someone do your fighting for you? Tell about the situation.
4. Write another scene for this play. You may choose one of the following situations or make up one of your own.
   a. The Villagers invite the dragon to a dance.
   b. The Boy and his family go to the dragon's cave for dinner.

In the Theater

There is much more to putting on a play than having a script, a cast, and a director. Many kinds of people work behind the scenes to make the play a smash hit.

The **set designer** plans the scenery. He makes sketches and often builds small models of a room, a street, or even a castle. Then **stage hands** get to work building and painting the sets that will serve as backgrounds for the action.

When the scenery is finished, the **lighting director** decides how and when the stage should be lit. She works out a cue sheet that shows when each light should be turned on and off.

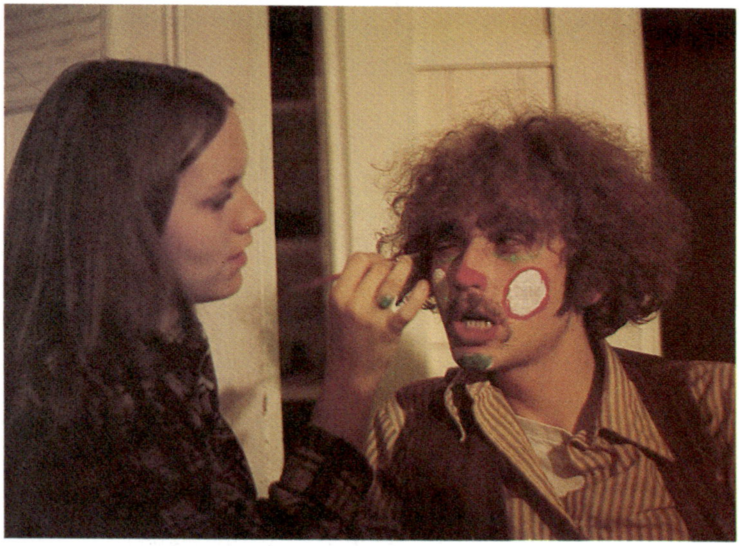

The **costume designer** *(above)* plans the clothes the members of the cast will wear. Patterns are made from drawings, and workers sew the costumes and make sure they fit.

A **makeup person** *(above)* plays an important part in changing an actor into a character in a play. Makeup can help turn a young woman into a grandmother and a young man into an aging clown.

In her large notebook, the **stage manager** *(left)* writes down everything that happens in the play. She keeps a record of the lighting and sound cues, where the actors stand, and when they speak. She supplies cues to whoever needs them.

The **ticket seller** closes the window; the **ushers** show the audience to their seats. The house lights dim. While the audience waits for the curtain to rise, all the people who helped stage the play stand in the wings and wish the actors good luck.

5 ENTRANCE PLACE OF WONDERS

I Am Glad Daylong

I am glad daylong for the gift of song
For time and change and sorrow;
For the sunset wings and the world-end things
Which hang on the edge of tomorrow.
I am glad for my heart whose gates apart
Are the entrance-place of wonders,
Where dreams come in from the rush and din
Like sheep from the rains and thunders.

William Stanley Braithwaite

The Dun Horse

GEORGE BIRD GRINNELL

Many years ago there lived in the Pawnee tribe an old woman and her grandson. These people were very poor. They were so poor that they were looked down upon by the rest of the tribe. They had nothing of their own. Whenever the village moved the camp from one place to another, these two would stay behind to pick up anything that the other Indians had thrown away. In this way they would sometimes get pieces of robes, worn-out moccasins with holes in them, and bits of meat.

One day, after the tribe had moved away from its camp, this old woman and her grandson were following along the trail behind the rest. Suddenly they saw a miserable old dun horse standing before them. They supposed he had been left behind by some Indians. He was thin and exhausted, and he was blind in one eye. He had a bad sore back, and one of his forelegs was badly swollen. In fact, he was so worthless that none of the Pawnees had wanted to drive him along with them. But when the old woman and her grandson came along, the boy said, "Come now, we will take this old horse. We can make him carry our pack." So the old woman put her pack on the horse and drove him along.

The tribe moved up the North Platte until they came to Court House Rock. The two poor Indians followed them and camped with the others. One day while they were here, a young Indian came hurrying into camp. He told the chiefs that a large herd of buffalo was near and that among the buffalo was a spotted calf.

When the Head Chief of the Pawnees heard this, he ordered the young man to go through the village and call out that the man who killed that spotted calf should have his beautiful daughter for his wife. A spotted robe is *ti-war'-uks-ti*—big medicine.

The buffalo were feeding about four miles from the village. The chiefs decided that the charge should be made from there. In this way the man who had the fastest horse would be the most likely to kill the calf. Then all the warriors and the young men picked out their speediest horses and made ready to start.

Among those who prepared for the charge was the poor boy on the old dun horse. But when all the rich young braves on their fast horses saw him, they pointed at him and said, "Oh, there is the horse that is going to catch the spotted calf." And they laughed at him, so that the poor boy was ashamed. He rode off to one side of the crowd, where he could not hear their jokes and laughter.

When he had ridden off a little way, the horse stopped and turned his head around. He spoke to the boy. "Take me down to the creek and cover me all over with mud." When the boy heard the horse speak, he was afraid. But he did as he was told.

Then the horse said, "Now mount, but do not ride back to the warriors. Stay right here until the word is given to charge." So the boy stayed.

Soon all the fine horses were lined up. The old crier gave the word, *"Loo-ah!"*—Go! Then the Pawnees all leaned forward on their horses and yelled, and away they went.

Suddenly, away off to the right, the old dun horse appeared. He did not seem to run. He seemed to sail along like a bird. He passed all the fastest horses, and in a moment he was among the buffalo. He picked out the spotted calf and charged up alongside of it.

U-ra-rish! The boy's arrow flew. The calf fell. Then the boy drew another arrow and killed a fat cow that was running by. He dismounted and skinned the calf and the cow. Then he packed all the meat on the horse and put the spotted robe on top of the load. He started back to the camp on foot, leading the dun horse.

Pretty soon the boy came to the lodge where he and his grandmother lived. When the old woman saw him leading the dun horse with the load of meat and the robes on it, she was very surprised. The boy said to her, "Here, I have brought you plenty of meat to eat, and here is a robe that you may have for yourself." Then the old woman laughed, for her heart was glad.

That night the horse spoke again to the boy. He said, "Tomorrow the Sioux are coming—a large war party. They will attack the village, and you will have a great battle. Now, when the Sioux are all ready to fight, you jump onto me. Ride as hard as you can, right into the middle of the Sioux. Go up to their Head Chief, their greatest warrior, and kill him. Then ride back. Do this four times to four of the bravest Sioux warriors. But don't go again. If you go the fifth time, you might be killed, or else you might lose me. Remember." So the boy promised.

The next day it happened as the horse had said. The Sioux came down and formed in line of battle. The boy took his bow and arrows and jumped on the dun horse. He charged into the midst of them. When the Sioux saw that he was going to strike their Head Chief, they all shot their arrows at him. The arrows flew so thickly across each other that they darkened the sky. But none of them hit the boy.

And he killed the Chief and then rode back. After that he charged again and killed the bravest Sioux warrior. He did this twice more until he had gone four times as the horse had told him.

But the Sioux and the Pawnees kept on fighting. The boy stood and watched the battle. At last he said to himself, "I have killed four Sioux, and I am all right. I am not hurt anywhere. Why may I not go again?"

So he jumped on the dun horse and charged again. But when he got among the Sioux, one Sioux warrior drew an arrow and shot. The arrow struck the dun horse, and he fell down dead. The boy jumped off and fought his way back through the Sioux. He ran away as fast as he could go to the Pawnees.

Now as soon as the horse was killed, the Sioux said to each other, "This horse was like a person. He was brave. He was not like a horse." And they took their knives and hatchets and cut him into small pieces.

The Pawnees and Sioux fought all day long. But toward night the Sioux broke away and rode off.

The boy felt very bad that he had lost his horse. After the fight was over, he went out to where it had taken place to mourn for his horse. He went to the spot where the horse lay, and he gathered up all the pieces of flesh. He put them all together in a pile. Then he went off to the top of a hill nearby and sat down. He drew his robe over his head and began to mourn.

As he sat there, he heard a great windstorm coming up. It passed over him with a loud rushing sound. After the wind came a rain. The boy looked down to the pile of flesh and bones, which was all that was left of his horse. He could just see it through the rain. And the rain passed by, and his heart was heavy.

Pretty soon came another rushing wind, and after it, a rain. The boy looked through the driving rain toward the spot where the pieces lay. He thought that they seemed to come together and take shape. The pile looked like a horse lying down, but he could not see well through the rain.

After this came a third storm like the others. Now when the boy looked toward the horse, he thought he saw its tail move. And it seemed to lift its head from the ground. The boy was afraid and wanted to run away, but he stayed.

As he waited, there came another storm. And while the rain fell, the boy saw the horse raise himself up on his forelegs and look about. Then the dun horse stood up.

The boy left the hilltop and went down to the horse. When he came near, the horse said, "*Ti-ra'-wa* has been good and has let me come back to you. After this, do what I tell you, not any more, not any less. Now lead me off, far away from the camp, behind that big hill. Leave me there tonight, and in the morning, come for me." The boy did as he was told.

When he went for the horse in the morning, he found with him a beautiful white horse, much more handsome than any horse in the tribe. That night the dun horse told the boy to take him again to the place behind the big hill and to come for him the next morning.

When the boy went for him again, he found with him a beautiful black horse. And so for ten nights he left the horse among the hills. And each

morning he found a different-colored horse. All of them were finer than any horses that the Pawnees had ever had in their tribe before.

Now the boy was rich, and he married the beautiful daughter of the Head Chief. When he became older, he was made Head Chief himself. He always took good care of his old grandmother and kept her in his own lodge until she died.

No one ever rode the dun horse. But he was always led about with the Chief wherever he went. The horse lived in the village for many years until he became very old. And at last he died.

Reflections

1. The other Pawnee Indians scorned the dun horse, but the boy found a use for him. What qualities do you think determine worth or value?
2. What did the dun horse do to help the poor boy become a rich and powerful chief?
3. What *two* things caused the death of the dun horse?
4. What do you think is the most exciting part of this story? What is the most mysterious part? Give reasons for your answer.
5. To judge from this story, how did the Pawnee Indians feel about people who are weak or poor? What did the Pawnees admire in a person? Skim the story again for clues before you express your opinion.
6. What might the boy have been saying to himself as he sat on the hill in the wind and the rain? Write a paragraph expressing some of his thoughts.

Pueblo Artist

Song of the Sky Loom

O our Mother the Earth,
O our Father the Sky,
Your children are we,
and with tired backs
We bring you the gifts
you love.
Then weave for us a garment
of brightness;
May the warp be the white
light of morning,
May the weft be the red
light of evening,
May the fringes be the
falling rain,
May the border be the
standing rainbow,
Thus weave for us a garment
of brightness,
That we may walk fittingly
where birds sing,
That we may walk fittingly
where grass is green,
O our Mother the Earth,
O our Father the Sky.

PABLITA VELARDE

The ancient artists and storytellers of the pueblos are gone, but painter Pablita Velarde has kept them alive in her art. From her father, she heard stories out of the Indian past. As a little girl, she learned the Tewa poems like "Song of the Sky Loom." Pablita Velarde's ancestors also spoke to her from the pictures painted on the flat rock walls of the ancient ruins on the Santa Clara pueblo where she was born. All of these influences have been incorporated by Pablita Velarde into her paintings.

A well-known painter, Pablita Velarde has captured the Pueblo present and past in oil paints and water colors. But her favorite source of color is the earth itself—natural colors from stones that she transforms into the form and feeling of Indian life.

The unusual technique Pablita Velarde uses is her own. She gathers stones and grinds them into powder on a *metate*—a stone with a concave surface that is used as a millstone for grinding corn. *(top right)*

She uses ordinary sea shells to hold the powdered stone—each color in its own shell. *(bottom right)*

Another common utensil—the muffin tin—is used to mix and hold the paints. (page 377, *top left*) Spooning out some of the colored powder, Pablita Velarde mixes it with water and glue in one of the cups of the tray.

Soon all the colors are ready and the artist goes to work. When her painting is finished, she uses a broad brush to add a background wash. *(top right)*

These ceremonial dancers and the traditional designs on their costumes *(bottom left)* are an example of Pablita Velarde's finished work. She has used the past to create a modern work of art.

Captain Stormalong Meets a Kraken

WALTER BLAIR

Captain Alfred Bulltop Stormalong was a seagoing Down East Yankee. He was a sailor in the days when wooden ships and iron-muscled men traveled over the seven blue seas. Where Alfred was born, nobody knows for sure. Some say Kittery, some say Kennebunkport, some say Nantucket. Wherever it was, at that time the land in New England wasn't too good for farming. That's why many of the Down Easters in those parts went away to sea. Among them was Alfred.

One morning in Ogunquit, the owner of the trim schooner called the *Silver Maid* was signing up hands for a voyage. The *Maid* was going to take a cargo of furs and hides to China. Then it was coming home with a cargo of silks and spices and tea. The owner wanted a crew that could step lively.

The owner looked up from his desk and saw a fellow standing there, about a fathom long.

"It seems my name is Alfred Bulltop Stormalong," said the fellow, "and I sort of think I want to be a cabin boy."

"A tall fellow like you?" said the owner.

"Well, I think maybe I'm a bit too big for my township. And maybe I'm a tiny bit overgrown for my age."

"How old are you?" asked the owner.

"My folks say that I'm twelve, sort of going on thirteen."

"Well, that's about the right age for a cabin boy, sure enough. Are you healthy?" asked the owner.

"Sort of," Alfred told him. "I can crack a coconut with one hand, if I can get a coconut. I can throw a salt mackerel a few feet farther than any young one in the township, they tell me. When it comes to swimming, I'm as slick as an eel in a keg full of oysters. I'm not considered sickly, by most people, that is."

"I see," said the owner. "You might do pretty well." And he signed him up as a cabin boy.

On that trip Alfred learned how to be an A.B.S.—able-bodied seaman. He learned how to climb up to the crow's nest. He found out the way to talk the seagoing lingo. And he took lessons in tying sailor knots. That was what led to his doing the first thing that won fame for him.

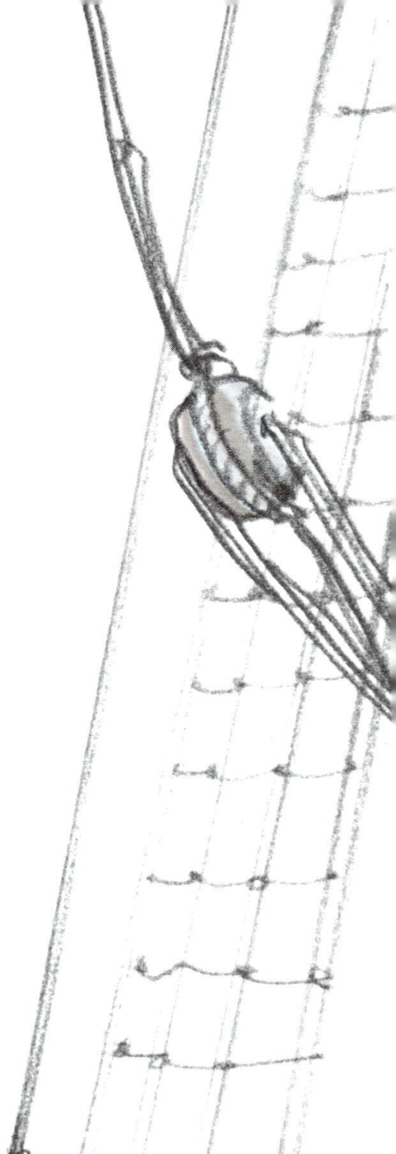

One day the *Silver Maid* was moving along under full sail, when all of a sudden—it stopped. The pans in the cook's galley clattered in a clutter on the floor. Some sailors scrubbing the deck went skidding along until they could grab a mast. And three sailors that had just come off watch and started to take a snooze were plunked out of their bunks.

The white sails bellied in the wind. The masts creaked. But the ship stood still as a picture.

Everybody who was on board—even the cabin boy—knew what was the trouble, quick as a wink. Either a Kraken had laid hold of the keel with his tentacles, or a Remora Monster had fastened on to the bottom of the vessel with his suckers. And there was no telling when the rascal would let go. Remora Monsters had been known to hold on to a vessel until everyone aboard had got mighty hungry. And Krakens had been known to hang on until everybody aboard had starved.

The captain trotted around, wringing his hands and carrying on. "What'll we do?" he moaned.

Nobody answered. But Alfred ripped off his jacket and then dived into the ocean. After he'd been under the water a minute or two, there was a big welling and swelling of waves under the ship. Then there was another and another, up to the number of ten. Then, after the tenth heave, the *Silver Maid* gave a jerk and started moving along over the water again.

When they looked, the crew saw Alfred Stormalong bob out of the ocean. He sputtered, took his bearings, and started swimming after the *Maid*. He reached her quicker than you could say "Mother Carey's chickens." He grabbed a rope and climbed aboard. He was panting a little when he stood dripping on the poop deck.

"What was it?" the crew asked him. "How'd you handle it?"

"Well," said Stormalong, "it appeared to be a Kraken. But I guess perhaps I fixed him. I tied

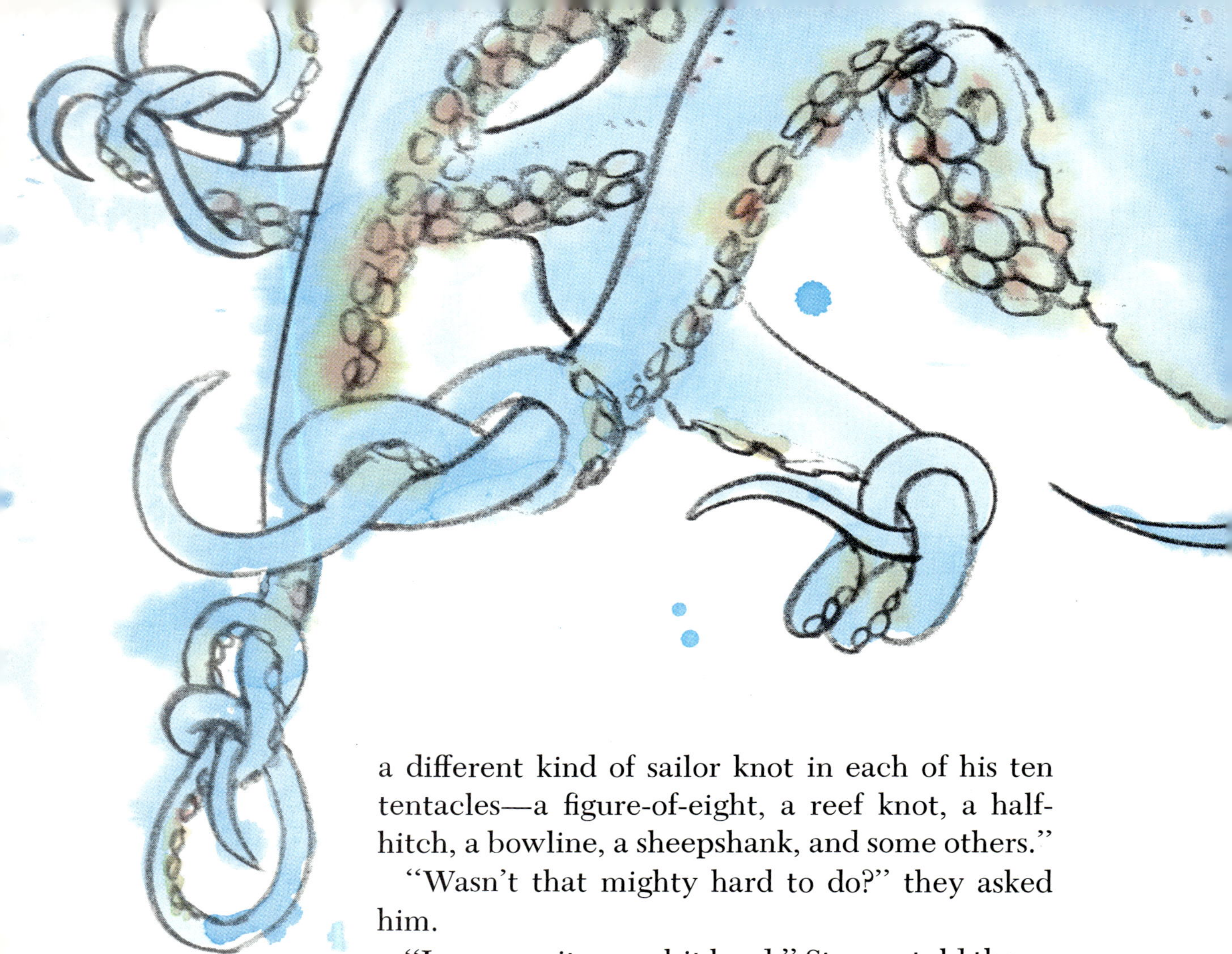

a different kind of sailor knot in each of his ten tentacles—a figure-of-eight, a reef knot, a half-hitch, a bowline, a sheepshank, and some others."

"Wasn't that mighty hard to do?" they asked him.

"I suppose it was a bit hard," Stormy told them. "I had to kind of hold my breath. There were a few sharks and whales and such that kept more or less bumping into me. And the Kraken wasn't what I'd call helpful. I tend to think that he may not be able to stop many ships for a while."

"How'd he take it?" the crew wanted to know. "Did he get snorting mad and tear around?"

"There's a bare chance, from the way he acted," Stormalong told them, "that the fellow was just a wee bit peeved."

Reflections

1. In what ways was Alfred unusual for a twelve-year-old boy?
2. Which words or phrases below would you use to describe Alfred? Support your choices in each case with evidence from the story.
   a. modest
   b. courageous
   c. slow-speaking
   d. timid
   e. strong
   f. excitable
   g. self-controlled
   h. boastful
   i. resourceful
3. In what way did Alfred's lessons in knot tying start him on the road to fame?
4. Which would be worse, to have a Kraken or a Remora Monster fasten itself to the bottom of your boat? Explain your answer.
5. At one point Alfred said that he was "as slick as an eel in a keg full of oysters." What other things can you think of that would be as slick as that?
6. What do you think a Remora Monster might look like? Write a vivid description of one, guaranteed to send chills down a sailor's spine!

Clipper Ships and Captains

ROSEMARY and STEPHEN VINCENT BENÉT

There was a time before our time,
It will not come again,
When the best ships still were wooden ships,
But the men were iron men.

From Stonington to Kennebunk
The Yankee hammers plied,
To build the clippers of the wave
That were New England's pride.

The *Flying Cloud*, the *Northern Light*,
The *Sovereign of the Seas*—
There was salt music in the blood
That thought of names like these.

Sea Witch, Red Jacket, Golden Age,
And *Chariot of Fame*—
The whole world gaped to look at them
Before the steamship came.

Their cargoes were of tea and gold,
And their bows a cutting blade;
And, on the poop, the skippers walked,
Lords of the China trade;

The skippers with the little beards
And the New England drawl,
Who knew Hong Kong and Marblehead
And the Pole Star over all.

Stately as churches, swift as gulls,
They trod the oceans, then;
No man had seen such ships before
And none will see again.

The Adventures of Paul Bunyan

DELL J. McCORMICK

The Red River

When Paul Bunyan arrived on the Big Onion, the first thing he set out to do was to build the largest logging camp in the world. People from miles around came to see it when it was finished. It was so big that when it was breakfast time in the kitchen, it was dinner time in the blacksmith shop at the other end of the camp.

Paul bought a great watch so that everybody would know when it was mealtime. It was four feet across the face, and he tied it to his trousers pocket with a logging chain. Of course, it cost a lot of money, but Paul said it gained enough time in the first three days to pay for itself.

At dinner time Hot Biscuit Slim, the cook, would blow a huge dinner horn. It was so large and made such a noise that he knocked down two hundred trees and started a windstorm on the Gulf of Mexico. After that they decided not to use it. Later they sold it, and the tin was used to put a new roof on the Capitol at Washington.

Day by day the camp covered more ground until the men had to take a week's food with them when they walked from one end of it to the other. Even the smokestack on the kitchen was so high, they had to have it hinged in the middle to let the clouds go by. The dining room

tables were two miles long. The cookhouse boys wore roller skates so they could serve the food quickly.

Everything was on a huge scale. Even those crumbs that fell on the floor were so big that the chipmunks who ate them grew as large as wolves. They chased all the bears out of the country. Later the settlers who came shot them for tigers!

Finally all the logs were cut and floated down the Onion River to the mills. Paul decided to move on into a new country directly west. The new country was later known as the Red River Valley.

The Red River got its name from Paul's camp. It seems one of Paul's cookhouse boys drove a catsup wagon in the dining room. Every meal the men ate so much catsup that the boy would only get halfway around when his wagon would be empty.

This made him so angry that one day he tipped the catsup wagon over and left camp. The catsup

ran down into the river and colored the water red. To this day, that part of the country is known as the Red River Valley.

When Paul moved his camp into the new country, he found that the dining room was still too small for all his men. Every day dinner would be from two to three hours late. Paul was angry and shouted, "Hot Biscuit Slim!" Three men who were standing beside him were blown over by the force of his voice.

Hot Biscuit Slim came on the run. Paul said, "I want a larger kitchen, where two hundred cooks can work at the same time. Also, build a larger dining room. Make the tables six miles long! Yesterday the men sat down to dinner, and it was lunchtime the next day before the food arrived. By that time the biscuits were cold, and who wants cold biscuits?"

So they cleared the forest for miles around and built a huge kitchen and dining room. Ole the Big Swede, the blacksmith, made a huge black kettle. It held eleven hundred gallons of soup.

When Hot Biscuit Slim made soup, he rowed out into the center of the kettle with boatloads of cabbages, turnips, and potatoes and shoveled them into the boiling hot water. In a few hours they had wonderful vegetable soup.

Next the blacksmith made a ten-acre griddle pan for hot cakes. Hot Biscuit Slim strapped flat sides of bacon on the feet of the cookhouse boys.

They skated back and forth over the huge griddle until it was well greased.

They thought it was great fun and played tag and crack the whip. The griddle was hot, and they sometimes fell and burned their trousers. When the griddle began to steam, it became so foggy, no one could see across it.

Every Sunday morning for breakfast, Paul's campers had hot griddle cakes. They were so large, it took five men to eat one. Paul himself ate twelve or fourteen. The cookhouse boys worked all day Saturday mixing dough and bringing in huge barrels of maple syrup.

Sunday dinner, however, was the biggest meal of the week. Hot Biscuit Slim would cook the very best soup and serve it with the finest vegetables and the nicest spring chickens.

One Saturday he said to Ole the Big Swede, "Tomorrow I am going to have the best Sunday

dinner of the year. When the men are through eating my hot biscuits with jelly, spinach, cucumbers, young red radishes, and chicken pie, they won't be able to eat a mouthful of dessert."

Cream Puff Fatty, who made the desserts, overheard this. He was very angry, for his pride was hurt. "So Hot Biscuit Slim thinks they won't eat any dessert. We shall see!" said he.

Cream Puff Fatty called the dessert boys together and said, "We will make cream puffs that will melt in your mouth! Light creamy ones, with whipped cream a foot high! We shall see if they refuse to eat dessert!"

The dinner hour arrived. The men sat down to eat. Soup, vegetables, and salads disappeared as the men ate and ate. When the chicken pie arrived, they were almost full.

"Oh, look! Chicken pie!" they shouted. They ate the chicken pie. Then the cookhouse boys on roller skates brought in more large platters of food.

"Hot biscuits and jelly! Hurrah!" they cried. They ate the biscuits, and there didn't seem to be room for another mouthful of food. Cream Puff Fatty was in despair. He looked down the long dining room. The men were almost finished. It looked as if they couldn't eat another mouthful.

"Now is the time, boys!" cried Cream Puff Fatty. The dessert boys strapped on their roller skates and started down the long tables.

"Cream puffs! Cream puffs!" the men shouted as they saw large plates of fluffy white cakes topped with whipped cream. With a shout they picked up their forks and started eating again. Not a man left the dining room! Every single cream puff was eaten!

"Three cheers for Cream Puff Fatty!" yelled the men.

The fat little dessert cook had tears of joy in his eyes. "It was a wonderful dinner!" said Cream Puff Fatty as he shook hands with Hot Biscuit Slim.

The Popcorn Blizzard

When Paul Bunyan had cut down all the trees in North Dakota, he decided to go west. It was summertime, and the forest was sweet with the smell of green trees. The spreading branches that reached toward the sky cast their cool shadows on the ground.

"We must cross vast plains," said Paul to his men, "where it is so hot that not even a blade of grass can grow. You must not become too thirsty, as there will be very little water to drink."

With Paul and Babe the Blue Ox leading the way, the camp then started across the plains on their long journey west. In a few days they had left the woods and were knee deep in sand that stretched out before them for miles and miles. The sun became hotter and hotter!

"I made some vanilla ice cream," said Hot Biscuit Slim one day, as he gave the men their lunch, "but the ice became so hot under this boiling sun that I couldn't touch it!"

Tiny Tim, the water boy, was so hot and tired that Paul had to put him up on Babe's back, where he rode the rest of the trip. Every time Babe took a step forward, he moved ahead two miles. Tiny Tim had to hold on with all his might. Even Ole the Big Swede, who was so strong he could carry a full-grown horse under each arm, began to tire.

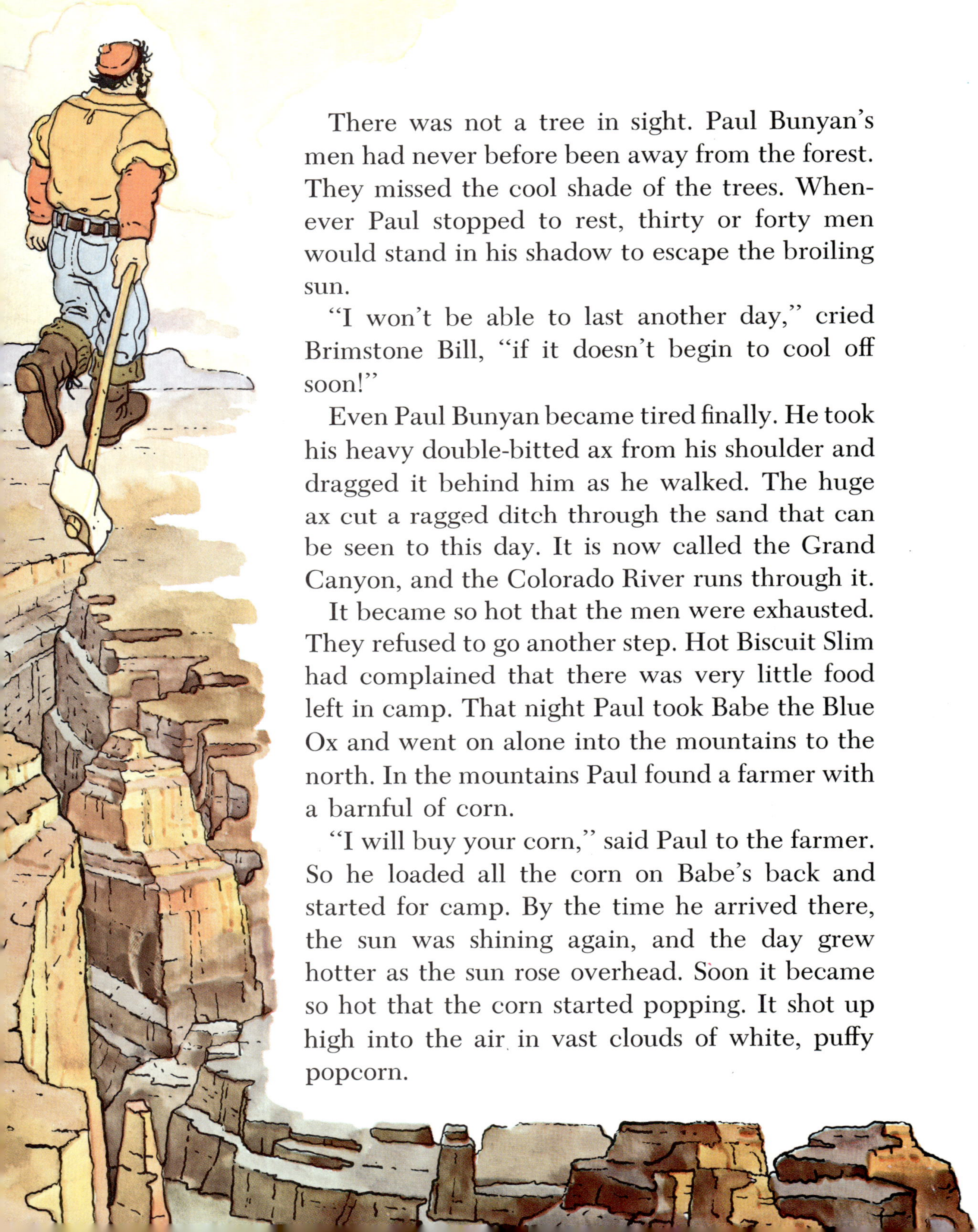

There was not a tree in sight. Paul Bunyan's men had never before been away from the forest. They missed the cool shade of the trees. Whenever Paul stopped to rest, thirty or forty men would stand in his shadow to escape the broiling sun.

"I won't be able to last another day," cried Brimstone Bill, "if it doesn't begin to cool off soon!"

Even Paul Bunyan became tired finally. He took his heavy double-bitted ax from his shoulder and dragged it behind him as he walked. The huge ax cut a ragged ditch through the sand that can be seen to this day. It is now called the Grand Canyon, and the Colorado River runs through it.

It became so hot that the men were exhausted. They refused to go another step. Hot Biscuit Slim had complained that there was very little food left in camp. That night Paul took Babe the Blue Ox and went on alone into the mountains to the north. In the mountains Paul found a farmer with a barnful of corn.

"I will buy your corn," said Paul to the farmer. So he loaded all the corn on Babe's back and started for camp. By the time he arrived there, the sun was shining again, and the day grew hotter as the sun rose overhead. Soon it became so hot that the corn started popping. It shot up high into the air in vast clouds of white, puffy popcorn.

It kept popping and popping, and soon the air was filled with wonderful white popcorn. It came down all over the camp and almost covered the kitchen. The ground became white with popcorn as far as the eye could see. It fell like a snowstorm until everything was covered two feet deep with fluffy popcorn.

"A snowstorm! A snowstorm!" cried the men as they saw it falling. Never had they seen anything like it before. Some ran into the bunkhouses and put on their mittens, and others put on heavy overcoats and woolen caps. They clapped each other on the back and laughed and shouted and jumped for joy.

"Let's make snowshoes!" cried Ole the Big Swede. So they all made snowshoes and waded around in the white popcorn and threw popcorn snowballs at each other. Everybody forgot how hot it had been the day before. Even the horses thought it was real snow. Some of them almost froze to death before the men could put woolen blankets on them and lead them to shelter. Babe the Blue Ox knew it was only popcorn and winked at Paul.

Paul Bunyan chuckled to himself at the popcorn blizzard. He decided to start west again while the men were feeling so happy. He found them all huddled around the kitchen fire.

"Now is the time to move on west," said Paul, "before it begins to get hot again." So they packed up and started. The men waded through the popcorn and blew on their hands to keep them warm. Some claimed their feet were frostbitten, and others rubbed their ears to keep them from freezing.

After traveling for a few weeks more, they saw ahead of them the great forest they had set out to reach. They cheered Paul Bunyan who had led them safely over the hot desert plains. Babe the Blue Ox laughed and winked at Paul whenever anyone mentioned the great blizzard.

Reflections

1. This selection is made up of episodes (separate happenings) concerning Paul Bunyan and his men. Which one of these episodes did you enjoy most?
2. Would you have enjoyed being a cookhouse boy in Paul Bunyan's camp? Why or why not?
3. Why did Babe wink at Paul every time the "blizzard" was mentioned.
4. Write a report on another legendary hero that you know about from books, movies, or television. Describe some of the strange and wonderful things that person does.

Johnny Appleseed
(1775–1847)

ROSEMARY and STEPHEN VINCENT BENÉT

Of Jonathan Chapman
Two things are known,
That he loved apples,
That he walked alone.

At seventy-odd
He was gnarled as could be,
But ruddy and sound
As a good apple tree.

For fifty years over
Of harvest and dew,
He planted his apples
Where no apples grew.

The winds of the prairie
Might blow through his rags,
But he carried his seeds
In the best deerskin bags.

From old Ashtabula
To frontier Fort Wayne,
He planted and pruned
And he planted again.

He had not a hat
To encumber his head.
He wore a tin pan
On his white hair instead.

He nested with owl,
And with bear-cub and possum,
And knew all his orchards
Root, tendril and blossom.

A fine old man,
As ripe as a pippin,
His heart still light,
And his step still skipping.

The stalking Indian,
The beast in its lair
Did no hurt
While he was there.

For they could tell,
As wild things can,
That Jonathan Chapman
Was God's own man.

Why did he do it?
We do not know.
He wished that apples
Might root and grow.

He has no statue.
He has no tomb.
He has his apple trees
Still in bloom.

Consider, consider,
Think well upon
The marvelous story
Of Appleseed John.

SAVE THE FOREST!

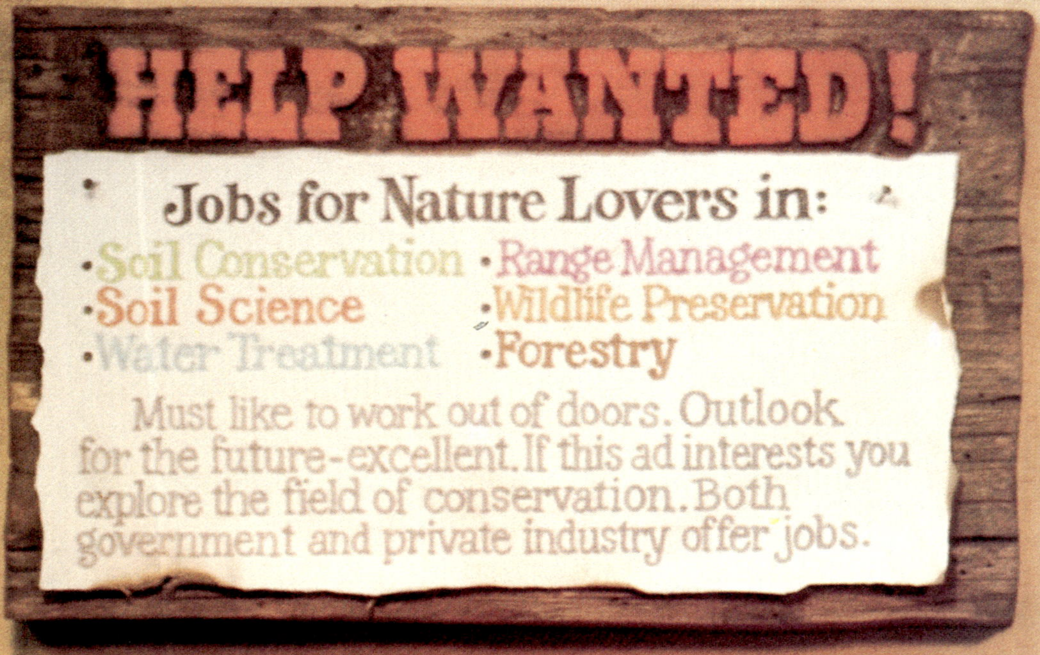

Soil conservation technicians survey the land. They make plans for protecting the soil from erosion and for keeping rivers from flooding.

Soil scientists make tests that will help farmers choose the crops that will grow best on their land. They also suggest ways to make the soil produce more and better crops.

Waste water treatment operators work in plants to develop ways of treating waste products and to keep our rivers and lakes clean.

(*top*) **Rangers** employed by the National Park System protect the wildlife and plants in the parks. They drop food to starving animals in winter and help them if they are injured.

Foresters plant new trees and inspect old ones. Some fight forest fires. This forester (*bottom*) works for a paper company. She is taking a sample from the core of a tree to check it for disease.

General Moses

DOROTHY STERLING

Harriet Tubman crossed the line dividing the free states from the slave six times, twelve times, eighteen times. The count of the men and women and children she led to the North ran into the hundreds. From Canada to the Gulf of Mexico, Americans knew of her plodding feet. They talked of her in the swamps of Virginia and the blue hills of Kentucky, and in Maryland's rolling fields. To the slaves, she became known as "Moses," and the many stories about her became legends.

"Moses is tall—wisest woman you ever did see," a man said.

"Her eyes can pierce the distance like an eagle. Like a cat, she can see on the darkest night," a woman boasted.

"Moses runs faster than the rabbits, climbs trees like the possums, jumps over fences, flies over streams," the children whispered, their eyes big with wonder.

"She can hear a patroller sneeze twenty miles away."

"The fiercest dog will lick her hand."

These are the things the slaves said about Harriet Tubman. When she headed South, three words went ahead of her, buzzing over the grapevine telegraph until they became a chant: "Moses is coming!"

Then, under the cover of night, dark forms stole to the woods to meet their deliverer. In marshes along the Bay, a slender ladies' maid named Tilly hid in the tall grass for days, on the watch for Moses. A husky field hand with a torn, bleeding back whispered in his neighbor's ear, "Next time Moses comes, let me know."

The slaveowners talked of Harriet Tubman too. "She has stolen thousands of dollars of my property," one said. "We've got to stop her."

"Every time she steals five slaves, ten more take to their heels on their own. We've got to stop her," the others agreed.

The cities of Maryland, Delaware, and Virginia were plastered with handbills describing

Harriet Tubman. Offers of rewards mounted from \$1,000 to \$5,000 to \$10,000, until she was worth \$40,000 to the man bringing her in, dead or alive.

These things made Harriet's friends proud and anxious. "What has become of Harriet Tubman?" they asked. "It would be a sorrowful fact if such a hero as she should be lost from the Underground Railroad."

But Harriet was not caught to be shot or hanged or burned alive. Fearless, she was never reckless. Each expedition into enemy territory was thoughtfully planned and carefully executed. She had a combination of courage and cunning which would have done honor to a general.

As a scout, she knew the hidden paths through forests and swamps, and the houses which offered shelter along the highway. She knew the potato holes in the cabins, the secret rooms in barns, the hollowed-out haystacks in the fields.

As a spy, she used disguises and passwords, forged documents and secret signals. But these weapons of warfare were always selected with

the greatest simplicity. A plain woman, she dressed plainly. Her disguise depended on a man's hat, an old lady's shawl, a hoe, a broom, a market basket. Passwords were drawn from the common speech of her people, or from the noises of the night birds in the woods. Her signals were carried by snatches of song, "Go Down, Moses" and "When That Old Chariot Comes," with a change in words or a verse sung twice to carry a warning to her listeners.

When she attacked, she made sure of taking the enemy by surprise. On Saturday nights and in the week between Christmas and New Year's Day there were gay parties in the big houses. Masters and overseers ate and drank and danced, giving little thought to their human property. It was on these nights that Harriet held her parties too, assembling them by the lights streaming from the curtained windows, marching them North with the music of the fiddlers in their ears.

Harriet knew when to advance boldly and when to retreat. If slaveowners hired men to tack up posters advertising her runaways, she paid

others to tear them down. If the hounds were baying in the woods and the roads blocked by posses, she turned her party around. For a few stops she rode with them on a southbound train, confident that people heading for the cotton fields would never be suspected of running away.

Strict military discipline was enforced while her infantry was on the march. Harriet was all kindness, yet as hard as granite. When slave mothers tired of carrying their babies on the long trek northward, she rocked them to sleep in the ticking bag tied to her waist, singing them lullabies as she strode along.

She would carry exhausted men or women in her arms, bind their wounds, and deny herself to feed them. But if terror made strong men weak and brave women faint of heart, Harriet permitted no turning back. With her pistol at their shoulder blades, her voice was firm and her meaning clear.

"There's no going back on this road. Move or die! Dead men tell no tales."

There were no traitors on Harriet Tubman's trips.

Harriet Tubman had crossed the line into enemy territory nineteen times, leading more than three hundred slaves to freedom.

"As a conductor of the Underground Railroad, I can say what most conductors can't," and she grinned. "I never ran my train off the track and I never lost a passenger."

Reflections

1. Why did the plantation owners offer rewards for the capture "dead or alive" of Harriet Tubman? What "property" of the plantation owners did they accuse her of stealing?
2. Moses in the Bible led his people out of slavery in Egypt. Why did people call Harriet Tubman "Moses"? In what ways was she like him?
3. Harriet Tubman was a real person. How did she become a legend?
4. Make a list of some problems and hardships Harriet Tubman and her people might have had on their way North. Then write an essay on this topic, using the items from your list.

Gretchen and the White Stallion

ARNOLD DOBRIN

"Children, children!" Gretchen's mother scolded. "I want you to stop your noise now!" Gretchen was not surprised that her mother was annoyed. It seemed that her brothers and sisters were always fighting or teasing or giggling or laughing.

The covered wagon, which had been their home for many weeks, was crowded. Inside were farm tools, furniture, clothing, and food. There was hardly any room left for Gretchen's big family. She was tired of the crowding and the noise. "Won't we ever get there?" she thought wearily.

They were all tired of traveling. The family had left Germany many months before, and the trip across the Atlantic Ocean was slow and hard. Many people were sick in the dark and crowded quarters below deck. When they finally docked in New York, the family boarded still another ship that took them to a Texas port on the Gulf of Mexico.

And now they were on the last part of their journey. The wagon was taking them to a town in central Texas where they would make their new home. Gretchen tried to think of something to do—some way to escape the stuffy wagon. She looked at Daisy, the old gray mare, loaded with sacks of corn meal, following the wagon. Gretchen had an idea. Perhaps—perhaps she could ride on Daisy instead of inside the crowded wagon. Yes, that was it!

Quickly she went to the front of the wagon where her father was in the driver's seat. "Papa," she said, "I'm tired of sitting in the wagon. Can I ride on Daisy's back for a while? Please?"

"Well now," Gretchen's father said, as he took off his hat and wiped his forehead. "Can't see what would be wrong with you sitting up on old Daisy. I'll put some good strong straps around you so you won't fall off."

The big sack of corn meal made a good platform for Gretchen to sit on. And when her father strapped her on she was much happier than in

the wagon. The wagon started to move once more, and Daisy and her passenger followed along behind.

Gretchen was staring dreamily into the distance when the wagons stopped suddenly. One of the wheels had broken. Gretchen's father slapped his thigh angrily and jumped down to the ground. While he set about to repair the old wooden wheel, Daisy nibbled at some grasses behind the wagon. As the old mare chewed contentedly, Gretchen's head began to nod. The sun made her sleepy. As Gretchen dozed, Daisy strayed further and further from the trail. Minutes passed. Suddenly, Gretchen awoke with a start and looked around her. Where was the wagon? Where was the wagon train? Daisy had wandered too far! All Gretchen saw around her were empty hills stretching into the distance.

"Where am I?" she cried aloud. Then she heard the sound of galloping hoofs. Maybe it was her father! Instead, a beautiful white horse with a

cream-colored tail and mane appeared. Daisy started to trot after him.

"Where are you going?" Gretchen cried. "Stop, Daisy, stop!" But Daisy paid no attention. Her trot turned into a canter and then into a gallop. Ahead flew the white stallion.

At sundown, they came to a green valley filled with wild horses. The herd ran up to the stallion and then surrounded Daisy as if to greet her. The sacks on Daisy's back began to tear and the horses greedily tasted the corn meal. Quickly, Gretchen tried to move her legs away from the sacks. But the horses pushed in closer and closer. Gretchen felt the horses' teeth nipping her legs. "Help!" she screamed. "Please help!"

The beautiful stallion raced into the group of horses. He tossed his head and mane. When he reared, the other horses moved away. The stallion gently chewed the ropes that bound Gretchen to Daisy. He carefully took her by the collar of her dress and set her on the ground. When he saw that she was all right, he galloped away, leading the herd toward the mountains.

Gretchen made a nest for herself in the tall grasses. She was very tired. All through the night she slept curled up in the grass. When she awoke, the sun was high in the sky and she was hungry and thirsty. She went to a nearby water hole and sipped some water from her hands. Hungrily she picked some bright red currants and ate them.

Gretchen thought sadly about her mother and father and little brothers and sisters. Where were

they now? If only she could be with them, she wouldn't care how noisy they were! Gretchen wondered if she should look for the wagon train. Then she remembered her mother telling her, "If you're ever lost, you be sure to stay put in one place." Gretchen looked around for Daisy but she had gone off with the other horses.

All that day and night Gretchen stayed near the water hole. She drank the water and ate currants. As the day ended, she fell asleep thinking of her mother and father.

When she awoke the next morning, Daisy was standing over her. "Wherever in the world have you been?" Gretchen asked as she jumped up and hugged the old mare. Gretchen tried to mount Daisy, but she was too short. She tried and then she tried again. She was leaning against Daisy's side when she heard hoofbeats in the distance.

It was the white stallion. How beautiful he was as he galloped toward her in the brilliant sunlight! He arched his neck and paced around Gretchen. There was something about him that kept her from being frightened. In a moment he gently grasped her by the collar of her dress and lifted her up onto Daisy's back. Then he looked at Gretchen, tossed his mane, and galloped away.

As soon as the stallion was out of sight, Daisy began to trot. The old mare seemed to know exactly which way to go. In a few minutes the

wagon train came into view. There were her mother and father running toward her with outstretched arms. "Oh, Gretchen!" her mother cried.

Gretchen hugged her mother and father and all of her brothers and sisters. Then she told them about her adventures and showed them the nips on her legs.

In later years, when she became a mother and a grandmother herself, Gretchen told the story of the white stallion many times. Often people said they didn't believe her. Then Gretchen would lift her long skirts a little and show them the scars on her legs where the horses had nipped her.

Reflections

1. Why do you think Gretchen's family decided to come to America? What did they hope to find in Texas?
2. Why did families travel together in wagon trains?
3. Why did Gretchen's mother advise her to stay in one place if she ever got lost? Do you think that is still good advice? Why or why not?
4. There are many legends in the West about wild horses. Why do you think this is so? What does this tell you about how the people living there felt about horses?
5. Do you believe Gretchen's story? Why or why not? Write a paragraph stating your opinion and giving reasons for it.

WYOMING PIONEER

ESTHER MORRIS (1814–1902)
When pioneers were settling the old West, Esther Morris was one of the sturdy women who left her mark on the Wyoming wilderness.

By 1869, the journey West was made by train and stagecoach—not by covered wagon. But South Pass City, for which Esther Morris was bound, was still only a town of rough shacks. And she traveled there alone. Her husband and sons, bitten by the gold fever, had gone on ahead. (Esther had stayed behind in Illinois to close out the family store.)

Arriving in Pass City, Esther quickly made the Morris shack a place of comfort and charm. People were drawn there by her friendliness, wit, and intelligence. Before long, it became a place where town problems were discussed.

Wyoming had become a territory in 1868, and it was soon to elect its first legislature. The two candidates were among the guests at the Morris home. Esther persuaded both men to promise to present a bill granting women the vote.

Thanks largely to pioneer Esther Morris, Wyoming women voted in 1870, the first women in our country to gain that right.

Stranger

ELIZABETH MADOX ROBERTS

When Polly lived back in the old deep woods,
Sing, sing, sing and howdy, howdy-o!
Nobody ever went by her door,
Tum a-tum and danky, danky-o!

Valentine worked all day in the brush.
He grubbed out stumps and he grubbed with
his ax.
He chopped a clear road up out of the branch;
Their horse made all the tracks.

And all they could see outdoors were the trees,
And all in the night they could hear the
wolves go;
But one cold time when the dark came on,
A man's voice said, "Hello, there, hello!"

He stood away by the black oak tree
When they opened the door in the halfway light;
He stood away by the buttonwood stump,
And Valentine said, "Won't you stay all night?"

He sat by the fire and warmed his bones.
He had something hidden down deep in a sack.
And Polly watched close while she baked her
    pones.
He felt of it once while she turned her back—
Polly had a fear of his sack.

Nobody lived this way or there,
And the night came down and the woods came
    dark.
A strange man sat by the fire that night,
And the cabin pane was one red spark.

He took the something out of his sack,
And the logs went dim and the light fell low.
It was something dark, as Polly could see—
Sing, sing, sing, and howdy, howdy-o!

He held it up against his chest,
And the logs came bright with a fresh new glow,
And it was a fiddle that was on his breast,
Tum tum a-tum and danky, danky-o!

He played one tune and one tune more.
He played five tunes all in a long row.
The logs never heard any songs before,
Sing, sing, sing and howdy, howdy-o!

The tunes lay down like drowsy cats.
They tumbled over rocks where the
waterfalls go,
They twinkled in the sun like little June gnats,
Tum a-tum tum and danky, dee-o!

The stumps stood back in Valentine's mind.
The wolves went back so Polly couldn't see.
She forgot how they howled and forgot how they
whined,
Tum tum tum and danky, danky-dee!

The tunes flew by like wild quick geese,
Sing, sing, sing and howdy, howdy-o!
And Polly said, "That's a right good piece!"
Tum tum tum and danky, danky-o!
Tum a-tum tum and danky dee-o!

The Fast Sooner Hound

ARNA BONTEMPS and JACK CONROY

No Grass Under His Feet

A railroad man was walking down the street with his hands in his overall pockets, and a long-legged, lop-eared hound trotted behind him. The man was smoking a pipe. After a while he stopped walking, took the pipe out of his mouth, and turned to the hound.

"Well, Sooner," he said, "here's the place."

They had come to a small building near the railroad tracks. Over the front door was a sign which said "Roadmaster." The dog called Sooner didn't seem to pay much attention to the man's words. But when the man opened the door, the hound followed him inside.

The man in the office looked up from his desk. "What do you want?" he asked.

"I'm a Boomer fireman," the railroad man said, "and I'm looking for a job."

"So you're a Boomer! Well, I know what that means. You go from one railroad to another."

"That's right," the man in overalls answered proudly. "Last year I shoveled coal on the Katy. Before that I worked for the Frisco line. Before that it was the Wabash. I travel light, I travel far, and I don't let any grass grow under my feet."

"We might be able to use you on one of our trains," said the Roadmaster. "Have you got some place you can leave the dog?"

"Leave my dog!" cried the Boomer, knocking the ashes out of his pipe. "Listen here, Mr. Roadmaster, Sooner always goes along with me."

"He does, eh? And why do you call him Sooner?"

"He'd sooner run than eat—that's why. I raised him from a pup, and he's never spent a night or a day or even an hour away from me. He'd cry fit to break his heart if we weren't together. He'd cry so loud, you couldn't hear yourself think."

"I don't see how I can give you a job with the hound," the Roadmaster said. "It's against all rules of the railroad to allow a passenger in the cab. Makes no difference if it's man or beast,

nobody is allowed to ride with the fireman and the engineer in the cab, and no passenger is allowed in the caboose. That's Rule Number One of this road, and it's never been broken yet. What's more, it never will be broken as long as I'm Roadmaster. So it looks as if Sooner is going to spoil things for you."

"Why, he's no trouble," said the Boomer. "He won't have to ride in the cab. He just runs alongside the train. When I'm on a freight train, he chases around a little in the fields to pass the time away. Sometimes he scares up a rabbit—just to play with when things get dull. But he's no trouble, and he won't have to ride in the cab or the caboose."

"You mean that old hungry-looking hound can outrun a freight train?" The Roadmaster laughed. "You can't make me believe that!"

"Shucks! He'll do it without half trying," said the Boomer proudly. "Matter of fact, it will be a little bit tiresome on him having to travel so slow, but Sooner will put up with anything just to stay close by me. He loves me that much."

"Oh, come now!" said the Roadmaster. "The dog isn't born that can outrun one of our freight trains. We run the fastest freights from coast to coast. That's why we get so much business. I'm sorry, we can't give you a job. You look like a man that could keep a boiler popping off on an uphill grade, but I just don't see how we can work it with the hound."

"Listen," said the Boomer, "I'll bet my first paycheck against a dollar bill that my Sooner will run circles around your freight train. What's more, he'll be fresh as a daisy when we pull into the junction, and his tongue won't even be hanging out. Of course, he'll want to trot around the station about a hundred times before we start—just to limber up, you know."

"It's a bet," said the Roadmaster, "and you can have the job. I'm not a mean man, you know, but Rule One has got to stick."

So the Boomer fireman climbed into a cab beside the engineer and began to shovel coal for all he was worth. The freight train pulled out of the station and started to pick up speed. Sooner loped along beside it. In no time at all he had left the freight train far behind. Sometimes he would pop out of sight in the underbrush along the tracks in search of rabbits or squirrels. But before long he could be seen up ahead, waiting for the train to catch up. Once the Boomer looked out of the cab and saw a strange look on the hound's face. The engineer noticed it, too.

"What's the matter with your Sooner?" the engineer asked. "He looks worried."

"That's right," the Boomer said. "He's worried about the law. The law says that we can't work more than sixteen hours on this run. If that happens, we'll have to stop this train in the middle of the fields and wait for a fresh crew to take our places. Sooner thinks we're going to get in trouble running so slow."

"Why, this is not at all slow!" exclaimed the engineer. "This engine is doing all it can. The boiler is hot enough to pop."

"Well, it's no speed for my Sooner," the Boomer laughed.

The freight train made its run and then returned, but Sooner led it all the way. When the dog trotted into the Roadmaster's office a mile ahead of the train, the Roadmaster got angry. He knew right away that he had lost his bet, but he didn't mind that. What he minded was what people would say about a freight train that couldn't keep up with a long-legged, lop-eared Sooner hound. They would say the train wasn't any good. The Roadmaster couldn't put up with such talk as that. No, sir. His freight trains must keep the name of being the fastest in the country.

Spoiling Everything

"Look here, Boomer," he said as the fireman climbed down from the cab. "You won the bet. That Sooner outran the freight train, but I'm going to transfer you to a local passenger run. What do you think about that?"

"Suits me," said the Boomer. "Me and my Sooner aren't choosy. We take the jobs we get, and we always stay together."

"You think the hound can keep up with our passenger train?"

"He'll do it easy," said the Boomer. "No trouble at all."

"If he beats our local, there'll be two dollars waiting for you when you get back. That Sooner is faster than he looks, but I don't believe he can beat a passenger train."

So the race was on again. Sooner speeded up to a trot as they pulled out of the station, and it seemed for a while that the passenger train might get ahead of him. But just as the race was getting exciting, the local train had to stop to pick up passengers. Then Sooner had to run around in the fields so he wouldn't get too far ahead of the engine. Even so, he won the race, and came into the station ten minutes ahead of the local passenger train.

The Roadmaster thought that maybe the stops were to blame for the local not keeping up with the Sooner hound. The next time he put the

Boomer in the cab of a limited passenger train that didn't make any stops till it got to the end of the line. So another race was on.

By that time people who lived along the railroad tracks were getting interested in the races. They came out of their houses to see the old Sooner hound that could outrun the trains and still come into the station without his tongue hanging out an inch and without his panting the least bit.

They began to think that something was surely wrong with the trains, but the trains were really right on schedule. They were keeping up their best speed. The trouble was with that old Sooner. He ran so fast, he made the trains seem slow. He did it so easily, you wouldn't think he was getting anywhere until you saw him pull away from the trains. But you couldn't tell that to the country people. They felt sure the trains were slowing down. And they began to talk about not riding on them any more.

When the Roadmaster heard that kind of talk, he got mad enough to bite the heads off nails. It would have to stop. Why, that old lop-eared Sooner was spoiling everything for the railroad. The people wouldn't ride the trains, and they were sending all their freight by trucks. The Roadmaster had half a mind to fire the Boomer and tell him to take his hound and go somewhere else, but he hated to own he was licked. He was a stubborn man, and he didn't want to admit that the Sooner was just too fast for his trains.

"Hey, Boomer," he said one day as the fireman climbed down from the cab at the end of a run. "That Sooner of yours is causing this road a lot of trouble. That hound makes our trains look like snails."

"It's not my Sooner that causes the trouble," said the Boomer. "It's that Rule Number One. My dog doesn't aim to give the road a black eye by outrunning the trains. He just aims to stay near me, that's all. Do away with the rule and let him ride with me in the cab, and everything will be okay."

"Not on your life. That's the oldest rule on this road, and I don't plan to change it on account of an old lop-eared Sooner hound."

The Boomer shrugged his shoulders as he turned to walk away. "It's your railroad, Mr. Roadmaster," he said. Then he reached down and patted Sooner's head. "Don't look ashamed,

Sooner," he told his hound. "It's not your fault at all."

Before the Boomer and the hound were out of sight, the Roadmaster had a fine idea. "I'll fix that Sooner," he said, snapping his fingers. "I've got what it takes to beat him. I'll put the Boomer in the cab of our *Cannon Ball.* That's the fastest thing on wheels. That Sooner hound is about the fastest thing on four legs, but if the fastest thing on four legs can beat the fastest thing on wheels, I'll admire to see it. That Sooner will be left so far behind, it'll take a dollar to send him a postcard."

"You're going to a lot of trouble," the Boomer said to the Roadmaster when he heard the plan. "There's no use for all this fuss. Just let my dog ride in the cab with me. That's all he wants, and it's all I want."

But the Roadmaster wouldn't change his plan. He was so sure the *Cannon Ball* would leave Sooner far behind that he smiled from ear to ear. "I aim to see this race from the cab myself," he said, "but if that Sooner beats the *Cannon Ball,* I'll walk back, and he can have my seat."

A Streak of Lightning

Word got around that Sooner was going to try to keep up with the *Cannon Ball.* Farmers left off plowing, hitched up, and drove to the railroad crossings to see the sight. The children were dismissed from school. So many men left the towns to see the race that the factories had to close down. It was like circus day or the county fair.

Just before the starting whistle blew, the Roadmaster climbed into the cab of the *Cannon Ball* with the Boomer and the engineer. He wanted to be sure that the Boomer shoveled plenty of coal and that the engineer kept the fast train moving at top speed. He also wanted to be close at hand to laugh at the Boomer when the *Cannon Ball* pulled away from the old lop-eared Sooner as he knew it would.

A clear track for a hundred miles was ordered for the *Cannon Ball,* and all the switches were spiked down. The train pulled out of the station like a streak of lightning. It took three men to see the *Cannon Ball* pass on that run: one to say, "There she comes," one to say, "Here she is," and another to say, "There she goes." You couldn't see a thing for steam, cinders, and smoke. The rails sang like a violin for half an hour after she had passed into the next county.

Every valve was popping off. The wheels rose three feet in the air above the roadbed. The

Boomer shoveled coal for all he was worth, but he worked with a smile on his face. He knew his hound, and he didn't mind giving the dog a good run. He worked so hard, he wore the hinges off the fire door. He wore the shovel down to a nub.

The Roadmaster stuck his head out of the cab window. *Whoosh!* Off went his hat—and he nearly lost his head, too. Gravel pinged against his goggles like hailstones. He peered through the smoke and steam. Where was the Sooner? The Roadmaster couldn't see hide nor hair of him anywhere. He let out a whoop of joy.

"The *Sooner!* The *Sooner!*" he yelled. "He's *nowhere* in sight! This is the time we outran that old lop-eared hound."

"I can't understand that," the Boomer said. "Sooner's never failed me before. It's just not like him to lie down on me. Let me take a look."

He dropped his shovel and poked his head out of the window. He looked far and wide. The Roadmaster was right. Sooner was nowhere to be seen. Where could he be?

The Roadmaster kept poking fun at the Boomer and laughing all the rest of the way to the station. But the Boomer didn't answer. Every moment or two he'd glance out of the window. Surely something was wrong. What had become of his Sooner?

Presently the station came into sight, and the *Cannon Ball* began to slow down. A short moment later the Boomer saw a crowd of people around the station. He supposed they were waiting to greet the *Cannon Ball* and to give it a cheer for making such a fast run. But no, they weren't even looking down the tracks. They were all watching something else.

"Those people aren't even noticing us," the Roadmaster said to the engineer. "Give a toot on the whistle."

The engineer blew the whistle just before he brought the *Cannon Ball* to a stop. Still nobody paid any attention. The people were all looking the other way and laughing. The Boomer and the Roadmaster and the engineer were all puzzled. They climbed down out of the cab.

"Well, here we are!" the Roadmaster cried, trying to get some attention. Nobody gave him any, so he pushed his way through the crowd. "What's going on here?" he insisted. "Didn't you people come down here to see the *Cannon Ball?*"

"Take it away," somebody answered. "It's too slow even to catch cold. Sooner's been here ten minutes and more."

The Boomer's heart gave a big jump when he heard that news. It seemed too good to be true. But a minute later he saw with his own eyes. Around the corner of the station came the old lop-eared hound, chasing a rabbit that he had rounded up along the way. Sooner was having so much fun playing with the rabbit and making the people laugh that he had forgotten about his race with the *Cannon Ball.*

"He's here!" the Boomer shouted. "He's here! My Sooner's true blue, and he's won again!"

The Roadmaster was so overcome, he chewed up his cigar like a stick of chewing gum and swallowed it. "P-p-put him in the cab," he sputtered. "P-p-put him in the cab and get going."

"But where will *you* sit?" the Boomer asked with a grin.

"I'll walk as I said I would," the Roadmaster answered as he started chewing on a fresh cigar. "Anything to stop that hound from outrunning our trains."

A few moments later the Boomer was back in the cab, his hound beside him. The big crowd of people let out a great cheer as the *Cannon Ball* pulled out of the station for the home trip. Sooner seemed to know whom the cheer was for. There was an unmistakable smile on his face. As the train gathered speed, his long ears flapped gaily in the breeze.

Just before the station went out of sight, the three in the cab of the *Cannon Ball* saw a man leave the crowd and begin to walk down the tracks. It was the Roadmaster starting for home.

Reflections

1. Why did the Roadmaster at first refuse to give the Boomer a job?
2. If you were the Roadmaster, how would you have reacted to the Boomer's statement that his hound could outrun a freight train?
3. Reread the part of the story that describes the last race and relate all the details that show that the *Cannon Ball* was going very fast.
4. The Roadmaster said, "I'm not a mean man, you know." Do you agree? Explain why or why not.
5. How many of the events that happened in this story could have happened in reality? What do you think makes the story a *tall tale?*
6. Pretend you had a dog like Sooner. Write a story telling what you would do with him.

The Bird of Seven Colors

RICARDO E. ALEGRIA

Because Americans came from so many different parts of the world, many of our folktales are similar to tales told in Europe, Africa, and Asia. Puerto Rico was an early stopping place for the Spanish who came to explore the New World. The Indians who lived there, and the people who were later brought from Africa, contributed their influence to tales that were brought from Spain. Here is a Puerto Rican tale that sounds very much like a European fairy tale, but it has many elements in it that make it Puerto Rican.

There was a mother who had two daughters. The elder, who resembled her mother, she loved very much, but she did not care for the younger daughter. One day she sent the younger daughter to the fountain for water, and on the way the girl dropped the water pitcher and it broke. The mother was furious. To punish her daughter, she sent her from home to look for the Bird of Seven Colors who would mend the pitcher, and she told her daughter that she could not come home again until the pitcher was mended.

The unhappy girl set out without knowing which way to go to find the Bird of Seven Colors. As she passed a mango tree, it spoke to her and asked where she was going. She said she was looking for the Bird of Seven Colors.

The tree said, "When you find him, ask him why I, who am so big and leafy, give no fruit."

The girl promised that she would and continued walking until she came to the seashore.

When the sea saw her, it asked where she was going, and she told it she was going in search of the Bird of Seven Colors.

The sea said, "When you find him, ask him why my waters, so vast and deep, hold no fish."

The girl promised she would; then she went on until she reached the King's house. The King's daughters asked her where she was going, and she told them her story. They asked her, if she found the Bird of Seven Colors, to ask him why they, being so beautiful, had no children. The girl promised she would, and went on her way in search of the bird.

Finally, she reached an enchanted mountain where the Bird of Seven Colors lived with the little old woman who was his mother. When the mother of the Bird of Seven Colors saw the girl, she asked what she was doing there, and the girl told her story again. The little old woman said that she would help her, but that she must hide, for her son was wicked, and if he saw her there, he would eat her. So that the Bird of Seven Colors would not see the girl when he came home, his mother hid her in a barrel.

It wasn't long before the Bird of Seven Colors arrived. When the bird was in bed, the mother called, "Birdling! Birdling!" and the bird asked what she wanted. She said that she had broken a pitcher and wondered if he could fix it. He did, in no time at all, and went back to bed. It wasn't

long before the mother called again, "Birdling! Birdling!"

He woke up and asked, "What is the matter, Mother?" The little old woman said that she had been dreaming about a very great mango tree, with luxuriant foliage, that bore no fruit. The Bird of Seven Colors told her that was because there was a treasure buried among its roots and, until the treasure was dug up, the tree would bear no fruit. The girl heard everything from her hiding place in the barrel. She rejoiced at having the answer to the mango tree's question.

Again the little old woman called, "Birdling! Birdling!" The bird woke up and asked what she wanted. The old woman asked why a great, deep sea might not have fish in its waters.

The bird grumbled, sleepily, "It has to swallow someone before it can have fish," and went back to sleep.

It wasn't long before the old woman called again, "Birdling! Birdling!" The Bird of Seven Colors grew furious. He sat up in bed and told her that if she didn't let him sleep, he would eat her! The little old woman said that she had been dreaming about the King's daughters who were very beautiful but had no children.

The angry bird snapped at his mother, "They'll have no children until they stop gazing at the moon!" And he went back to sleep.

The girl was overjoyed. Now her pitcher was mended and she knew the answers to the questions that had been asked her. In the morning, after the Bird of Seven Colors left, the little old woman took her out of the barrel. She gave her something to eat and said, "Now that you have what you came for, go, before my son returns!"

The grateful girl kissed the little old woman who had done so much for her and went home along the road by which she had come. When she reached the King's house, his daughters asked her if she had the answer to their question. "Yes, I have," she answered. And she told them what the Bird of Seven Colors had said. The King's daughters were so pleased that they gave her many pretty clothes and pieces of jewelry. When she came to the sea, it asked her if she had the answer to its question. "Yes, I have. Wait a minute, and I'll tell you," and she turned around and walked far, far from the shore. Then she called back. "The Bird of Seven Colors says that, in order to have fish, you must swallow someone." Then she ran away as fast as she could for she knew that the sea is treacherous and would try to swallow

her. The sea reached out a great, long wave, trying to catch her, but she was too far away.

After walking a long time, the girl reached the mango tree and told it what the Bird of Seven Colors had said. Then the tree begged her to dig at its roots and remove the treasure. She did, and she found enough gold coins to fill her pitcher.

After she left the tree, it did not take her long to reach home. Her mother was very surprised when she saw her dressed in pretty clothes, and even more surprised when she saw the mended pitcher filled with gold coins. The girl told her everything. Immediately, the vain woman set out for the house of the Bird of Seven Colors to see if there was another treasure hidden somewhere. She was thinking so hard about the riches she would find that she forgot what her daughter had said about the sea, and as she passed by on the shore, it reached out a great, long wave, pulled her in, and swallowed her.

Reflections

1. What did the mango tree, the sea, and the king's daughters want to know? Can you think of anything these three questions have in common?
2. If you had met the younger daughter, what question would you have given her to ask for you? How might the bird have answered your question?
3. Reread the last paragraph of the story. Then write a different ending.

Theater on Wheels

You don't always have to go indoors to see a play. In spring, when flowers come out in city parks, the Puerto Rican Traveling Theater takes to the streets. An acting company founded by Miriam Colon, it gives performances in both English and Spanish. And the producer, Miriam Colon, often directs and acts in the plays too.

The Puerto Rican Traveling Theater sets itself smack down in the middle of the city. The arrival of the truck and the setting up of the stage is a joyful street scene in itself. Children, pets, and grown-ups watch as the microphones are connected and the scenery put in place. They come as close as they can and wait for the performance to begin.

LITERARY DIALECTS

People from many lands settled in America. They often settled in communities far away from each other. They had no radio or television and few newspapers. These people inherited their speech, their vocabularies, and their pronunciations from their parents and grandparents. The speech of one community was quite often very different from the speech of another community.

Differences in pronunciation, in usage, and in the choice of words make dialects. The dialects of people in the backwoods of Florida, on the plains of Texas, or in a New England town may differ very much from the dialects in West Virginia, in New Orleans, or in San Francisco. All of these dialects have contributed to the variety of American English.

Writers often try to capture the speech of a dialect by respelling words. You have seen this happen in some books and many comic strips.

The *Yearling* by Marjorie Kinnan Rawlings is about a family living in the backwoods of Florida. Here is a conversation between the father and his son, Jody:

"Pa, you recollect the doe and the fawn?"

"I cain't forget 'em. The pore doe saved me, and that's certain."

"Pa, the fawn may be out ther yit. Hit's hongry, and likely mighty skeert."

"I reckon so."

"Pa, I'm about growed and don't need no milk. How about me goin' out and seein' kin I find the fawn?"

"And tote it here?"

Discuss each word that is spelled differently from the way you would spell it. What word might be used instead of *tote?*

Here are some words used by characters in *The Yearling.*

mebbe	fur (for *far*)	h'ep
jest (for *just*)	kilt (for *killed*)	shore (for *sure*)
git	leetle	figgered

Read each of the words aloud; then tell why you think Marjorie Kinnan Rawlings respelled these words in her story. If you were Jody's brother or sister, why do you think you might pronounce *sure* as *shore* or *get* as *git?*

Many years ago the Pennsylvania Dutch came from Germany and settled in parts of Pennsylvania. When the Pennsylvania Dutch speak English, they use the word order of German and bring to English words a "German" pronunciation. Read aloud the following sentences about the weather. Then decide how you would speak these same ideas.

1. Ain't it wonderful how it keeps makin' down?
2. It's going to give thunder gusts—it looks chust like.
3. This hands-in-the-pocket weather contraries me, and it's slippy (icy) out there yet.
4. Chris, look the window out and see if it's putting down somesing, still. I hope it don't give more down than what iss already.

These examples of American dialects that you have just read are only a few of the many dialects used in our country. As you read, you will find many other examples. Learn to recognize and appreciate dialects, and your reading skills will improve.

6 TO SEE THE LAND

Night Journey

Now as the train bears west,
Its rhythm rocks the earth,
And from my Pullman berth
I stare into the night
While others take their rest.
Bridges of iron lace,
A suddenness of trees,
A lap of mountain mist
All cross my line of sight,
Then a bleak wasted place,
And a lake below my knees.
Full on my neck I feel
The straining at a curve;
My muscles move with steel,
I wake in every nerve.
I watch a beacon swing
From dark to blazing bright;
We thunder through ravines
And gullies washed with light.
Beyond the mountain pass
Mist deepens on the pane;
We rush into a rain
That rattles double glass.
Wheels shake the roadbed stone,
The pistons jerk and shove,
I stay up half the night
To see the land I love.

Theodore Roethke

The City: San Francisco

San Francisco

LANGSTON HUGHES

I went to San Francisco.
I saw the bridges high
Spun across the water
Like cobwebs in the sky.

Magic and Some Black and Blue

ZILPHA KEATLEY SNYDER

According to the Great Swami's prophecy, Harry Houdini Marco thought he was destined to become a great magician. But at the age of twelve, he was only the "World's Clumsiest Kid," who helped his mother maintain Marco's Boardinghouse.

Harry sympathized with anyone else who was clumsy. Mr. Tarzack Mazzeeck, a temporary boarder at Marco's, was just such a person. Before leaving Marco's late one foggy night, Mr. Mazzeeck insisted on giving Harry a gift.

After helping Mr. Mazzeeck with his bags, Harry sat on his bed looking at his gift. It was a silver bottle containing Volo Oil. Harry followed Mr. Mazzeeck's instructions, rubbed a drop on each shoulder, and repeated the incantation on the label. Imagine Harry's thrill when he discovered he had grown wings. But as soon as Harry tried flapping his wings, he bumped his head on the bedroom ceiling and became completely discouraged with flying.

Proceeding with Caution

Harry's complete discouragement with flying didn't last very long. As a matter of fact, it really only lasted until the pain had faded from the bump on the top of his head. It left behind, though, a very vivid reminder of what Mr. Mazzeeck had said about proceeding with caution and of his own promise to be careful.

After his head began to feel better, he got up and went to his window. He leaned out and looked into the foggy night. Below, fading away from down the hill, were streetlights and lights of houses, blurred and pale through the drifting fog. To climb out on his windowsill and take off into the blinding mist would be stupid, to say the least. He would have to think of a safer place to learn.

Just then he noticed the roof of the Furdells' carriage house, and he knew right away where it was going to be. He got out his flashlight, the extra big one that Mr. Brighton had given him for his birthday, and cautiously opened the door of his room. Marco's Boardinghouse slumbered in an after-midnight kind of quietness. On the stairs Harry kept close to the wall, where the old boards were less likely to squeak. When he reached the ground floor hall, he headed for the kitchen and the back door and made a short dash through the foggy yard to the carriage house.

Once inside, Harry stopped to catch his breath and turn on his flashlight. There were overhead lights, but it would be a risk to turn them on. One of the windows faced the house, and too much light might bring someone to investigate. At night, the carriage house had always seemed a spooky place to Harry. Even with the lights on, the immensely high ceiling where the hayloft used to be was full of shadows. But tonight Harry wasn't a bit frightened. Somehow having wings made a difference.

Except for Lee Furdell's beat-up, old automobile, the carriage house was empty, so there was plenty of floor space. Harry walked to one end of the building, grasped his flashlight firmly in both hands, and spread his wings.

At first he didn't try to go very far or very high. He fanned his wings hard, took off, and tried stopping right away. He soon learned that a quick run forward helped him to get under way and that in order to stop, all he needed to do was make huge cups of his wings to catch the air. The cupped wings slowed him up and at the same time acted as a kind of parachute to bring him down easily. Once or twice he didn't come down quite easily enough to keep himself from collecting a couple of new reminders to "proceed with caution." One time it was a skinned knee, and another a bruised heel.

When he finally felt ready to try it from one end of the barn to the other, he made a marvelous discovery. He found that once he was really under way, his body leveled out into a kind of swimming position, with his toes trailing along behind. When that happened, the flying became much easier. Balancing, which had been a problem before, was suddenly almost automatic, and he no longer had to beat the air frantically to stay up. Once his body leveled out, it took only long, gentle strokes to keep him gliding smoothly through the air.

From one end of the barn to the other he went, over and over again, getting more confident with every flight. He kept at it until it was perfect.

Two or three fast hard beats to get airborne and leveled out, and then a swooping, breathtaking glide to the far wall. Once there, he simply cupped his wings, backpedaled, and came down gently, feet first. Finally he got so confident that he tried a quick pinpoint landing on the roof of the automobile. He came down perfectly, feather light and right in the middle of the roof. And that made him so confident that he decided to fly straight up and land on the huge crossbeam, high up under the roof of the barn.

After that he practiced a few more spirals until he got the knack of slanting his wings into a turn and knew just how much to slant to sharpen a turn or smooth it out. Then he felt ready to go outdoors.

In the tiny backyard Harry looked around him and up at the sky. There was certainly no room for a running takeoff. He would have to climb very steeply and would be fanning his wings very hard—if he could make it at all—just as he was going past the windows of the boardinghouse. The motion or the rustle of feathers might bring someone to the window.

It was just about then that he thought of the perfect takeoff spot—the flat roof of the carriage house. He could take off away from the buildings on Kerry Street and climb over the roofs of the houses on the street below.

He ducked back into the Furdells' yard and climbed the outside stairway to the roof. Once there he stopped for a minute to look and listen. All the windows in the boardinghouse were dark; and in the Furdells' house, only one small light was on somewhere on the second floor. There was no sound but the faraway honking of car horns and no movement except the slow drift of the fog. At last Harry took a deep breath, spread his wings, and took off into the blinding fog.

Up and up he went, in a wide circle, his heart pounding with a crazy excitement that was more than half fright. The wind was wet against his face, and his ears were full of the breathy whirr of feathers. It was a pretty frantic and frightening few minutes until at last he broke out above the fog into the clear open starlit sky.

Coming up so suddenly out of the damp, gray blindness, Harry was amazed to see how bright it was and how clearly he could see. As he climbed higher into the starlit brightness, the fog became only a rolling gray river beneath him. It poured in through the Golden Gate in great billows, spread out over the water of the bay, and spilled up onto the surrounding land. To the south the tops of some of the tallest buildings looked like the last remains of a sunken city. As Harry turned in his circling flight, he caught a glimpse of the twin towers of the Golden Gate Bridge, barely showing above the foggy flood. Farther north small patches of the hills of Marin could be seen through the fog breakers.

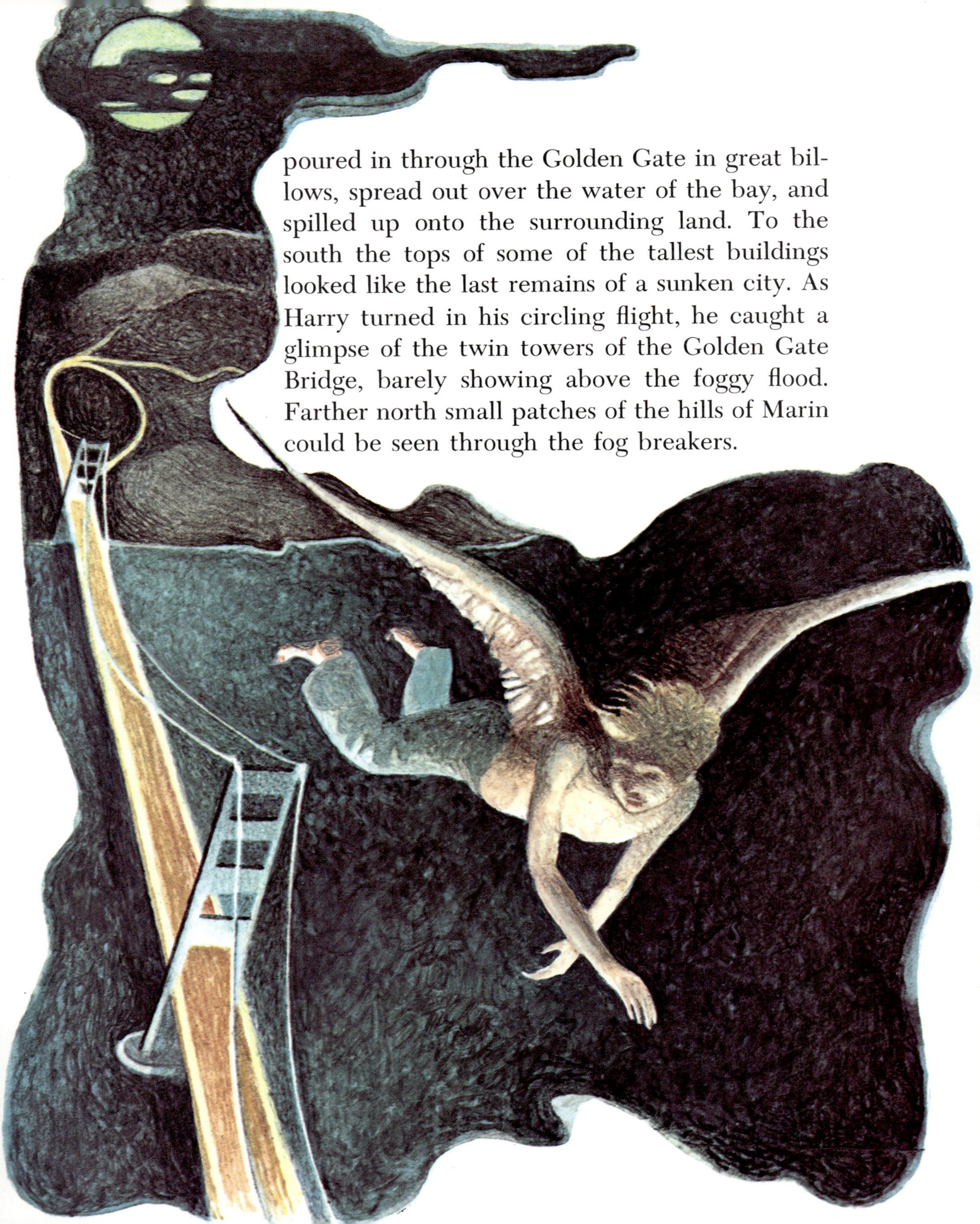

A Wonderful Feeling

As Harry went on climbing up and up, he suddenly noticed a wonderful feeling of warmth. The air above the fog blanket was a whole lot warmer than it had been further down. It was the good feel of sudden warmth that made Harry realize how cold he'd been for a long time. All that time in the carriage house he must have been freezing, but he'd been too excited to notice. He decided right then that flying around San Francisco without a shirt on wasn't a good idea.

The warm air above the fog blanket was so comfortable, and the fog-flooded world beneath him was so fascinating that Harry stopped being even the least bit afraid. In fact, for a few minutes he came close to forgetting where he was and what was keeping him up there. Without intending to, he had been flying slower and slower. It all came back as quickly as anything, though, when he suddenly started to fall.

Right then Harry learned two things in a hurry. If you fly too slowly, you begin to sideslip—and you will only make things worse if you panic and try to climb too steeply. His feet dropped down, and he began to slide downwards and backwards toward the water of the bay. It wasn't until he had spun through a heart-stopping tailspin and several hundred feet of air that he managed to get his balance back and catch the wind under his wings. With a huge gulp of relief, he started back up to the warm upper air. After that he kept his mind strictly on his flying.

As time passed and Harry flew and flew, he forgot all about the fog, the city below him, and just about everything. Nothing in the world seemed to matter but wings and sky and motion —the free and endless kind of motion that people are always looking for in hundreds of ways.

Flying was the way a swing swoops up and the glide down a slide. It was the shoot of a sled downhill without the long climb back up. It was the very best throat-tightening thrills of skates, skis, surfboards and trampolines, diving boards, merry-go-rounds, Ferris wheels, roller coasters, skate boards, and soapbox coasters. It was all of them, one after the other, all at once and a thousand times over.

Harry didn't have any idea how much time had passed when, during a long quiet glide, he noticed that the sky above the Berkeley hills had turned the pale green color that it often was just before dawn. Morning wasn't far away. The thought brought Harry back to earth with a jolt —mentally anyway. How to get back home was the problem.

As he slanted into a sharp turn and a long slow glide towards home, he realized that it wasn't going to be easy. By taking his bearings from the bay and the hills and the few tall buildings that stuck up through the fog, he would be able to come down in the general vicinity. But it wasn't very likely that he would be able to go straight down to his own backyard.

For a minute or two he felt panicky, but then he managed to calm down enough to think it over carefully. He drifted in a big circle over the general area of home and tried to figure something out. He finally decided to make as good a guess as he could and go straight down and land. If he could hit a rooftop, it would be a good place to get his bearings.

He picked his spot carefully. Fortunately the fog had begun to thin a bit, and more buildings and hilltops were visible. Twin Peaks were in the clear now, and the bridge towers reached high above the fog. Harry located a tall apartment building that looked like one he could see from his window, and if the blinking green glow to his left was what he thought it was—the drive-in just two blocks from home—he wasn't going to be far wrong. He cupped his wings just a bit and started down in as small and slow a spiral as he could manage. Once inside the fog belt, he was blind and helpless. Straining his eyes until they hurt, his heart thumping wildly in his throat, he drifted down and down until suddenly a dark surface rushed up beneath him. Desperately he reversed his wingbeat, but it was too late to keep him from landing with a thud that sent him to his hands and knees.

"Ouch," he said and then, "Oh, for Pete Squeaks!" He'd torn a big hole in the knee of his pajama pants. Mom wasn't going to like that. He stood up and looked around. Now that he was down, there was some reflected glow in the air from the streetlights, and he could tell that he was on the flat roof of a large building. By some rare good fortune, he had come down in a rather small open area between a long clothesline and a very fancy TV antenna. A little bit more to one side or the other and he'd have messed up somebody's wash or else their TV reception, not to mention what it might have done to him.

All of a sudden he realized that there was something familiar about the whole thing. He made his way carefully to the edge and looked over, and sure enough there, right next door, was Marco's Boardinghouse. Harry had come down right smack dab on top of Madelaine's School of Ballet.

The rest was easy. He walked along the edge of the roof until he was exactly opposite his own window on the third floor. From there it took only a couple of flaps of his wings to take him across the alley. Of course, he did get sort of jammed in the window for a moment because he forgot to fold his wings before he tried to go through. But he got them down all right and climbed into the room, with nothing more than a few splinters from the window frame. He felt pretty lucky about that because he'd thought for a second that he was going to fall out again, backwards.

Because he'd made a few whacking and thudding noises getting into the room, he didn't waste any time about saying the reverse incantation. It wouldn't do to have Mom come in to investigate before he got rid of his wings. The incantation worked fine. The feeling wasn't quite as violent as when the wings grew. It was more of a shrinking sensation. The dizziness came down like a dark curtain, and when it was over, the wings were gone.

Harry couldn't help having a feeling of loss—a sharp stab of regret—even though he knew that his wings had to go, for the time being at least. He reached back suddenly and touched the spot where the wings had been. As he ran his fingers across his back, he had a strange sensation that in some unexplainable way the wings were still there. It was as if he would always be able to feel them there, now that he knew about them—deep inside his back, tiny wings or maybe only wing buds. Probably they'd always been there. Maybe everybody had wing buds or at least the possibility of wings, only they just didn't know it. Maybe people had really been meant to have wings.

All of a sudden Harry realized that he was shivering violently. It had been very cold coming down through the fog belt, and it wasn't much warmer in his room. He pulled on his pajama top and then his robe for good measure and jumped into bed.

Only a few hours later Harry woke up in a glorious glow of sunshine and excitement. He had extremely stiff shoulder muscles, a bump on his head, two skinned knees, a bruised heel, several splinters, torn pajama pants, and the beginning of a cold in the head—not to mention the most marvelous, wonderful, super-colossal secret in the whole world.

Reflections

1. Why do you suppose Mr. Mazzeeck made Harry promise to be careful? What steps did Harry take to make sure he "proceeded with caution"?
2. Look at the last paragraph of the first section. To what is the fog compared? How is the comparison continued throughout the whole paragraph?
3. What have you ever done that has thrilled you so much that you forgot about any discomforts at the time? What discomforts did Harry forget about when he was flying?
4. Suppose that, like Harry, you have been given the magical gift of wings but that if you reveal the gift, the wings will be taken away forever. Would you be able to keep the secret? Explain why or why not. If not, to whom would you first reveal it and why?
5. Pretend that you have wings and can fly. Write a description of the way your community looks from the air. Be sure to mention the features you think would stand out the most.

In San Francisco

Close up, some of the scenes of San Francisco shown on pages 448 and 449 take on a more personal look. When the camera zeros in, a city of landmarks and points of interest becomes a city of people at work.

That delicious fish dinner in one of San Francisco's many restaurants began in a fishing trawler. Sailing back at dawn under the Golden Gate Bridge, the **fisherman** has plenty of time to prepare his catch for this **chef** and others working in restaurants all over the city.

The **driver** of the cable car that goes up and down steep Nob Hill carries not only workers traveling to and from their jobs but most visitors to San Francisco as well.

On assignment for a TV station, this San Francisco **reporter** is talking to people on the street about their jobs. In this city of more than 800,000, how many different kinds of work do you think the people do?

The City : Houston

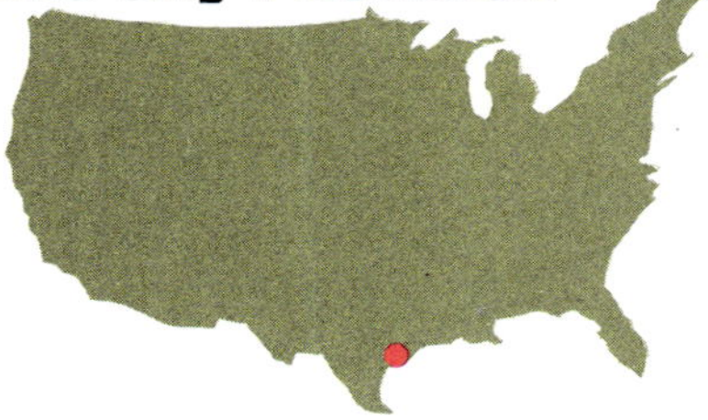

Houston

HELEN HAVEMANN, A Student at Lamar High School, Houston

A big bulky hand with "Howdy!"
    stamped inside;
Shake it!
        Meet Houston . . .

Camp Miller School

DORIS GATES

"Camp Miller School" takes place somewhere in the southwestern United States. The time is the 1940's. The people in the story barely earn a living by picking crops of fruits, vegetables, and cotton. Some, like Janey's family, are people who lost their own farms. Others are migrant workers. They move around from place to place, trying to find work as the crops ripen. They live in camps near the fields where they are working. Special camp schools are set up, but the migrant children never can stay in one place long enough to feel they really belong.

Janey and Dad were on their way to the cotton fields. Dad was going to work. Janey was going to school. It was October now. The sun, though bright and warm, was not hot as it had been a month ago. Wild sunflowers turned bright faces to the east. But Janey, huddled in a corner of the ragged front seat, was not aware of the world around her. The corners of her mouth sagged, and her eyes glowered darkly. She wasn't glad to be going to school, not this school! The town school was the one where all the other children of the district went. That is, they did if they belonged to the district. Janey was well aware that she could have attended that school, too. There was no law forbidding it. But she would have been unwelcome. And Dad, knowing this, had made his own law about school.

"We'll keep with our own kind," he said. "The camp schools are put there for us to use, and so we'll use them and be thankful. Besides, a person can learn anywhere if she's a mind to."

Janey didn't argue with her father. She knew that going to the "regular" school would no longer satisfy her anyway. Just going there couldn't make her really belong. Since she had begun to want to stay in this place, merely going to the district school was no longer enough. What Janey wanted was to belong to this place. She wanted to go to the district school because, as a member of the community, it was her right to go there. The camp school would now be a daily reminder that she didn't belong. And so she dreaded it.

She knew what the camp school would be like. No two of the children would have learned the same things, and it would all be a jumble. In some lessons Janey would find herself way ahead of most of the boys and girls her age. But she would be expected as a matter of course to learn. Most of the time she wouldn't know whether she was going or coming. There would be endless questions and much tiresome fussing.

Besides, it was much too early in the day for school to start. She would have to wait around until it did. She would have asked Dad to let her go into the field with him if she had thought it would do any good. But she knew from past experience that it wouldn't. Never had she been allowed to do any field work. Other children did, and sometimes Mom, but never Janey. Dad, so easygoing about most things, was firm on this. So Janey sat with a frown on her face. As the old car jolted along its way, she came very near to feeling sorry for herself.

She would have known the schoolhouse as soon as they came in sight of it, even if Dad hadn't bothered to point it out. She had seen many of them before. They all looked alike. Some were newer than others, and that was about the only difference. This was one of the newer ones. It was

a rather large square building. Its unpainted boards gleamed in the bright light. Janey's father let her off at the front step. Then he drove over to park beside a row of cars that looked as if they might all have come from the same junk pile. Janey sat down to wait, her package of lunch beside her.

Across from her were the cottages, row upon row, that made up the camp. Looking at these little one-room sheds so close together, she was thankful for their own shack and the spreading country around it. Of course there was plenty of country spread around here. But the camp itself was squeezed into as small a space as possible, so as not to use up any more of the cotton ground than was absolutely necessary. The deep green of the cotton plants reached in every direction almost as far as the eye could see. And here and there against the green of every bush, a gleam of white showed clearly. That was where a cotton boll had burst open to free the fluffy fibers. The fibers would be thousands, perhaps millions, of these little white bunches. It would take many fingers working many hours a day to pick all the ripening cotton. That is why there was a village of little houses at this place with a schoolhouse at hand. During the picking season hundreds of people lived here. They worked here until all the cotton was harvested. Then they loaded their cars with what household goods they owned and moved on to some other part of the country.

For perhaps ten minutes Janey sat on the steps of the schoolhouse. She was a figure of gloom. Then all at once she caught a movement in the dust in front of her. It was so slight a movement that at first she thought her eyes were playing tricks on her. But in the next second the dust was again stirred. And then she was off the schoolhouse steps in one lunge. Flat on the ground she hurled herself, one arm reaching out ahead of her. Slowly she drew in her arm, her hand tightly closed, and gathered herself up. From head to foot she was coated with fine dirt, but she didn't care. She didn't even stop to brush herself off before she slowly began to open her fingers. She squinted closely at what she held there. A smile widened across her face, for in her

MOTHER'S
OATS

palm was a small horned toad. Its eyes stared fiercely at her. Its mouth was set grimly. But Janey was not alarmed. She had captured many horned toads before this. She knew that for all their fierce expression and spiky covering, they were quite harmless creatures. To most people it would have appeared far from beautiful, but to Janey it seemed an object of delight. She loved it at once and began cautiously to draw her finger across its hard little head.

Suddenly an idea occurred to her. She would use this horned toad to test the new teacher. In every school she had ever been, someone had always told her whenever she happened to mention a "horned toad" that she should call them "horned lizards." They were not really toads at all. Janey knew that they were not, strictly speaking, "horned toads." But to call them anything else just wasn't possible. The minute you said "horned lizards," you turned a perfectly good horned toad into a new and unattractive animal. She would hate having anyone refer to her new pet as a horned lizard. If the new teacher did so, Janey's respect for her as a human being would be completely shattered.

She and the horned toad had not long to wait. Janey had hardly gotten some of the dirt brushed off when a dusty car rolled to a halt in the shade of the schoolhouse. A smiling woman got out of it. Janey felt hopeful.

"Hello," called the woman. "No ten-o'-clock-scholar about you, is there?"

Janey felt increasingly hopeful as she rose to meet this teacher. Surely no one who quoted Mother Goose to you before she had asked your name would call a horned toad a horned lizard. More than that, she would know what to do with you if you were good in reading and poor in arithmetic. Suddenly the whole tone of the day was changed. But the final test was yet to come.

"Look," said Janey, holding out her captive.

"Well, bless my soul," said the woman heartily. She bent over Janey's hand. "A horned toad! Did you catch it?"

Janey nodded, too delighted for the moment to speak.

The woman looked at Janey with eyes that were merry and direct.

"I am Miss Peterson," she said.

"I'm Janey Larkin."

"Welcome to Camp Miller School, Janey.

Come on inside. We'll start the day together."

No questions, no fussing. Just "Come on in," as if she had known you always. Janey was thrilled because she was certain that this very morning she had discovered the most wonderful teacher in the world.

During the next half-hour Janey helped Miss Peterson prepare for the day's work. Soon the boys and girls began to arrive, and at nine o'clock the school day started.

As the morning advanced, Janey's regard for Miss Peterson increased, if that were possible. Because they were crowded on the benches and because their legs were not all long enough to reach the floor, she saw to it that the children were given time to move around and rest. And it seemed to be the custom for two or three of the

children to tell the others each day which part of the country they had thought the most interesting in their traveling around. Janey decided that when her turn came, she would tell about the place by the river that she had discovered the other day.

Right in the middle of one of these recitals, there was a sudden disturbance outside. A covered truck stopped in front of the door. Miss Peterson's face seemed to light up at the sight of it. She stopped the boy who was talking and said to the room, "This is our lucky day. The library people are here." But though she sounded as if it were something especially fine, none of the boys and girls appeared interested. And this was not surprising, since none of them knew who "library people" were.

"The library truck has brought us some books," Miss Peterson explained. "We'll have recess while I pick them out."

Immediately the children wiggled off their benches and filed out. They circled the truck, their glances frankly admiring. That was the sort of thing to travel around in. It had room. Janey wasn't interested in the truck, but she hung around in the hope of seeing what sort of books were coming out of it. She could hardly wait for the library people to go so she could see what they would leave behind.

But when they had finally gone, Janey's high hopes were dashed. The books were old and ragged, with some of the pictures torn out. But they were all good stories, she discovered on looking them over. And once upon a time they had been new. Janey picked up a copy of *King Arthur* and returned to her bench with it. As she opened the book's worn cover, she tried very hard to remember that in the beginning it, too, had been new and shiny. Then she began to read. And soon she forgot everything but the shining splendor of its pages.

Then school was over for the day. It ended sooner than most schools, for the boys and girls worked in the cotton fields. Janey walked into the cotton patch and let the horned toad go. The toad had had an exciting day, and it would be cruel to keep the tiny creature longer. Besides, horned toads were fairly common. She could catch another one almost any time. Then she curled up in the shade, her back resting against the schoolhouse wall, to wait for Dad. She knew she would have to wait a long time. But now she didn't care. Miss Peterson had let her keep *King Arthur* until tomorrow.

Her father had been grinning down at her for several seconds before Janey became aware of him. She looked up, startled to find Dad instead of a knight in armor standing before her.

"Think you can get your nose out of that long enough to ride home with me?" he asked.

Without answering, she got dreamily to her feet. The spell of *King Arthur* still held Janey, and she moved quietly so as not to shatter it. For the moment the little girl on the edge of the cotton patch had become the Lady Guinevere. The man beside her had assumed the figure of a noble knight.

But as they reached the row of parked cars, Janey became herself again. It was beyond even her power to imagine the Lady Guinevere climbing into an automobile.

"I wish we lived back in olden times when everything was an adventure. You just had to be brave or it was the end of you."

Dad was silent for so long following her words that Janey glanced at him. She was surprised to discover a sober expression on his face. The teasing smile was gone entirely. Had she said something wrong? She waited a little anxiously for him to speak.

At last he cleared his throat and began to talk. His hands tightened on the steering wheel, and his eyes looked straight ahead.

"Some day, Janey, perhaps when you're grown up, you'll realize that every day you've been living these last five years has been an adventure. You know, an adventure is just something that comes along that's not expected. You don't know

for sure how it will turn out. Sometimes there may be danger mixed up in it. And it doesn't matter whether it happened a thousand years ago or right this minute. It's still an adventure. Every day that comes along is an adventure to us. And every day may be dangerous because we don't know for sure what it's going to bring. Perhaps I'm wrong, but I've got a hunch that it takes just about as much courage to live like that without losing your grip on things as ever it took to buckle on armor and go out to fight."

Janey considered Dad's words and found them very puzzling. It was hard to discover anything adventurous in the way they lived. Her notions of adventure were quite different. She looked at

Dad. She tried to see in his seamed and suntanned face the look of a hero, but she couldn't. It was a kind face and the dearest one in the world to her, but she had to admit that Dad in armor would have looked strange rather than noble.

It required, too, considerable effort for her to think of him as being brave. Yet she supposed he must be. He had just said it took courage to live the kind of life they lived without losing your grip on things. Certainly Dad hadn't yet lost his grip. When the car broke down, as it frequently did, he simply went quietly about the business of fixing it. And after a long day in the fields, he was never too tired to tease her when he came home. But was this really being brave? Janey hardly thought so. Still, Dad had as much as said it was. And Dad couldn't be wrong.

Then a surprising thought occurred to her. Why, she must be brave too. After all, she was living the same kind of life. That settled it. Dad was wrong after all. She was dead certain that whatever other qualities she might possess, bravery was not one of them. What had Dad meant? Could there be more than one kind of courage in the world? Janey considered this possibility for a moment. But she found it too confusing.

"I guess I won't understand it till I'm grown up," she thought. She was relieved when Dad asked her to tell him what had happened at school that day. For the rest of the ride home Miss Peterson crowded all other topics out of the conversation.

Reflections

1. Why does Janey dread going to the camp school? Why doesn't she go to the district school instead?
2. What does Janey think class at the camp school will be like?
3. How does Janey test the teacher?
4. What is Janey's opinion of Miss Peterson? What is the basis of Janey's opinion? (Name at least five things.)
5. What is Janey's idea of courage and adventure? What is her dad's idea of courage and adventure? Do you think there is more than one kind of courage in the world? Explain your answer.
6. Write a short story about a time when you or someone you know acted bravely. Your story might be about a daring act, or it might be about a quiet, everyday kind of courage.

My Uncle Joe

LOIS LENSKI

Oh, do you know my uncle Joe?
He used to live in Buffalo;
He had a car, he rode all day
Until he came to Santa Fe.

His car broke down, he let it go,
And then he walked to Idaho;
His feet got tired and that's why he
Just took a boat to Kankakee.

The boat went down with all but Joe;
He hitched a ride to Ko-ko-mo;
He bought a bike, away rode he,
He pedaled hard to Cher-o-kee.

His legs got tired, he had a flat,
He wrecked his tire at Medicine Hat;
He left his bike, away he flew—
He took a plane to Kalamazoo.

The plane it crashed, he ate some beans
And took the train to New Orleans;
The train it bumped, he could not sleep,
So off he jumped and got a jeep.

The jeep it smashed into a truck,
Said Uncle Joe, That's just my luck!
A car, boat, bike, a train or plane,
I will not ride in them again.

He walked as fast as he could go,
Came back again to Buffalo;
And now he stays at home all day,
And says he'll never go away!

The City: New York

The New Colossus

EMMA LAZARUS

Give me your tired, your poor,
Your huddled masses yearning to be free,
The wretched refuse of your teeming shore.
Send these, the homeless, tempest-tossed to me—
I lift my lamp beside the golden door!

Davie's Wonderful Summer

MARIO PUZO

When Davie Shaw's parents left their home in Los Angeles one summer for a round-the-world cruise, they thought their son would stay with his uncle. And Davie did do that, but only for a few weeks. Then he decided that it would be a good idea to travel cross-country to New York alone and be there to meet his parents when they returned from their trip. Davie's uncle gave him all his spare cash and Mustang, a pony that would not carry anyone who could walk. With the aid of friendly people they met along the way, Davie and Mustang finally reached New York City very early one morning. They had come on foot, by boat, and by railroad. On the few occasions Davie had had to ride Mustang, he had bandaged his foot to fool the pony.

In the Big City

Davie felt like a prince riding Mustang across the George Washington Bridge. He took the avenue next to the river and headed downtown because he knew his parents would be stopping at the Plaza Hotel when they arrived in New York.

It was a beautiful ride.

Then he rode east on Fifty-ninth Street, passing Eleventh Avenue, Tenth Avenue, Ninth Avenue, all the way to Fifth Avenue. He rode alongside Central Park until he came to the square that held the Plaza Hotel. On one side of the square were coaches and coachmen lined up waiting for business.

They all looked at Davie and his pony in a very interested way. Davie got off Mustang to give him a rest, and one of the men said, "Hey, kid, if you got a coach, you could get into this business with that pony. He's pretty big."

The other men laughed, and Davie knew the man was just making a joke. Mustang wasn't big enough to pull a coach.

But one of the men, with a great stovepipe hat and scarf, said, "Son, if you can get yourself a real saddle and blanket, you could sell rides up here to the kids. You could make some eating money."

Davie started thinking very hard. He had exactly $2.43 in his pocket. Today was Sunday, and his parents would not arrive in New York until the following Friday. He would have to eat and pay for a place to sleep, and he just didn't have enough money. And then he realized something else. He would have to pay for Mustang's food and find a place for Mustang to sleep.

But Davie knew Mustang wouldn't let anybody ride him. So he asked the man, whose name was Josh Pringle, but was usually called Big Josh, "Is there some place where I can leave my pony and have him taken care of for a few days, for $2.43 worth?"

"I can take care of your pony, young feller," answered Big Josh. "But what will you do in the meantime?"

Davie said, "I can sleep in the park, and I don't need much to eat. I can take care of myself."

Big Josh thought that over. "Hitch your pony to my hansom cab," he said. "Then come up here on the driver's seat to keep me company. I'm going to take you to the only house in New York that has hay for horses."

They went through the streets of the city, with all the automobiles and buses honking their horns at them. Then they were over by the Hudson River, going along a line of tenements and warehouses. Big Josh reined to a halt in front of a long, barracklike building fronted by a roll-down iron door. He let out a long yodel that sounded like "Halloo," and the iron door began to slide into the top of the warehouse. His dapple-gray horse trotted inside.

And so, on Davie Shaw's first night in New York City, he slept on a coach seat, surrounded by horses, coaches ranging up to three hundred years old, and coachmen only a little younger. Outside the warehouse, the stone city encased them like the shell of a nut, and Davie fell into the best sleep he'd had since his trip started.

Early the next morning, Davie woke to the delicious smell of frying steak and eggs. He found that Big Josh had already cooked breakfast and was waiting for him to get up. Davie first went to see if Mustang was all right.

The whole vast warehouse floor was bustling. Coachmen were hitching their horses to coaches,

giving their wheels a final brush, putting back the leather seats they had used as beds.

As he watched the coaches rumbling out the raised iron door, Big Josh shook his head and waved an arm around the almost empty warehouse. "This is all that's left of a great Old World," he told Davie. "In a few years it will all be gone."

Davie helped him put the coach seats back into the hansom cab. Then Big Josh said, "All right, Davie, hop up here beside me, and I'll teach you how to manage the reins. Then maybe tomorrow you can do a few jobs for me."

Davie felt a thrill of delight when the great coach wheels rumbled beneath him and Big Josh guided his horse through the traffic. Taxis, buses, private cars eddied around them, but they were above everything on their high seat.

They pulled up at the end of the cab line waiting near the Plaza Hotel entrance to Central Park. While they waited for customers, Big Josh told Davie, "I'll teach you to drive. Then when we see your mother and father come out of the Plaza Hotel on Friday, you can bring the coach right up to them. What a surprise that would be!"

Davie liked the idea. He was worried about his parents being angry because of his trip across the country. But if he surprised them in such a nice way, how could they get mad?

They spent a wonderful morning. To Davie it was the greatest way of earning a living that anybody could find. By noon they were both very hungry, and Big Josh stopped the coach beside a mobile frankfurter cart.

On the umbrella was a sign printed in pale blue: "Gourmet Franks by Emil." The owner of the stand was a very neat man with a very neat moustache. He had a paper baker's hat on his balding head and special tissue-thin paper gloves on his hands. He wore a very neat white serving jacket with his name in red thread script over its left breast pocket. His name was Emil. He said politely to Davie, "Onions or sauerkraut?"

Davie didn't know what he meant, since he had never heard of onions on hot dogs.

"I make the best hot dogs in New York, the finest grade," said Emil. "I buy the best rolls. I cook my sauerkraut and onions myself in my own special sauce. My mustard jar contains the finest mustard ever mixed. Quality is all. Onions or sauerkraut?"

"Onions," Davie said.

"Sauerkraut," Big Josh boomed.

And the frankfurters were delicious. Davie ate five more and washed them down with orange soda pop.

Big Josh had three hot dogs, and then he and Davie staggered back to the coach so full they could hardly walk.

A Noble Gesture

That night after supper, Big Josh took Davie out of the warehouse through a side exit that led into a street filled with people. There were boys playing box-ball, girls playing jacks, men sitting on brownstone stoops reading the paper, women leaning on their arms in windows and peering down on their children. Davie had never seen so many people crammed into such a little space.

When Big Josh appeared, a bunch of boys who had been running around playing ring-a-lievo stopped playing and surrounded him. Davie was surprised when they called him Coach. Then he saw some boys marking bases in white chalk on the street stones and sidewalks, while others pushed parked cars farther down toward the avenue to make a clear playing field. Then the stickball game started. It was just like baseball

except that the boys used a rubber ball and a thin, sawed-off broomstick for a bat.

Davie watched Big Josh coaching his team. He was fascinated because he had never heard of stickball in California.

Finally he asked timidly, "Can I try?"

They all looked at Davie. He didn't *look* like a stickball player. He didn't *talk* like a stickball player. He just didn't.

Even Big Josh was a little doubtful, but he said very kindly, "All right, Davie, go in there and hit for the pitcher."

Davie stood over home plate (an iron sewer cover in the middle of the street) and waved the

thin bat. The opposing pitcher threw the red ball on an easy bounce, but then the ball did a tricky curve. Davie took a level, calm swing. The red ball hung in the air like a big balloon. The thin stick whipped it high into the air over the roof of a building and into the next block. There was an astonished silence as Davie ran around the bases for a home run.

The next time Davie was up, he did the same thing, but this time over the right-field roofs because he swung a little late. It was another home run. This time everybody cheered, the kids sitting on the curb, the women at the windows, the men reading their papers on the stoop.

The third time Davie was up, he hit the ball right down the middle but far over the head of the center fielder and into the next block. The people really went wild over the third home run.

Big Josh held up his hands for silence. He lifted his top hat in a respectful salute. Then he said, "Davie, you are a natural."

Everybody tried to shake Davie's hand, and the captain of the team asked him if he would play with them in the championship game. Davie said that he couldn't because he had to meet his parents and go back to California. Still, he felt very pleased to find out that he was a natural, though it wouldn't do him much good in California because nobody ever played stickball there.

When Davie got up on Wednesday morning, he started to worry about what his parents would say. He would have to give them some reason for coming all the way across the United States to New York. And he really couldn't think of a good reason. He had just done it. However, he had two more days to think of what to tell them, since they would not arrive from Europe until Friday.

As he rode on the driver's seat, Davie told Big Josh about his worries.

Big Josh just laughed and said, "Your folks will be so glad to see you, nothing will bother them."

It was a slow day because of the heat, and they stopped by Emil's gourmet frankfurter stand for lunch. They saw a sign on the umbrella that read, "Gourmet Hot Dog Cart For Sale—Cheap—Owner Retiring Because of Illness."

"Yes," Emil said. "The doctor has advised me that my health is too delicate to let me drag my cart through the streets. So I must sell the cart."

Davie couldn't bear to think of not eating those delicious frankfurters every day. He had a brilliant idea.

"If I lent you my pony, couldn't he drag the cart for you?"

Emil beamed. "A pony! That is perfect. I thought of a horse, but a horse is too big for my cart. But I never thought of a pony. Davie, if you do this, you can eat free hot dogs as long as I stay in business."

So Davie took a bus back to the warehouse and then brought Mustang to the Central Park corner where Emil kept his cart. Mustang was glad to get out into the fresh air.

"Mustang likes to eat hot dogs, too," Davie told Emil. "So you won't have to worry about carrying special food for his lunch. I'll give him his oats and hay during the night and morning."

"When must I give him back?" Emil asked, in the meantime serving Mustang a hot dog with onions.

Davie hesitated. "Well, I have to find my parents on Friday, but we may stay in New York another week. I'll let you know when I want him."

Thursday night Davie felt very gloomy. He had already decided to reclaim Mustang on Friday. He would also have to explain things to his parents. They would check into the Plaza, call his uncle, and learn that their son had been left on his own for the summer.

The Reunion

Friday morning dawned bright and clear. It was a beautiful August day. Big Josh guided his hansom cab through the huge iron door of the warehouse and guided the horse toward Central Park. Davie knew that it was the last time he would ever see the strange warehouse full of its antique stagecoaches and aging horses, so he took a long look. He knew he would remember it forever.

Noontime came, and Mr. and Mrs. Shaw had still not arrived. Davie decided to walk over to Emil's gourmet frankfurter stand and get Mustang back. Big Josh promised to look out for Mr. and Mrs. Shaw. Davie gave him a very good description of his mother and father so that he would recognize them.

When Davie got to Emil's stand, he saw Mustang tied to a nearby tree. "I'm sorry Emil, I have to take my pony back," he said.

Emil gave Davie a hot dog with onions. Then he said, "Davie, why don't you let your pony stay with me? I'll give him a good home, and he likes hot dogs. We'll both be very happy together. And remember, Davie, without a pony I'll have to go out of business."

Now Davie was by no means a selfish boy, but Mustang was his pony, and it was unfair for anybody to ask another person for his most precious possession. He went over to the tree and untied

Mustang. As he led the pony past the frankfurter cart, Emil held out a hot dog for Mustang to eat on the way. Mustang stopped. He nuzzled Emil. He put his muzzle into Emil's neck. He snuffled the tins boiling with water and sauerkraut. Emil gave him another hot dog with all the trimmings.

Davie pulled at Mustang's bridle, but Mustang wouldn't budge. Davie pleaded with him, but Mustang wouldn't budge.

Finally Emil said sadly, "Don't you see that Mustang wants to stay with me? He likes pulling the cart; he likes being tied to a tree; he likes my hot dogs with onions. He doesn't want to leave me."

At first Davie couldn't believe it, but then he saw it was true. Mustang would rather stay with Emil than go with him. Davie was sure it was because of the hot dogs. Mustang had always liked them, and he just wasn't leaving a man who made the most delicious hot dogs in the world. And maybe it was all for the best. Emil did need Mustang more than he did.

Davie went back to the coach. Big Josh was just pulling away from the curb, so Davie knew there must be some passengers inside. He swung up on the high driver's seat beside Big Josh.

They made a tour of Central Park and around the lake. Davie felt really terrible now. He had lost his pony, he still had not found his parents, and he couldn't think of an explanation for being in New York when he did find them. He told Big Josh about how Mustang had deserted him.

They were near the end of the trip, and Big Josh said to Davie, "Be a good lad and hop down to open the door for the passengers, please."

Big Josh had a smile on his face, and Davie wondered what he was smiling at. Davie swung off the coach and opened the door with a flourish. A woman stepped out backwards, and a man followed her, his head peering down at the steps.

They both straightened up, and the woman gave a little scream and said, "Davie! What are you doing here?"

The man turned around and said, "Davie! What are you doing here?"

And then, for the first time, Davie knew what to say to his parents. For the first time he really knew why he had traveled all across the United States of America from California to New York.

"I missed you," he said to his mother and father. "I wanted to see you again as soon as I could."

He was surprised when his mother didn't scold him but, instead, gave him a hug and a kiss. He was even more surprised when his father clapped him on the back, shook his hand, and said, "I'm proud of you, son."

Davie Shaw and his parents spent the next week together in New York, and it was the happiest week in Davie's life. His parents took him to Coney Island, the American Museum of Natural History, the Bronx Zoo, and the most famous restaurants in New York City. Davie took them to Emil's gourmet frankfurter stand.

Before they left New York, Mr. and Mrs. Shaw gave a party for Big Josh, Emil, and Mustang.

Finally it was time to go home. Davie said good-by to all his new friends. When he stroked Mustang's soft nose, the pony whinnied and pushed his head against Davie's chest. Then he walked back over to where Emil was standing. Big Josh drove Davie and his parents out to the airport and waved good-by as the Shaws got on the plane.

Six hours later the Shaw family was home. The big jet plane had been up in the clouds for more than three thousand miles, and it was the first time Davie had ever flown. There was nothing to see, and there were no people to meet, no roads to walk, no food to cook, no strange adventures. It was the most uninteresting part of Davie Shaw's summer, and he never talked about it.

Reflections

1. What do you think Big Josh meant when he said, "This is all that's left of a great Old World"? Why did he say, "In a few years it will all be gone"?
2. Which sides of New York City life did Davie get to see? Which sides did he miss?
3. If you were Davie, would you have given Mustang to Emil? If not, what would you have done with him?
4. Why do you think Davie's father was proud of him? Give as many reasons as you can.
5. Do you agree with Davie's opinion about flying across the continent on a jet? Write a paragraph giving your reasons.

Master Builders

LOUIS SULLIVAN (1856–1924)
Louis Sullivan designed the first modern skyscraper. The Wainwright Building in St. Louis is an expression of his belief that a skyscraper "must be every inch a proud and soaring thing."

FRANK LLOYD WRIGHT (1869–1959)
Frank Lloyd Wright is considered the greatest architect that America has produced. His daring imagination came up with the design for the Guggenheim Museum in New York City.

EERO SAARINEN (1910–1961)
Eero Saarinen employed the best principles of modern design in his architecture. Perhaps his favorite building was the Dulles International Airport in Washington, D.C.

IEOH MING PEI (1917–   )
The East Building of the National Gallery of Art in Washington, D.C., is an example of the work of the modern architect known to the world as I. M. Pei.

The City of Tomorrow

ALVIN SCHWARTZ

Of all human creations, the city is one of the most remarkable. For over five thousand years it has served as a crossroads where people come together to buy and sell, to work and seek their fortunes, to learn, to be entertained, and to live their lives as best they can.

For many years, however, the good life has been hard to find in some American cities. Many of the houses are old and shabby. Slums have spread. Schools and libraries have worn out. Business districts have run down. Streets are clogged with traffic.

To make our cities better places to live and work in, many of them are being rebuilt. To provide for a growing population, many new cities and new towns are being planned. In both cases exciting changes are being considered.

One plan would reduce the number of cars on city streets. Cities would rise from spacious, landscaped platforms well above street level. Cars, buses, trucks, and trains would operate below. To reach a platform, drivers would park in a garage. Then they would take an elevator or escalator up one level. The idea already is in use on a small scale in Hartford, Connecticut.

But architects and planners are already thinking about far more imaginative structures—single buildings containing cities that would extend for miles. Because they would be long and narrow, they are called *linear cities.*

Older cities have, of course, often grown in a circular pattern. Important activities are found at the center, from which the city extends in all directions. Early cities grew this way because they were easier to defend. But even when defense was not needed, this pattern continued to work as long as the city was small enough so that the center could be reached easily.

In recent years, however, cities and their suburbs have spread over such large areas that it has become far more difficult to reach the center in a reasonable time. As the suburbs continue to expand, the situation can only grow worse.

The linear city is seen as one solution. It would make it far easier to reach important activity

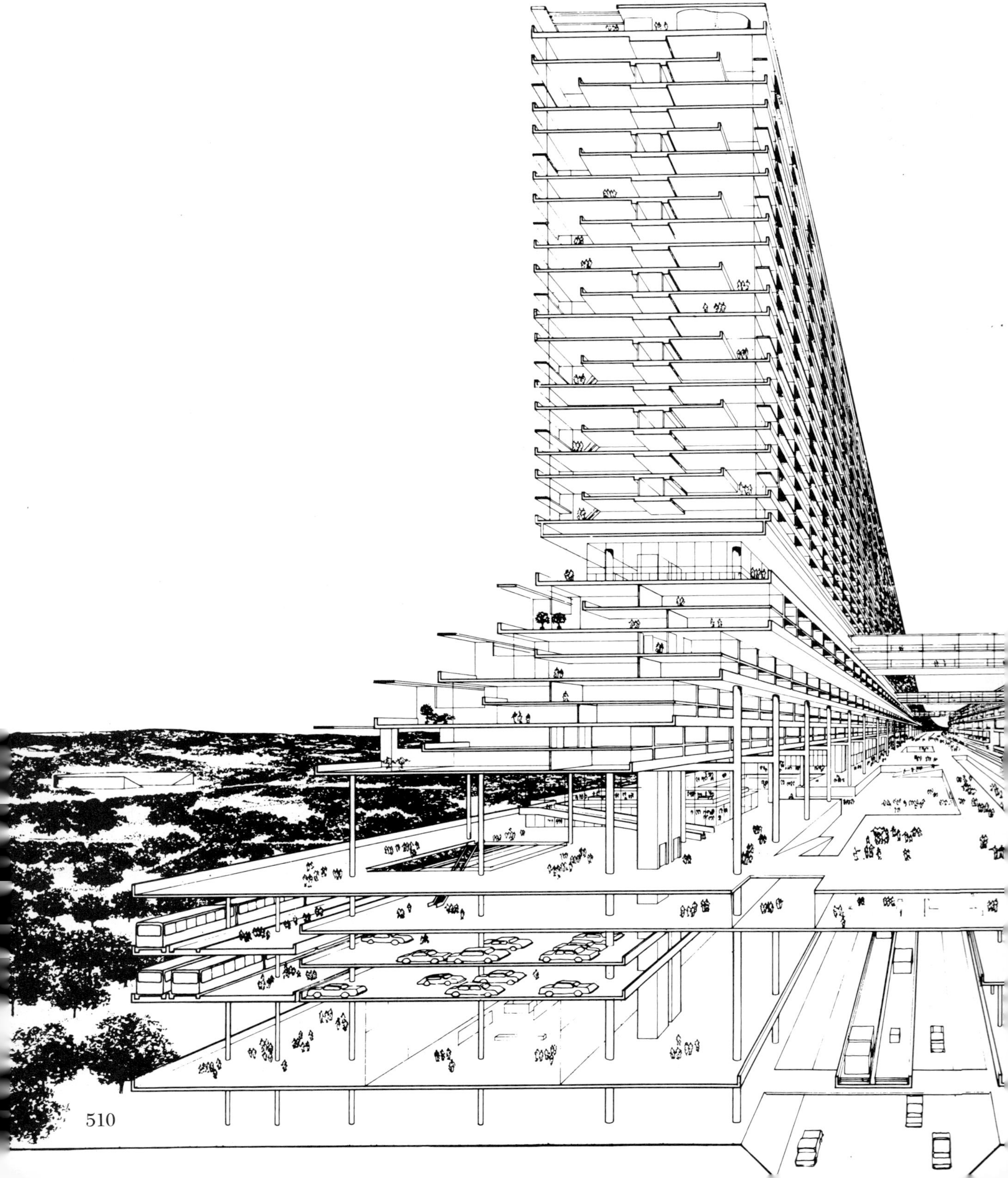

centers. It would also stop sprawl and once again bring the countryside close to the city. The illustration shows a linear city designed by two Princeton University architects.

The possibility of climate control is also being explored. Many planners foresee a day when it will be practical to cover a city with giant domes and thereby control the weather inside. Inside the city there would no longer be a need for heavy clothes, umbrellas, and snow-removal equipment. In addition, buildings could be made

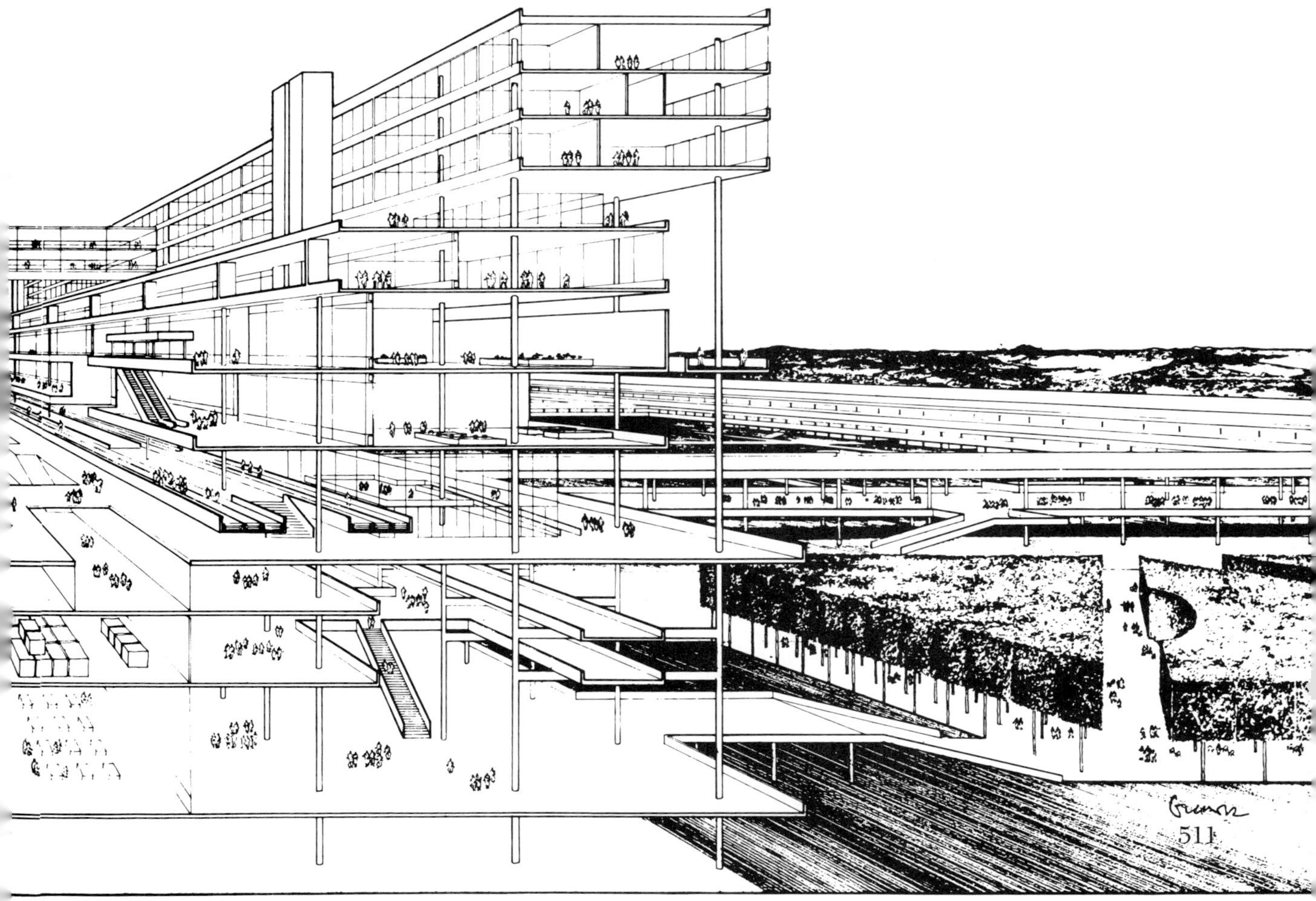

of cheap, lightweight materials, and roofs would not be needed. The drawing below shows how Poughkeepsie, New York, might appear with a set of domes.

New kinds of transportation also may be on the way. A small electric car called an *Urbmobile* is one idea. It is seen as an answer to traffic jams of the future. For trips of more than a few miles, it would use a highway with an electric guide rail. The guide rail provides the car with power. It keeps it on course at 96 kilometers (about 60 miles) an hour. Its drivers, meanwhile, are free to read their newspapers. Whenever they want to, they can switch over to a battery. Then they can drive off under their own power.

There are plans for a hovercraft that travels only inches above the earth on a cushion of air. A giant helicopter might fly from city center to city center. A train may travel at hundreds of miles an hour through tunnels hundreds of miles long.

A single building large enough to be a complete town or city is another plan that has taken shape. Architects call such buildings *megastructures.* One of the first steps toward the use of a megastructure was taken in Chicago where a

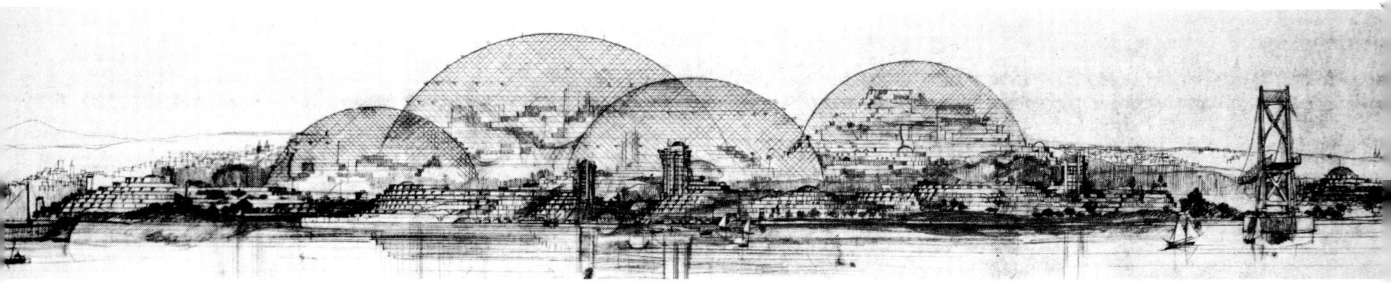

100-story building, almost four hundred meters ($\frac{1}{4}$ mile) high, now stands. It has seven hundred apartments, twenty-eight floors of offices, parking space for twelve hundred cars, five floors of shops, a swimming pool, a health club, and an ice-skating rink. It is pictured below at the left.

The building in the picture bottom right is a *Modemixer*. It is placed over a picture of Buffalo, New York. By the year 2000 it may be in use in a number of cities. Its purpose is to bring together all forms of transportation that serve a city. In this version, helicopters land on top, Urbmobiles and standard cars are parked inside, and hovercraft and high-speed ferries use the lower areas.

Another experimental city would have a great many of its facilities underground. As a result, there would be very little noise.

All cars and trucks would be required to travel through the city by tunnels from which deliveries and shipments would be made. Travel from place

to place within the city would be by some new form of underground transportation, such as an automated subway which would take travelers in small "pods" directly to their destinations.

All wires and pipes would be installed in easily reached tunnels. Underground pipes would carry smoke and fumes from factories to an air-cleaning plant.

Traffic and air pollution would be ended. Noise would be reduced. Then it would be possible to mix homes with shops, theaters, schools, and even factories far more than is now done in most communities. This, in turn, would reduce the need for public transportation.

Planning new cities and improving those we have means learning to see things in a new way. It means seeing things not only as they are, but as they could be. It also means doing everything possible to bring about needed changes.

Reflections

1. What do you think is meant by the phrase "the good life" in the second paragraph?
2. Which plan for cities of the future do you feel is the most imaginative? What would be the advantages of the plan? What might be some disadvantages?
3. Would you like to live in a perfectly run and completely controlled city? Explain why or why not?
4. If you could design and build the "perfect city of the future," what would it be like? Write and illustrate a report describing your city.

Concrete Mixers

PATRICIA HUBBELL

The drivers are washing the concrete mixers;
Like elephant tenders they hose them down.
Tough gray-skinned monsters standing
    ponderous,
Elephant-bellied and elephant-nosed,
Standing in muck up to their wheel-caps,
Like rows of elephants, tail to trunk.
Their drivers perch on their backs like mahouts,
Sending the sprays of water up.
They rid the trunk-like trough of concrete,
Direct the spray to the bulging sides,
Turn and start the monsters moving.
        Concrete mixers
        Move like elephants
        Bellow like elephants
        Spray like elephants,
    Concrete mixers are urban elephants,
    Their trunks are raising a city.

WORD ORDER IN SENTENCES

When we write the twenty-six letters from *A* to *Z*, we usually arrange them in alphabetical order. When we write the numbers from 1 to 100, we usually arrange them in numerical order. When we write or read a sentence, we use an arrangement of words. Words are grouped together in most of the sentences we read. This arrangement of words in sentences is called word order. To see how this works, let's examine one sentence. Begin with the following:

The boy eats breakfast.

Here we have the word *the*, a noun (*boy*), a verb (*eats*), and another noun (*breakfast*).

Let's arrange this into a pattern.

⟶	NOUN	VERB	NOUN
The	boy	eats	breakfast

Now let us take the first part of the sentence and make this arrangement, or pattern:

	⟶	NOUN
A		boy
An		American boy
A		young American boy
One	noisy,	young American boy
A	somewhat noisy,	young American boy
This	somewhat noisy,	young American boy

In this way, we can tell more about *boy.* We can think of other words to use instead, but the important thing here is that any words we use will fit a pattern. In this pattern *a, an, one,* and *this* come first. It is not natural to say, "Somewhat noisy young this American boy." The words that describe *boy* follow words like *this* or *the.* As long as the other words fit before *boy,* you can change the word order: *young, noisy, American boy,* or *noisy, young American boy,* but not *a somewhat boy.* The words are arranged, or ordered, to describe *boy.*

We can tell more about *boy* by doing something like this:

NOUN	⟵
boy,	John Blair,
boy,	John Blair, who lives down the street,
boy,	John Blair, who plays baseball,
boy,	John Blair, the champion tennis player,
boy,	John Blair, my cousin,

We could then add other words. But the addition of other similar word groups would be in the order shown above. The words would be grouped together after *boy.* So now instead of *The boy* to begin our sentence *The boy eats breakfast,* we have the following:

This somewhat noisy, young American boy, *John Blair, my cousin, the champion tennis player who plays baseball and lives down the street,* eats breakfast.

The words are ordered and grouped to give you more information about *boy.*

Now let's take a look at *eats.*

	VERB	
slowly quickly quietly noisily	eats	slowly quickly quietly noisily

We might choose other words to describe how the boy eats, and we may say either "eats slowly" or "slowly eats." Words like *slowly, quickly, quietly,* and *noisily* are adverbs. They are sometimes used to go along with verbs. We may generally place them wherever we wish in a sentence. Since natural word order here permits a choice, we might then expand our sentence to this:

This somewhat noisy, young American boy, John Blair, my cousin, the champion tennis player who plays baseball and lives down the street, *slowly and quietly* eats breakfast (or eats breakfast *slowly and quietly* or, if we wish, we could begin or end the sentence with *slowly and quietly*).

Now take a look at *breakfast:*

⟶	NOUN	VERB	⟶	NOUN
The	boy	eats	his that tasty an appetizing, tasty a hot, appetizing, tasty	breakfast breakfast breakfast breakfast

⟶	NOUN	VERB	NOUN	⟵
The	boy	eats	breakfast	of bacon, eggs, and pancakes of crisp bacon, fried eggs, and golden pancakes

So our original sentence, *The boy eats breakfast,* has become the following:

This somewhat noisy, young American boy, John Blair, my cousin, the champion tennis player who plays baseball and lives down the street, slowly and quietly eats a hot, appetizing, tasty breakfast of crisp bacon, fried eggs, and golden pancakes.

We have now seen some ways to arrange words in sentences. But look what happens if we follow no order.

Noisy and the somewhat Blair John baseball boy young champion cousin this my eggs fried plays bacon crisp slowly tennis who player and lives street quietly the eats hot a pancakes golden of tasty appetizing and.

See what you can do with one of these sentences by expanding it as *The boy eats breakfast* was expanded.

A girl eats dinner.
The dog chases a cat.
The man drives a car.

Watch out for the order of words, because in English, word order is an important clue to meaning.

Glossary

FULL PRONUNCIATION KEY

The pronunciation of each word is shown just after the word, in this way: **ab•bre•vi•ate** (ə brē′ vē āt).

The letters and signs used are pronounced as in the words below.

The mark ′ is placed after a syllable with primary or heavy accent, as in the example above.

The mark ′ after a syllable shows a secondary or lighter accent, as in **ab•bre•vi•a•tion** (ə brē′ vē ā′ shən).

a	hat	i	it	p	paper	v	very
ā	age	ī	ice	r	run	w	will
ä	father			s	say	y	young
		j	jam	sh	she	z	zero
b	bad	k	kind	t	tell	zh	measure
ch	child	l	land	th	thin		
d	did	m	me	ŦH	then		
		n	no			ə	represents:
e	let	ng	long	u	cup		a in about
ē	equal			u̇	full		e in taken
ėr	term	o	hot	ü	rule		i in pencil
		ō	open				o in lemon
f	fat	ô	order				u in circus
g	go	oi	oil				
h	he	ou	house				

The pronunciation key, syllable breaks, and phonetic respellings in this glossary are adapted from the second edition of the *Thorndike Barnhart Intermediate Dictionary.* Users of previous editions or of other dictionaries will find other symbols for some words.

ab•bre•vi•a•tion (ə brē vē ā′ shən) short form of a word: *Mr. is an abbreviation of Mister.*

ab•so•lute•ly (ab′ sə lüt′ lē) completely; without doubt

ac•cu•rate (ak′ yə rət) free from mistakes; correct

a•cre (ā′ kər) measure of land equal to 4,840 square yards

ac•ro•nym (ak′ rə nim′) word made up of the first letter or letters of a many-worded term: *UNESCO is an acronym for the United Nations Educational, Scientific, and Cultural Organization.*

Ad•am (ad′ əm) in the Bible, the name of the first man

ad•van•tage (ad van′ tij) reason for preferring something; reason for choosing something

aer•o•nau•tics (er′ ə nô′ tiks) flying and space travel

ail (ā′ əl) to feel sick

air•borne (er′ bôrn′ *or* ar′ bôrn′) up in the air; carried by the air

air clean•ing (er *or* ar klēn′ ing) taking dirt out of the air; cleaning the air

Aire•dale (er′ dāl *or* ar′ dāl) large curly-coated brown and black terrier

air raid (er *or* ar rād) an attack by airplanes

A•kar•ram (ak′ ə ram) river in east Africa

al•ge•bra (al′ jə brə) branch of mathematics dealing with unknowns

a•li•as (ā′ lē əs) otherwise; also known as

al•tar (äl′ tər) a place used as a center of religious ceremonies

am•a•teur (am′ ə chər *or* am′ ə tər) person who does something for pleasure or fun, rather than for money

a•maze (ə māz′) to surprise; to cause wonder

am•bu•lance (am′ byə ləns) a vehicle, like a wagon or truck, that carries sick or injured persons

a•mid (ə mid′) in the middle of

an•ces•tor (an′ ses′tər) a parent, grandparent or relative from the past

an•ces•try (an′ ses′ trē) all of one's ancestors or parents, grandparents, great grandparents, etc.

an•chor (ang′ kər) pronged piece of iron used to hold a ship in place: *To weigh anchor is to lift the anchor before departure.*

an•cient (ān′ shənt) relating to an early time in history; very old

an•noy (ə noi′) to bother; to disturb

an•nu•lar (an′ yə lər) shaped like a ring; round

an•te•lope (an′ tl ōp) swift African animal with horns, something like a deer

an•ten•na (an ten′ ə) wires or rods used to tune in radio or television waves

an•tique (an tēk′) very old

anx•ious (angk′ shəs *or* ang′ shəs) uneasy about something; worried

ap•par•ent (ə par′ ənt) easily seen

ap•pe•tiz•er (ap′ ə tī′ zər) food or drink served before a meal

ap•proach (ə prōch′) to come near or close

Ar•a•bic (ar′ ə bik) language spoken in parts of the Middle East

ar•chi•tect (är′ kə tekt) one who designs buildings

ar•chi•tec•ture (är′ kə tek′ chər) the art or science of building

ar•roy•o (ə roi′ ō) term used in the Southwest for a ditch or groove in the earth with steep sides, often having a stream running through it in the rainy season

hat, āge, fär; let, ēqual, tėrm; it, īce; hot, ōpen, ôrder; oil, out; cup, pu̇t, rüle; ch, child; ng, long; sh, she; th, thin; ᴛʜ, then; zh, measure; ə represents *a* in about, *e* in taken, *i* in pencil, *o* in lemon, *u* in circus.

as·bes·tos (as bes′ təs) fabric made of fire-resistant fibers

a·ston·ished (ə ston′ isht) very surprised; amazed

as·tro·naut (as′ trə nôt) person trained to pilot or to act as a member of a crew of a spacecraft

as·tron·o·mer (ə stron′ ə mər) expert in astronomy

as·tron·o·my (ə stron′ ə mē) science that deals with the physical and chemical characteristics of heavenly bodies

at·mo·sphere (at′ mə sfir) layer of air or gases above the earth

au·di·ence (ô′ dē əns) people who watch or attend something, such as a television program, movie, play, or lecture

Au·du·bon (ô′ də bon) John James (jon jāmz)

au·to·mat·ed (ô′ tə māt id) running by itself; not powered by a person

au·to·mat·ic (ô′ tə mat′ ik) done without thinking

a·venge (ə venj′) to correct a wrong; to hurt someone because the person has hurt someone else

Bac·chus (bak′ əs) ancient Greek god of celebration

badg·er (baj′ ər) gray animal that lives underground

baf·fler (baf′ lər) something that puzzles or is hard to understand

ba·gel (bā′ gəl) hard roll, shaped like a doughnut

Ba·ja Cal·i·for·nia (bä′ hä kal′ ə fôr′ nyə) lower California; part of Mexico directly south of California

bal·let (bal′ ā *or* ba lā′) a flowing kind of dance made up of special steps; often telling a story set to music

ban·dit (ban′ dit) a robber

bane·ful (bān′ fəl) destructive

ban·tam (ban′ təm) a small fowl, like a small chicken

ba·roque (bə rōk′) kind of pearl that is shaped unevenly

bar·rack·like (bar′ ək līk′) plain; like an army building

bear·ings (ber′ ingz *or* bar′ ingz) sense of direction; knowledge of where one is

be·hold (bi hōld′) to look; to see

bel·ly (bel′ ē) to swell; to bulge

Ben·ton (bent′ ən) Thomas Hart (tom′ əs härt)

Ber·keley Hills (bėr′ klē hilz) hills north of San Francisco

be·wil·dered (bi wil′ dərd) confused and puzzled

Big Dip·per (big dip′ ər) group of stars that can be seen in the sky in the North

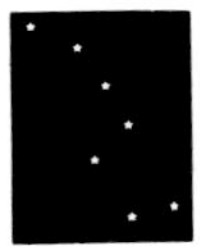

bill (bil) the jaws or beak of a bird

bil·low (bil′ ō) rolling high wave

bit (bit) the cutting edge of a tool

black·smith (blak′ smith′) one who makes or fixes things of iron

bliss·ful·ly (blis′ fəl ē) very happily

bliz·zard (bliz′ ərd) large snowstorm with high winds

bloom·ers (blü′ mərz) loose pants formerly worn by women under a skirt

blue·bot·tle (blü′ bot′ l) kind of large bluish fly

blue·grass (blü′ gras′) grass with bluish-green stems that grows in Kentucky

bluff (bluf) steep hill or cliff

board·ing·house (bôr′ ding hous′) house where owner rents rooms to people and serves meals

boll (bōl) the seed or pod of a plant

bon•fire (bon′ fīr′) large fire built outdoors
boom•er (büm′ ər) one who travels from place to place and takes different jobs
borscht (bôrsht) soup made from beets
box-ball (boks bôl′) game played by throwing a ball against a wall and trying to get it to bounce in certain squares on the sidewalk
Braille (brāl) alphabet of raised dots that can be felt by running the fingers over the page, used by the blind, named after the blind Frenchman Louis Braille who developed the system
break•er (brā′ kər) large wave that breaks into foam
bril•liant (bril′ yənt) very smart
brim•stone (brim′ stōn′) sulfur
brooch (brōch or brüch) piece of jewelry, such as a pin, usually worn near the neck
Brook•lyn (brůk′ lən) a part of New York City
brown•stone (broun′ stōn′) kind of narrow house with no more than five stories, built of brown stone
bruise (brüz) a bump that discolors the skin
Brus•sels (brus′əlz) capital city of Belgium
Bud•dha (bü′ də *or* bůd′ ə) religious leader who lived in Asia about 2,300 years ago
buff (buf) dull yellow
bung (bung) to toss *slang*
bun•ga•low (bung′ gə lō) small house or cabin
bunk•house (bungk′ hous′) one-roomed building with many beds; building in which a lot of people sleep
bur•den (bėrd′ n) something that makes trouble or gets in the way; load
bush cow (bůsh kou) a large, short-horned member of the antelope family
bush•whack•er (bůsh′ hwak′ ər) one who lives in the woods and attacks and robs passers-by
but•ton (but′ n) kind of pearl that is flattened like a disc, not round
ca•ble car (kā′ bəl kär) a car that moves on a railway by an overhead cable
ca•boose (kə büs′) last car on a freight train, in which the crew sleeps
Cair Par•a•vel (ker par′ ə vel)
cal•cu•late (kal′ kyə lāt) to figure out by arithmetic
cal•cu•la•tion (kal′ kyə lā′ shən) result found by careful figuring or calculating
cal•i•co (kal′ ə cō) cotton cloth with a pattern printed on it
cam•phor (kam′ fər) a chemical from camphor wood used in medicine
can•ter (kan′tər) a three-beat walk that is slower than a gallop
can•yon (kan′ yən) narrow valley with high sides, often with a river running at the bottom
cap•sule (kap′ səl) container, such as the part of a rocket that holds the crew
car•at (kar′ ət) unit of weight used for jewels and precious metals
car•a•van (kar′ ə van) group of people traveling together for safety through dangerous country
car•go (kär′ gō) goods carried on a ship
car•ni•val (kär′ nə vəl) program of games and amusements
Car•thage (kär′ thij) ancient city in north Africa
Cas•satt (kə sat′) Mary (mer′ ē *or* mar′ ē)
cast (kast) the characters in a play
cat•sup (kech′ əp *or* kat′ səp) sauce made of tomatoes, onions, vinegar, and spices
cav•i•ar (kav′ ē är′) fish eggs
Cen•tral Park (sen′ trəl pärk) large park in the middle of Manhattan Island in New York City

hat, āge, fär; let, ēqual, tėrm; it, īce; hot, ōpen, ôrder; oil, out; cup, půt, rüle; ch, child; ng, long; sh, she; th, thin; ᴛʜ, then; zh, measure; ə represents *a* in about, *e* in taken, *i* in pencil, *o* in lemon, *u* in circus.

cer•e•mo•ny (ser′ ə mō′ nē) special act or acts to honor someone

cham•ber•lain (chām′ bər lən) one who manages the household of a king or nobleman

check•book (chək′ bu̇k′) a book that has blank checks in it

choke•cherry (chōk′ cher′ ē) bitter wild cherry

chop•sticks (chop′ stiks) sticks held between the thumb and fingers, used to lift food to the mouth

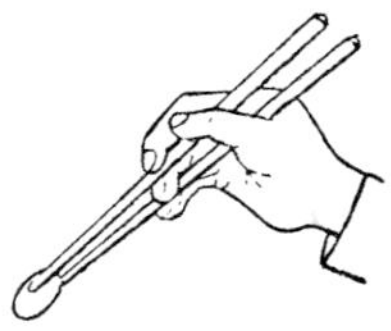

chow mein (chou mān) a Chinese dish made of sliced vegetables, meat, and crisp fried noodles

chro•nom•e•ter (krə nom′ ə tər) clock, watch, or other timepiece that keeps very accurate time

cin•der (sin′ dər) ash; burned piece of wood or coal

ci•pher (sī′ fər) kind of secret writing; code

cir•cuit (sėr′ kit) a closed path followed by an electric current

cir•cu•lar (sėr′ kyə lər) shaped like a circle; round

Cle•o•pat•ra (klē′ ə pat′ rə *or* klē ə pā′ trə) ancient Egyptian queen

clin•ic (klin′ ik) a place where doctors treat sick people

clip•per (klip′ər) cutting tool similar to an electric razor

clogged (klogd) crowded; stopped up

clo•ven (klō′ vən) divided into two parts, as a hoof

clus•ter (klus′ tər) to come together; to make a group

coach (kōch) **1.** four-wheeled cart pulled by one or more horses **2.** adviser to a sports team

coach•man (kōch′ mən) man who drives a coach

co•co•yam (kō′ kō yam′) tropical yam

code (kōd) kind of secret writing that substitutes other letters or symbols for those in the message

coif•fure (kwä fyu̇r′) hairstyle; hairdo

Col•o•rad•o Riv•er (kol′ ə rad′ ō *or* kol′ ə rä′ dō riv′ ər) river in the Southwest that forms the Grand Canyon

co•los•sal (kə los′ əl) very big

com•bi•na•tion (kom′ bə nā′ shən) one whole made by joining two or more items or objects

com•mand mod•ule (kə mand′ moj′ül *or* mod′ yül) the part of a spacecraft in which astronauts command a space flight

com•mer•cial (kə mėr′ shəl) a break in a regular TV show to sell something

com•mu•ni•ty (kə myü′ nə tē) group of people living together

com•par•i•son (kəm par′ ə sen) finding out how objects are like or unlike each other

com•put•er (kəm pyü′ tər) machine that computes; electronic machine that solves problems when given certain coded information

con•cave (kon kāv′) hollow; rounded inward

con•cen•tra•tion (kon′ sən trā shən) careful attention; thinking about one thing at a time

Co•ney Is•land (kō′ nē ī′ lənd) beach and amusement park in Brooklyn in New York City

con•jure (kon′ jər *or* kun′ jər) to cause to appear or disappear by saying certain words

con•nec•tion (kə nek′ shən) place where two things join or come together

con•ser•va•tion (kän′ sər vā′ shən) protecting something, such as natural resources

con•stel•la•tion (kon′ stə lā′ shən) group of stars that seem to form a picture

con·trap·tion (kən trap′ shən) gadget; complicated thing; clumsy object

con·ven·tion·al·i·ty (kən ven′ shə nal′ ə tē) usual way everyone acts; customary behavior

Cop·ley (kō′ plē) John Singleton (jon sing′ gəl tən)

co·ro·na (kə rō nə) a ring around a heavenly body

'cos (kôz) because

coun·cil (koun′ səl) a group of wise people who give advice

cov·ered wag·on (kuv′ ərd wag′ ən) wagon having a canvas cover that can be taken off

coy·o·te (kī ō tē *or* kī′ ōt) small wolf

cra·ter (krā′ tər) a bowl-shaped depression or pit

cres·cent (kres′ ənt) something shaped like the moon in its first quarter

crev·ice (krev′ is) crack

croc·o·dile (krok′ ə dīl) large African lizard that lives in rivers and swamps

crop (krop) all of something that a farmer raises; whole amount of something raised at one time: *Last year we raised a large crop of corn and hogs.*

cross·beam (krôs′ bēm′) beam that runs across a ceiling

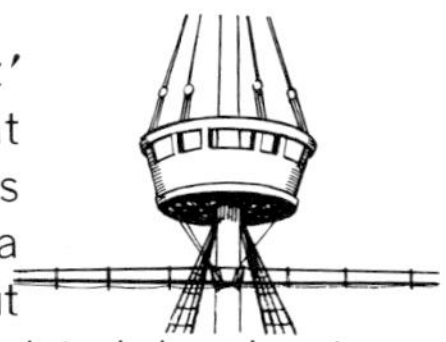

crow's nest (krōz′ nest) platform at the top of a ship's mast, used as a place to look out

crul·ler (krul′ ər) twisted doughnut

cryp·tog·ra·pher (krip tog′ rə fər) one who works with codes, either making or breaking them

cue (kü) a word or phrase in a play that serves as a signal for a speech or action

cu·lotte (kü′ lot *or* kü lot′) women's pants, cut loose and full to look like a skirt

cun·ning (kun′ ing) skill or cleverness

cur·rant (kər′ ənt) small seedless raisin

cyc·la·men (sik′ lə mən) kind of plant with red, pink, purple, or white nodding flowers

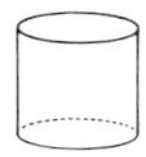

cyl·in·der (sil′ ən dər) object shaped like a tin can or roller

dam·sel (dam′ zəl) old-fashioned word for girl; maiden

dash (dash) to destroy or ruin: *Her hopes were dashed.*

da·ta pro·ces·sing (dā′ tə *or* dat′ ə präs′ es ing *or* prōs′ es ing) acting on some information or facts, like taking two numbers (the data) and adding them together (processing)

de·but (dā′ byü *or* dā byü′) first performance; first time a person performs

de·ci·pher (di sī′ fər) to figure out a coded message; to break a code

ded·i·cate (ded′ ə kāt) to name something after a person to show respect or admiration

de·moc·ra·cy (di mok′ rə sē) kind of government in which each citizen has a vote

de·ny (dē nī′) to refuse

de·sign (di zīn′) **1.** to make plans for **2.** a pattern or arrangement of things

des·o·late (des′ ə lit) without people; lonely

de·spair (di sper′ *or* di spar′) loss of hope; state of feeling that nothing good will happen to one

des·ti·na·tion (des′ tə nā′ shən) place where one is going

hat, āge, fär; let, ēqual, tėrm; it, īce; hot, ōpen, ôrder; oil, out; cup, pu̇t, rüle; ch, child; ng, long; sh, she; th, thin; ᴛʜ, then; zh, measure; ə represents *a* in about, *e* in taken, *i* in pencil, *o* in lemon, *u* in circus.

de•ter•mi•na•tion (di tėr′ mə nā′ shən) deciding to do something and sticking to it; great firmness and decision
de•vel•op (di vel′ əp) to treat film to make the image on it appear
di•am•e•ter (dī am′ ə tər) the thickness or width of something
di•a•ry (dī′ ə rē) account written down each day of what has happened to one, or what one has done or thought, during that day
di•no•saur (dī′ nə sôr) any of a group of reptiles now extinct, some of which were larger than elephants
di•rec•tor (də rek′ tər) one who tells the actors what to do in a play
dire•ful (dīr′ fəl) frightening; terrible
dis•ci•pline (dis′ ə plin) **1.** condition of obedience or order **2.** system of rules of conduct
dis•cour•age (dis kər′ ij) to depress; to deprive of confidence
dis•guise (dis gīz′) clothes, masks, and/or actions used to change one's appearance to hide who one really is
dis•tinc•tion (dis tingk′ shən) something that shows that someone or something is special
dis•trict (dis′ trikt) area
doc•ile (dos′ sel) quiet; obedient; doing what one is told
doc•u•men•ta•ry (däk′ yə ment′ ə rē) a factual film or photograph
do•nate (dōn′ āt) to give
Down East (doun ēst) Maine
downs (dounz) hilly grassland having few trees
draft board (draft bôrd) a government office that picks people to be soldiers
dry•ad (drī′ əd) wood nymph; spirit
dug•out (dug′ out′) a pit in the ground used as a shelter
dun (dən) a drab, dull color
Du•rand (də rand′) John (jon)
Ea•kins (ēk′ inz) Thomas (tom′ əs)
e•clair (ā kler′ *or* ā klar′) long, thin pastry filled with cream and covered with icing
e•clipse (i klips′) partial or complete blocking of light that occurs when one heavenly body passes another
ed•dy (ed′ ē) to move back and forth; to swirl
E•den Val•ley (ēd′ n val′ ē)
eel (ēl) a snakelike fish
eer•ie (ir′ ē) strange; weird; mysterious
Ein•stein (īn′ stīn) Albert (al′ bėrt′) genius who made many important discoveries in mathematics and physics
E•koi (ē′ koi) a tribe of East Africa
el•der•ly (el′ dər lē) old
El Di•a•blo (el dē äb′ lō) Spanish: the devil
e•lec•tric•i•ty (i lek tris′ ə tē) kind of energy in the form of a current: *Lightning is a natural form of electricity.*
e•lec•tro•car•di•o•gram (i lek′ trō kär′ dē ə gram) vertical lines made by a machine that records a heart's beat and rhythm
elk (elk) large deer of northern Europe and Asia
E•mil (ā′ mēl′)
en•cased (en kāst′) surrounded by
en•core (än′ kôr) an additional performance
en•cy•clo•pe•di•a (en sī′ klə pē′ dē ə) set of books containing articles, alphabetically arranged, giving information about many subjects
en•er•gy (en′ ər jē) power
en•gi•neer (en′ jə nir′) **1.** one who makes the plans for machines, buildings, bridges, roads, etc. **2.** one who runs a railroad engine
e•nor•mous (i nôr′ məs) very big; huge
e•ro•sion (i rō′ zhən) wearing away
es•ca•la•tor (es′ kə lā′ tər) moving staircase
e•ter•nal (i tėr′ nəl) endless
E•tuk (ē′ tük)
Eve (ēv) in the Bible, the name of the first woman
ex•e•cute (ek′ sə kyüt) **1.** to kill **2.** to put into effect

ex·pe·di·tion (ek′ spə dish′ ən) journey made for a special purpose
ex·per·i·ment (ek sper′ ə mənt) test to learn something new or prove a theory
ex·per·i·men·tal (ek sper′ ə men′ tl) as a test, to see how it will work out
ex·ploit (ek′ sploit) important, wonderful, or brave deed that someone has done
ex·ter·min·ate (ek stėr′ mə nāt) to kill; to wipe out
ex·tinct (ek stingkt′) no longer existing, such as certain kinds of animals: *All dinosaurs are now extinct.*
fa·cil·i·ties (fə sil′ ə tēz) equipment that makes living easier
fal·ter (fôl′ tər) to hesitate; to run out of energy
fas·cin·ate (fas′ n āt) to make very interested in something
fa·tal (fāt′ əl) causing death
fath·om (faŦH′ əm) unit equal to six feet, used for measuring the depth of water
faun (fôn) in Roman stories, imaginary creature that looked human but had the ears, horns, legs, and tail of a goat
fe·ver·ish·ly (fē′ vər ish lē) excitedly; very quickly
fi·ber (fī′ bər) a threadlike part
fir (fėr) kind of pine tree, often used as a Christmas tree
fleet (flēt) swift; fast
flour·ish (flėr′ ish) decoration; fancy way of doing something
foal (fōl) baby horse
fo·li·age (fō′ lē ij) leaves of plants
fore·cast·er (fôr′ kast ər) one who tells what is coming in the future
fore·leg (fôr′ leg′) either front leg of a four-legged animal
fore·see (fôr sē′) to see ahead of time
forged (fôrjd) made or wrote something false for the purpose of deceiving or fooling someone; signed falsely
for·te (fôr′ tā) loudly
fran·tic (fran′ tik) very excited; extremely worried
fre·quen·cy (frē′ kwən sē) the number of times something appears or happens in a given time or space
fri·jol·es (frē′ hōlz *or* fri hō′ lēz) Spanish: beans
Fris·co (fris′ kō) nickname for the St. Louis and San Francisco Railroad
frost·bit·ten (frôst′ bit′ n) drained of blood by very cold weather; frozen
fume (fyüm) bad smell; gas
Gal·i·le·o (gal′ ə lā′ ō)
gal·ley (gal′ ē) kitchen of a ship
gal·lop (gal′ əp) to move very fast; to run so that all four feet are off the ground at the same time
gar·ment (gär′ mənt) a piece of clothing

ga·zelle (gə zel′) small, swift antelope of Africa
ge·fil·te fish (gə fil′ tə fish) ball of chopped fish, served cold
gen·ius (jē′ nyəs) very smart person; person who can do things most people cannot do
Glack·ens (glak′ ənz) William (wil′ yəm)
glow·er (glou′ ər) to stare with anger
goat·herd (gōt′ hėrd′) one who takes care of goats
Go·bi (gō′ bē) desert in Asia
gog·gles (gog′ əlz) protective glasses
gold leaf (gōld lēf) gold that is painted on a surface
gou·lash (gü′ lash) stew of meat, onions, and other vegetables, flavored with paprika
gour·met (gür′ mā) **1.** one who is fond of delicious food and drink **2.** the kind of food such a person would enjoy
Grand Can·yon (grand kan′ yən) deep gorge formed by the Colorado River, located in Arizona
grape·vine (grāp′ vīn) a rumor; report

hat, āge, fär; let, ēqual, tėrm; it, īce; hot, ōpen, ôrder; oil, out; cup, pu̇t, rüle; ch, child; ng, long; sh, she; th, thin; ŦH, then; zh, measure; ə represents *a* in about, *e* in taken, *i* in pencil, *o* in lemon, *u* in circus.

grid·dle (grid′ l) piece of flat metal that is heated and used to fry foods

griev·ance (grē′ vəns) reason for being angry; cause for complaint

gum·bo (gum′ bō) stew or soup made with okra and chicken or fish

hag·gle (hag′ əl) to bargain

hai·ku (hī′ kü′) a Japanese poem of a fixed 17-syllable form

hail·stone (hāl′ stōn′) a lump of ice or snow

half·hitch (haf′ hich′) kind of knot

han·som (han′ səm) kind of horse-drawn coach used for hire

har·mo·ny (här′ mən nē) different notes that when played or sung at the same time, sound good together

har·vest (här′ vist) to gather a crop

head·land (hed′ lənd) point of land that sticks out into the water

hes·i·tate (hez′ ə tāt) to hold back; to pause; to be doubtful

hi·ba·chi (hi bäch′ ē) small portable charcoal grill, used for cooking meat

Hicks (hiks) Edward (ed′ wôrd)

high·land (hī′ lənd) mountain land

hinged (hinjd) fitted with a hinge; arranged so that one part can swing back and forth

Ho·mer (hō′ mər) Winslow (win′ slō)

ho·ri·zon (hə rī′ zn) line in the distance where the sky seems to meet the earth or sea

horned toad (hôrnd tōd) a small, harmless lizard with scales and hornlike growths

hors d′ oeuvres (ôr′ dėrvz′) small snacks or appetizers, served before the main meal

Hou·di·ni (hü dēn′ ē) Harry (har′ ē) famous stage magician

hov·er·craft (huv′ ər *or* hov′ ər kraft′) car or boat that is supported on a column of air produced by its fans or by jets

hud·dle (həd′ əl) to draw oneself together; to crouch

hy·giene (hī′ jēn′) science of health and conditions needed to avoid disease

ig·nit·er (ig nīt′ ər) something that sets something else on fire

il·lus·tra·tion (il′ ə strā′ shən) picture of something

im·mense·ly (i mens′ lē) greatly; very much so

im·mi·grant (im′ ə grənt) one who moves from one country to another

im·pa·la (im pa′ lə) kind of antelope

in·can·ta·tion (in′ kan tā′ shən) magic spell; words said to do magic

in·com·plete (in′ kəm plēt′) not finished

in·cor·por·ate (in kôr′ pə rāt′) to include

in·fan·try (in′ fan trē) foot soldiers

in·fec·tion (in fek′ shən) sickness

in·fir·ma·ry (in fėr′ mä rē) place where sick people are cared for

in·no·cent (in′ ə sənt) good; blameless: *A person who has not done anything wrong is innocent.*

in·quis·i·tive (in kwiz′ ə tiv) curious; looking into things

in·sist·ent (in sis′ tent) continuing to ask for something; unwilling to take no for an answer

in·stalled (in stôld′) set in place for use

in·ter·na·tion·al (in′ tər nash′ ə nəl) having to do with more than one country

in·ter·pret (in tėr′ prit) to translate; to explain the meaning of something in another language or other words

in·ter·rupt (in tə rupt′) to break in on a speech or activity

in·trude (in trüd′) to break in; to go where one has not been invited

in·ves·ti·gate (in ves′ tə gāt) to look into closely; to study

ir·re·sist·i·ble (ir′ i zis′ tə bəl) not resistible; unable to be resisted

Is•la Cer•ral•vo (ēs′ lä se räl′ vō) island off Baja California just east of La Paz

ivo•ry (īv′ rē) a creamy white color

jacks (jaks) game played with small pieces of metal and a rubber ball

Juil•li•ard (jül′ yärd) a famous school of music in New York City

junc•tion (jungk′ shən) place where two or more railroad lines meet

ka•ra•te (kä rä′ tē) very formal method of fighting that uses blows with open hands and feet

Ka•ty (kā′ tē) nickname for the Missouri, Kansas, and Texas Railroad

keel (kēl) a plate along the center of the bottom of a ship

keg (keg) small barrel

ker•nel (kėr′ nəl) a grain or seed

ki•mo•no (kə mō′ nə) a Japanese robe

King Ar•thur (king är′ thər) a British king of the sixth century who is the subject of many legends

knack (nak) trick; way of doing something

knight (nīt) in the Middle Ages, a soldier of noble birth who served a king or lord

Ko•re•a (kô rē′ a) country in southeast Asia

Kra•ken (krok′ n) imaginary sea monster that looks like a giant squid or octopus

Kwa•ki•utl (kwä kē ü′ l) group of people or related Indian tribes of southwestern Canada

lab•o•ra•to•ry (lab′ rə tôr′ ē) place where scientists work

lac•quer (lak′ ər) coating for wood, like paint but smoother and shinier

La•dy Guin•e•vere (lād′ ē gwin′ ə vēr) in legend, the wife of King Arthur

la•goon (lə gün′) small body of water partly cut off from the ocean

Lange (lang) Dorothea (där′ ə thē′ a)

La Paz (lä päz′) port city in southeastern Baja California

launch (lônch) to start moving

Law•rence (lôr′ əns) Jacob (jā′ kəb)

league (lēg) unit equal to three miles, used for measuring distance across water

ledg•er (lej′ ər) book used for keeping accounts or records

leg•end (lej′ ənd) story passed down from the past, often based on an actual event but not provable

leg•end•ar•y (lej′ ən der′ ē) having to do with a legend passed down from the past

le•gion (lē′ jən) group of people of similar interests; kind of club, such as the American Legion

leg•is•la•tor (lej′ ə slāt′ ər) one who makes laws

leg•is•la•ture (lej′ ə slā′ chər) the law-making body of a state or nation

lex•i•cog•ra•pher (lek′ sə kog′ rə fər) one who makes dictionaries

lex•i•cog•ra•phy (lek′ sə kog′ rə fē) the art or science of making dictionaries

light•weight (līt′ wāt′) not heavy

lim•ber (lim′ bər) loose; able to bend easily

Lind•bergh (lind′ bėrg′) Charles (chärlz) first person to fly across the Atlantic Ocean alone

lin•e•ar (lin′ ē ər) in a line

lin•go (ling′ gō) special way of talking

lin•gon (ling′ gən) kind of berry

li•quid ox•y•gen (lik′ wid ok′ sə jən) result of cooling and compressing oxygen so that the gas becomes a liquid

Lith•u•a•ni•a (lith′ ü ā′ nē ə) country in eastern Europe

lob (lob) to throw gently in a high curve

lodge (loj) kind of house in the woods; Indian house

log•ic (loj′ ik) science of reasoning

hat, āge, fär; let, ēqual, tėrm; it, īce; hot, ōpen, order; oil, out; cup, pu̇t, rüle; ch, child; ng, long; sh, she; th, thin; ᴛʜ, then; zh, measure; ə represents *a* in about, *e* in taken, *i* in pencil, *o* in lemon, *u* in circus.

lop (lop) to flop; to hang down
lope (lōp) to run easily with long steps
Lo•re•to (lôr āt′ ō)
loy•al•ty (loi′ əl tē) remaining true to someone or something
lu•nar mod•ule (lū′ nər moj′ ül *or* mod′yül) the part of a spacecraft used for landing on the moon
lunge (lənj) to make a thrust or forceful forward movement
lute (lüt) musical stringed instrument that is played by plucking the strings
lux•u•ri•ant (ləg′ zhůr′ ē ənt) lush; full
Lu•zon (lū zōn′) Soto (sōt′ o)
mack•er•el (mak′ ər əl) kind of edible fish that lives in the Atlantic
mag•ni•fi•cent (mag nif′ ə sənt) very rich; grand; wonderful
Mal•do•na•do (mäl dō näd′ ō) cape in southwestern Mexico
mane (mān) long, heavy hair growing on the back or around the neck of a horse, lion, etc.
man•go (mang′ gō) yellowish-red tropical fruit
Man o' War (man′ ə wôr′) a famous racehorse
Man•ta Di•ab•lo (män′ tä dē äb′ lō) Spanish: devil blanket: *A manta is a kind of fish shaped like a triangular blanket.*

mare (mer *or* mar) female horse
ma•rim•ba (mə rim′ bə) a musical instrument with a row of wooden bars played with small hammers; a large xylophone
mar•vel (mär′ vəl) to admire; to be surprised by
mast (mast) long pole that holds up the sails of a ship
math•e•ma•ti•cian (math′ ə mə tish′ ən) one who studies numbers, numerals, and measurements
mat•zoth (mät′ sōt′) pieces of flat, hard bread, like crackers, made with no yeast
M•bui (m bü′ ē)
meg•a•struc•ture (meg′ ə struk′ chər) very large building
mel•an•chol•y (mel′ ən kol′ ē) sad
men•u (men′ yü) list of foods a restaurant serves and their prices
Mes•ca•le•ro Ranch (mes′ kə ler′ ō ranch)
mi•cro•phone (mī′ krə fōn′) an instrument that strengthens or passes along sound waves by means of electricity
mil•li•me•ter (mil′ ə mē′ tər) unit of measurement in the metric system equal to $\frac{1}{25}$ of an inch
mill•stone (mil′ stōn′) a stone used for grinding grain
min•e•stro•ne (min′ ə strō′ nē) thick soup
min•gle (ming′ gəl) to mix
mir•a•cle (mir′ i kəl) a rare and outstanding thing or event
mis•er•a•ble (miz′ ər ə bəl) very poor; in very bad shape
mis•er•y (miz′ ə rē) pain; suffering
mo•bile (mō′ bəl) movable; able to be moved about
moc•ca•sin (mok′ ə sən) soft leather shoe that can be slipped on like a slipper

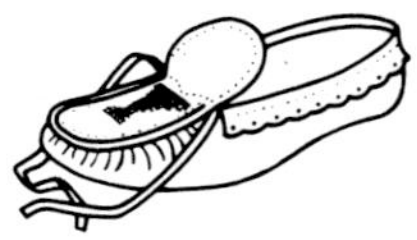

mock•up (mäk′ əp *or* mok′ əp) a full-sized model
Mode•mix•er (mōd′ mik′ sər) a junction for many types of transportation
mol•ten (mōlt′ n) melted; made liquid by heat: *molten metal*
mon•as•ter•y (mon′ ə ster′ ē) special house where monks live
Mon•gol (mong′ gəl) person who lives in Mongolia, a part of central Asia
monk (mungk) man who has given up worldly possessions for religious reasons and lives in a monastery with others like him
mo•not•o•nous (mə not′ n əs) always the same; boring

Mon·ti·cel·lo (mon′ tə sel′ ō *or* mon′ tə chel′ ō) Thomas Jefferson's home in Virginia

Mor·gan (môr′ gən) short stocky breed of horses developed in America and named after a schoolteacher who owned the first one

Moth·er Ca·rey's chick·en (muth′ ər ker′ ēz *or* kar′ ez chik′ ən) a sea bird

mot·ley (mot′ lē) **1.** mixture of different things **2.** costume of more than one color worn by clowns

mourn·ful·ly (môrn′ fəl lē) sadly

muz·zle (muz′ əl) front part of the face of an animal

mys·ter·i·ous·ly (mi stir′ ē əs lē) strangely; in a way hard to understand or explain

Narn·ia (närn′ yə)

Na·va·jo (nav′ ə hō *or* näv′ ə hō) an Indian tribe of northern Mexico and Arizona

neg·a·tive (neg′ ə tiv) film having the light and dark parts in the reverse order of the original subject

nick·er·ing (nik′ ər ing) neighing; friendly noise made by a horse

Nîmes (nēm) city in southern France

nin·com·poop (nin′ kəm püp) stupid person; idiot

no·mad (nō′ mad) one who does not live in one place but moves around all the time

North Platte (nôrth plat) river flowing through Colorado, Wyoming, and Nebraska

nos·tril (nos′ trəl) opening in the nose through which air passes

no·tion (nō′ shən) an idea: *I have a notion that you're not happy.*

nuz·zle (nəz′ əl) to rub with one's nose: *The horse nuzzled her owner.*

nymph (nimf) in Greek and Roman stories, a spirit that looked like a beautiful woman who lived in seas, rivers, forests, trees, etc.

Oa·xa·ca (wä häk′ ä) city in southeast Mexico that is famous for its ancient ruins

o·bi (ō′ bē) wide sash, worn by Japanese women around their kimonos

o·blige (ə blīj′) to please; to do what is wanted: *If you want some help, I'd be only too happy to oblige you.*

o·blit·er·ate (ə blit′ ə rāt) to wipe out; to erase

O·gun·quit (ō gun′ kwit) fishing village in Maine

o·ka·pi (ō kä′ pē) African antelope that looks something like a giraffe

O'Keeffe (ō kēf′) Georgia (jôr′ jə)

o·kra (ō′ krə) vegetable that looks like a fat string bean

om·elette (om′ lit) kind of pancake made of eggs beaten and fried, usually filled with meat, cheese, or vegetables

op·er·a (op′ ər a) play with music, in which almost all the words are sung

op·e·rat·ic (op′ ə rat′ ik) having to do with opera

op·er·a·tion (op ėr ā′ shən) treatment by a doctor to remove diseased parts, fix parts of the body, etc.

op·e·rat·or (op′ ə rāt′ ər) one who makes something work: *A telephone operator puts calls through.*

o·ri·gin (ôr ə jin) beginning; start

O·ri·on (ə rī′ ən)

out·land·er (aůt′ land ər) a person from another part of the country: *The outlander teacher is strange to this town.*

o·ver·se·er (ōv′ vər sē′ ər) supervisor: *The ranch was run by an overseer.*

oys·ter (oi′ stər) a type of shellfish

hat, āge, fär; let, ēqual, tėrm; it, īce; hot, ōpen, order; oil, out; cup, pu̇t, rüle; ch, child; ng, long; sh, she; th, thin; ᴛʜ, then; zh, measure; ə represents *a* in about, *e* in taken, *i* in pencil, *o* in lemon, *u* in circus.

Pal·la·di·o (pal äd′ ē ō) Andrea (äṅ drā′ ə)

palm (päm) kind of tree that grows in hot climates, usually having its leaves at the top

pan·ick·y (pan′ ə kē) scared to the point of not being able to act sensibly

par·a·chute (par′ ə shüt) umbrella-shaped piece of cloth, used to bring things or people down safely from great heights

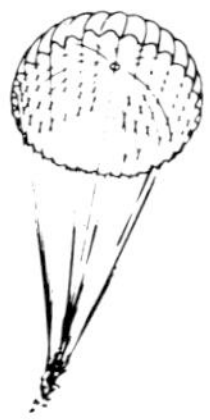

par·a·me·ci·um (par′ ə mē′ shē əm) very simple animal, having only one cell, too small to be seen without help of a microscope

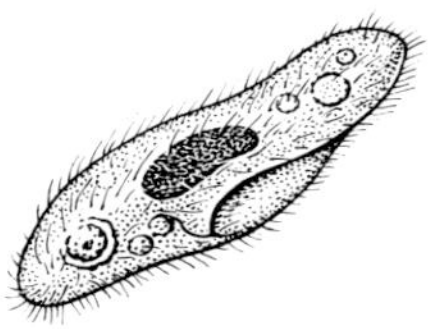

par·cel (pär′ cəl) a package

parch·ment (pärch′ mənt) skin of goats or sheep, prepared for writing or painting upon

par·lor (pär′ lər) room in a house used for entertaining guests; sitting room

pa·sa·da (pä säd′ dä) Spanish: walk; custom of walking around the main square in the afternoon; often called *paseo* (pä sā′ ō)

pa·tient (pā′ shənt) one under the care of a doctor

pa·tri·ot·ic (pā′ trē ot′ ik) showing love of one's country

Paw·nee (pô nē′) tribe of Indians once common in Nebraska and Kansas

peaked (pēkt) pointed; ending in a peak

peeved (pēvd) annoyed; irritated

Pei (pā) I. M.

Pe·king (pē′ king′) capital city of People's Republic of China

pe·sos (pā′ sōs) Mexican units of money, similar to dollars

pes·ti·len·tial (pes′ tl en′ shəl) causing diseases; very harmful

pet·its fours (pet′ ē fôrz) small cakes

Phil·ip·pines (fil′ ə pēnz′) group of 7,083 islands in the South Pacific

pho·tog·ra·phy (fə täg′ rə fē) the art of creating pictures with a camera

phy·si·cian (fə zish′ ən) medical doctor

phys·ics (fiz′ iks) science that studies matter and forms of matter

pi·an·o (pē ä′ nō) softly

pin·na·cle (pin′ ə kəl) high, thin piece of rock that looks like a tower

Pin·ney (pin′ ē) Eunice (yü′ nis)

piz·za (pēt′ sə) flat pie

plat·form (plat′ fôrm) raised level surface to sit or stand on

pol·lu·tion (pə lü′ shən) dirt; filth

pol·y·glot (pol′ ē glot) speaking many languages; made up of many languages

poop·deck (püp′ dek′) raised deck at the back of a ship

por·trait (pôr′ trət) a picture

pos·i·tive·ly (poz′ ə tiv lē) really; for sure

pos·se (pos′ ē) a group of people a sheriff or other peace officer calls to help keep the peace

pot·latch (pät′ lach′) a ceremonial feast of Indians of the northwest U.S.

Pough·keep·sie (pə kip′ sē)

prair·ie (prer′ ē) area of flat land covered with long grass but few or no trees

pre·cious (presh′ əs) very dear; extremely valuable

prej·u·diced (prej′ ə dist) disliking something or someone without cause

Price (prīs) Leontyne (lē′ ən tēn)

prim·i·tive (prim′ ə tiv) very early; very simple

pro·cess con·trol (präs′ es *or* prōs′ es kən trol′) system for checking a process or action

pro·duc·er (prə dü′ sər *or* prō dü′ sər) one who presents a play

pro·fes·sor (prə fes′ ər) one who teaches in a college or university

pro•gram•mer (prō′ gram′ ər) one who tells a computer what to do

pro•nun•ci•a•tion (prə nun′ sē ā′ shən) how a word is said

proph•e•cy (prof′ ə sē) prediction; telling what will happen in the future

prose (prōz) writing that is not poetry

pros•pec•tor (pros′ pek tər) one who searches for jewels or precious metals

pro•test (prə test′) to object

pro•vi•sions (prə vizh′ ənz) supply of food and other needs

Pueb•la (pweb′ lä) city in Mexico southeast of Mexico City

pueb•lo (pü eb′ lō *or* pweb′ lō) an Indian village of the southwest United States

Pu•get Sound (pyü′ jit sound) arm of the Pacific Ocean extending into the state of Washington

push•cart (pu̇sh′ kärt′) light cart or wagon that is pushed by hand

puz•zle•ment (puz′ əl mənt) confusion; lack of understanding

pyr•a•mid (pir′ ə mid) building with triangular sides that meet in a point

py•thon (pī′ thon) large African snake that kills its prey by crushing

Quak•er (kwā′ kər) a member of a religious group that is against war

quar•tet (kwôr tet′) a musical group made up of four people

qua•sar (kwā′ zär) a very bright starlike form that gives off radio waves

quince (kwins) hard sour fruit

ram•page (ram pāj′) to move around wildly and destructively

ramp•ing (ramp′ ing) moving as if one were angry

ran•som (ran′ səm) the release of a person or thing for payment

Ra•pal•je (rap′ ə lē) Garrett (ger′ ət)

rav•age (rav′ ij) to destroy all in one's path; to cause much destruction

re•cep•tion (ri sep′ shən) the way a picture comes in on television

re•cit•al (ri sīt′ əl) a telling of the details of an event

reck•on (rək′ ən) to think; to suppose

rec•re•a•tion (rek rē ā′ shən) a way to relax, such as a game or hobby

Red Riv•er Val•ley (red riv′ər val′ ē) river valley that forms the border between Minnesota and the Dakotas

reed (rēd) kind of hollow tall grass that is common near water

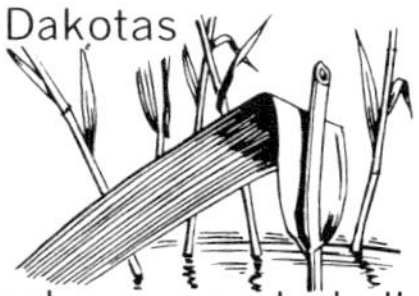

reef (rēf) ridge of rocks or coral shells lying just below the surface of the water

ref•er•ence (ref′ ər əns) source of information needed to answer questions

reign (rān) to rule; to exist everywhere

rein (rān) a line fastened on each side of an animal used to control the animal

re•luc•tant (ri luk′ tənt) unwilling

Re•mo•ra Mon•ster (rə môr′ ə mon′ stər) imaginary monster that has suckers it uses to attach itself to ships

re•nowned (ri nound′) famous

re•pub•lic (ri pub′ lik) government made up of elected representatives

re•sem•ble (ri zem′ bəl) to look like

re•spect•ful•ly (rē spekt′ fə lē) politely

re•spon•si•ble (ri spon′ sə bəl) trustworthy: *Responsible people can be trusted to complete their tasks.*

res•taur•ant (res′ tər ənt) place where meals are sold and eaten

re•u•nion (rē yü′ nyən) the act of coming together again

Rev•o•lu•tion•ar•y War (rəv′ ə lü′ shə ner′ ē wär) war from 1775–1783 in which the thirteen American colonies won independence from Britain

rhy•thm (riꟛH′ əm) regular beat

ri•dic•u•lous (ri dik′ yə ləs) very silly

ring-a-lie•vo (ring′ ə lēv′ ō) game that is something like tag

hat, āge, fär; let, ēqual, tėrm; it, īce; hot, ōpen, ôrder; oil, out; cup, pu̇t, rüle; ch, child; ng, long; sh, she; th, thin; ꟛH, then; zh, measure; ə represents *a* in about, *e* in taken, *i* in pencil, *o* in lemon, *u* in circus.

road•mas•ter (rōd′ mas′ tər) a person in charge of 50–150 miles of railroad line
Ro•a•noke Is•land (rō′ ə nōk′ ī′ land) an island off the coast of North Carolina
rush (rush) **1.** to push with speed or violence **2.** a kind of hollow tall grass
rus•tle (rəs′ əl) to make small sounds
Saar•i•nen (sär′ ə nən) Eero (ar′ ō *or* er′ ō)
sa•fa•ri (sə fär′ ē) long trip; trip to some wild place
Sa•la•zar (säl ə zär′) Ramón (rä mōn′)
Salz•burg (sôlz′ bėrg) city in Austria famous for its music festivals
sa•ri (sär′ ē) woman's dress of East India made by wrapping a long strip of cloth around the body

sat•el•lite (sat′ əl īt) something that orbits a larger heavenly body, either natural, such as the moon, or made by people
sauer•kraut (sour′ krout′) pickled shredded cabbage
sce•ner•y (sēn′ ə rē) the painted scenes on a theater stage
scent (sent) a smell
sched•ule (skej′ ül) set time for things to happen; list of times that trains will come and go
schol•ar (skäl′ ər) one who studies; a student
schoon•er (skü′ nər) sailing ship with sails set lengthwise on two or more masts

Scot•tish (skot′ ish) from Scotland
scourge (skėrj) something that causes trouble or disease
script (skript) **1.** the written text of a play **2.** handwriting
seamed (sēmd) lined; wrinkled
sem•i•nar•y (sem′ ə ner′ ē) boarding school for girls
se•ñor (sā nyôr′) Spanish: mister; sir
sen•si•bil•i•ty (sen′ sə bil′ ə tē) artistic feeling; feeling for the finer things in life
ser•geant (sär′ jənt) police officer lower in rank than a captain
set (set) a stage setting for a play
Shahn (shän) Ben (ben)
shan•ty (shan′ tē) shack; hut; small, badly built house
sheep•shank (shēp′ shangk) kind of knot

Shet•land po•ny (shet′ lənd pō′ nē) one of a breed of small ponies that come from the Shetland Islands off Scotland
shish ke•bab (shish kə bob′) meat and vegetables stuck on a spike and broiled
Si•a•mese (sī′ ə mēz′) from Thailand, which was formerly called Siam
Sic•i•ly (sis′ ə lē) island near Italy
sick•le (sik′ əl) crescent in shape
Si•le•nus (sī lē′ nəs) in Greek and Roman stories, the oldest of the forest spirits
sil•ver•smith (sil′ vər smith′) an artist who makes things out of silver
Sing•a•pore (sing′ ə pôr) island near China; city on this island
Sioux (sü) tribe of Plains Indians
si•ren (sī′ rən) a warning sound
si•tar (si tär′) a musical stringed instrument
skir•mish (skėr′ mish) to fight in a small way; to start a fight as a test
Slav•ic (släv′ ik) of or related to a certain group of languages and the people who speak them: *The Slavic languages of the Czechs and Poles have a common ancestor.*
slug (slug) slow-moving animal like a snail, without a shell or with a partially developed shell
slum (sləm) a rundown area of a city
smor•gas•bord (smôr′ gəs bôrd) meal of meats, fish, salads, pickles, and cheese, like a buffet
snow•shoe (snō′ shü′) a wooden frame with strips of leather that is used to walk on snow without sinking

snuf•fle (snəf′ el) to sniff
so•ber (sō′ bər) serious; thoughtful
so•lu•tion (sə lü′ shən) answer
son•net (son′ ət) a poem of a fixed fourteen-line form
so•pra•no (sə pran′ ō) high female voice
souf•flé (sü flā′) fluffy dish made of eggs that are beaten and baked
spa•cious (spā′ shəs) roomy
spi•ky (spī′ kē) having sharp points
spi•ral (spī′ rəl) gradually widening coil

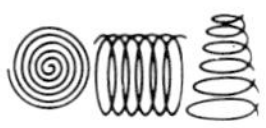

sprawl (spräwl) a careless spreading out
squaw (skwô) American Indian woman
stag (stag) male deer
stage•coach (stāj′ kōch′) a horse-drawn coach for carrying passengers and mail
stal•lion (stal′ yən) mature male horse
stan•za (stan′ zə) one section of a song or poem consisting of several lines
stark (stärk) plain; harsh
stat•ue (stach′ ü) a likeness or model
stee•ple (stē′ pəl) pointed tower such as on the top of a church; anything that looks like such a tower
St. George (sānt jôrj) a legendary hero who killed dragons
stir•rup (stėr′ əp *or* stir′ əp) rounded support for a rider's foot that hangs from the saddle
stove•pipe (stōv′ pīp′) a tall silk hat
stra•mash (stram′ əsh *or* strə mash′) commotion; much noise
stray (strā) to lose one's way; wander: *Our dog strayed off somewhere.*
sub•tract (sub trakt′) to take away
sub•urb (sub′ ërb′) area just outside a city
suc•co•tash (suk′ ə tash) lima beans and corn cooked together
sulk•i•ly (sul′ kə lē) in an annoyed way
Sul•li•van (sul′ ə vən) Louis (lü′ əs)
surf•board (sėrf′ bôrd′) narrow board used for riding on waves
sur•feit (sėr′ fit) too much; excess
sur•geon (sėr′ jun) a doctor trained to perform operations
sur•ren•der (sə ren′ dər) to give up
sus•pi•cious•ly (sə spish′ əs lē) believing that something is wrong; not trusting
swa•mi (swä′ mē) one who can tell what the future will be; magician
swirl (swėrl) twist; curl
syl•lab•i•ca•tion (sə lab′ ə kā′ shən) dividing words into syllables
Ta•ho•ma (tə hō′ mä) Quincy (kwin′ sē)
tar•pau•lin (tär pô′ lən) waterproof cloth
tart (tärt) pastry that is filled with fruit
tat•tered (tat′ ərd) ragged; torn
tech•nique (tek nēk′) a way of doing something; method
tel•e•scope (tel′ ə skōp) a tube with lenses in it, used to make faraway objects appear larger and clearer
tem•ple (tem′ pəl) a building in which to worship or pray
tem•po•rar•y (tem′ pə rer′ ē) for a short time
ten•e•ment (ten′ ə mənt) poor, ill-kept, or old apartment building
ten•ta•cle (tent′ i kəl) a long, sensitive arm coming out of an animal's head
theft (theft) stealing or act of stealing
threat•en (thret′ ən) to frighten
tick•ing (tik′ ing) a strong linen cloth
tin•gle (ting′ əl) stinging feeling
Ti•ra•wa (tir′ ə wä *or* ti rä′ wə) a Pawnee god
tis•sue (tish′ ü) very thin cloth or paper
tor•til•la (tôr tē′ yə) flat pancake made from corn meal
to•tem pole (tō′ təm pōl) pole carved and decorated with symbols, built by the Indians of northwestern America
town•ship (toun′ ship) unit of government in New England similar to a town
tram•po•line (tram′ pə lēn′) sheet of canvas on a frame, used for jumping
tran•quil•li•ty (tran kwil′ ə tē) calmness

hat, āge, fär; let, ēqual, tėrm; it, īce; hot, ōpen, order; oil, out; cup, pu̇t, rüle; ch, child; ng, long; sh, she; th, thin; ᴛʜ, then; zh, measure; ə represents *a* in about, *e* in taken, *i* in pencil, *o* in lemon, *u* in circus.

trans•fer (tran sfėr′ *or* tran′ sfėr) to move
trans•form (trans fôrm′) to change
trap•door (trap′ dôr′) hinged opening that drops down in a floor
trawl•er (träl′ ər) a boat equipped with a net for catching fish
treach•er•ous (trech′ ər əs) not to be trusted; dangerous; deceiving
tre•men•dous (tri men′ dəs) very big; huge; very good; wonderful
tri•bal (trī′ bəl) of a tribe or group of people living together under a leader
tri•umph (trī′ umf) success; victory
trot (trot) a medium-fast walk
Tum•nus (tum′ nəs)
twi•light (twī′ līt′) faint light in the sky before dawn and after sunset
U•lys•ses (yü lis′ ēz)
un•a•bridged (un′ ə brijd′) not shortened
un•at•trac•tive (ən′ ə trak′ tiv) not charming
un•der•brush (un′ dər brush′) small low bushes that form a ground covering
Un•der•ground Rail•road (un′ dər ground′ rāl′ rōd) a system before 1863 by which people secretly helped slaves to reach the northern U. S. or Canada
U•NES•CO (yü nes′ kō) acronym for United Nations Educational, Scientific, and Cultural Organization
u•nique (yü nēk′) rare; one of a kind
u•ni•verse (yü′ nə vėrs′) everything there is; everything that exists
un•us•u•al (ən yüzh′ ə wəl) not common
us•u•al (yüzh′ ə wəl) normal
u•ten•sil (yü ten′ səl) a tool
ut•most (ut′ mōst) best
valve (valv) movable part that controls the flow of a liquid or gas
vane (vān) the fin-like part of a rocket that helps to control movement

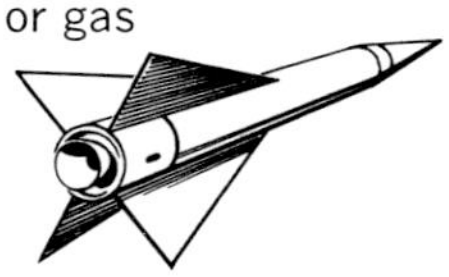

van•quish (vang′ kwish) to beat someone in battle
var•i•ous (ver′ ē əs) different kinds
vault (vôlt) room with an arched ceiling
veer (vir) to change direction; to swerve
Vel•ar•de (və lär′ dā) Pablita (päb lēt′ ə)
Ve•ro•na (və rō′ nə) city in north Italy
ver•sion (vėr′ zhən) one type within a related class; an account of an event
ves•sel (ves′ səl) a boat; a ship
vi•cin•i•ty (və sin′ ə tē) area
Vi•en•na (vē en′ ə) capital city of Austria
vit•tle (vit′ l) variant spelling for victual; food
viv•id (viv′ id) very strong; very clear
vo•cab•u•lar•y (vō kab′ yə ler′ ē) all the words of a language; all the words known by a person
vol•un•teer (vol′ ən tir′) one who offers to do something without being asked
Wa•bash (wô′ bash) Wabash Railroad
ward•robe (wôrd′ rōb′) closet; room for hanging clothes
wash (wäsh) a thin coat of paint
wa•ter•col•or (wät′ ər kəl′ ər) a paint with a water base
weird (wird) strange; mysterious
whin•ny (hwin′ ē) a soft neigh; a soft noise made by a horse
Whist•ler (hwis′ lər) James McNeill (jāmz mək nēl′)
White (hwīt) John (jon)
wind•mill (wind′ mil′) a wheel-shaped device that captures the energy of wind
wire•less (wīr′ lis) British English word for radio
with•er (with′ ər) to dry up
wretch•ed (rech′ id) poor; unhappy
Wright (rīt) Frank Lloyd (frangk loid)
Wy•eth (wī′ eth) Andrew (an′ drü)
yam (yam) edible root, like a sweet potato
yo•del (yō′ dl) high shrill call
yoke (yōk) something that weighs one down
ze•ro in (zē′ rō *or* zir′ ō in) to come in close; to focus